Which School ?
for A Levels
and
Education after Sixteen
1997/98

Editor: Derek Bingham

John Catt Educational Ltd

Published 1997 by John Catt Ltd, Great Glemham,
Saxmundham, Suffolk IP17 2DH.
Tel: 01728 663666 Fax: 01728 663415.

© 1997 John Catt Educational Ltd.

Which School? is a trade mark owned by **Which? Limited** and licensed to John Catt Educational Ltd.

All rights reserved. No part of this publication may be reproduced, stored in a retrieval system, transmitted in any form or by any means, electronic, mechanical, photocopying, recording, or otherwise, without the prior permission of the publishers.

Opinions expressed in this publication are those of the contributors, and are not necessarily those of the publishers or the sponsors. We cannot accept responsibility for any errors or omissions.

The Sex Discrimination Act 1975. The publishers have taken all reasonable steps to avoid a contravention of Section 38 of the Sex Discrimination Act 1975. However, it should be noted that (save where there is an express provision to the contrary) where words have been used which denote the masculine gender only, they shall, pursuant and subject to the said Act, for the purpose of this publication, be deemed to include the feminine gender and vice versa.

A CIP catalogue record for this book is available from the British Library

ISBN: 1-869863-98-4
ISSN: 1365-9618

Set and designed by John Catt Educational Ltd,
Great Glemham, Saxmundham, Suffolk IP17 2DH.

Printed and bound in Great Britain by Bell and Bain Ltd, Glasgow, Scotland.

Contents

Introduction	1
How to use the Guide	3
The future shape of GCE AS and A levels	4
A levels: the traditions of academia or the development of our next generation?, *David Prichard MA, Andrew Gillespie MA and J N D Gray BA*	7
Delivering what the examiner wants, *James Burnett*	11
The British Accreditation Council for Independent Further and Higher Education, *Robin Laidlaw*	13
Finding the fees, *Anne Feek*	15
Display Listings of Independent Tutorial and Sixth Form Colleges	19
Directory of Independent Tutorial and Sixth Form Colleges	D31
Display Listings of Independent Schools with Sixth Form entry	39
Directory of Independent Schools with Sixth Form entry	D79
Display Listings of Schools and Colleges offering the International Baccalaureate	147
Display Listings of Professional Schools and Colleges	151
Directory of Professional Schools and Colleges	D157
Directory of Colleges of the Arts	D165

Contents

Examinations and qualifications:

GCSE	170
AS courses	172
A levels	173
SCE	174
CSYS	176
Examination dates	177
The International Baccalaureate	180
Schools affiliated to the International Baccalaureate in the United Kingdom	183
BTEC Qualifications	192
National Vocational Qualifications	196
SCOTVEC Awards	198
RSA Examination Board	200
City & Guilds	202
Schools offering entry at 16 to Vocational Courses	204
Educational Associations	209
Glossary of Abbreviations	221
Map	224
General Index	225

Introduction

by the Editor

At a conservative estimate one pupil in four now either changes or leaves independent school at the age of 16.

The reasons are many. For some a long stay at one school may induce a staleness which can be overcome by the challenge of a move to another; for parents with children at a single-sex school there may be a wish for them to learn to associate with the opposite sex; for those with children at a day school, two years at a boarding school could help them get used to being away from home.

There may also be matters of subject choice, of finance, or of location. Whatever the reason, in part it is recognition of change, the start of the transition from pupil to student.

But these factors do not obscure two revolutions which have been taking place in education. The one in schools - National Curriculum, league tables, vocational courses, the future of A levels *etc* - has been well documented; the one within homes much less so.

Parents no longer regard GCSEs and subsequent exams as an automatic rite of passage for their children in which they have little say. To them the equation is simple: good exam results = better job prospects.

Indeed such are the pressures nowadays that a degree alone may not suffice; ever more graduates find that when they reach the job market they have not necessarily acquired what employers want. There may be a need for further studies and qualifications after that, or to diversify to cope with the modern trends in employment.

But before the job interviews can begin the right choices of A level and AS subjects, Scottish Highers or IB, of degree or other courses, of university or college, must be made.

To these must be added the confidence, character, poise, presentation, attitudes and achievements which, from their own experience, parents know employers look for. They know, too, that the foundations of these are acquired in a few, critical, teenage years. If the options and advantages are greater at another school or college - especially if university places become more difficult to secure - why not move your child there if you can ?

Little wonder that, in an area of such student movement and competition, schools and colleges aim to provide as comprehensive and effective an education as possible. This is reflected in that when we launched **Which School ? for A Levels and Education after Sixteen** three years ago, we had no idea of the overwhelming reception it would receive from parents and schools.

How to use this Guide

Welcome to the fourth edition of **Which School ? for A Levels and Education after Sixteen**, in which we aim to provide as much information as possible about the A level - and other - choices available at independent schools and colleges after GCSE.

Whatever you are looking for - the Sixth Form of an independent school or tutorial college - you will find the information in these pages. There is also information about schools teaching Scottish Highers and a separate section providing information about those which offer the International Baccalaureate.

Which School ? for A Levels and Education after Sixteen is divided into four main sections. Before the first are articles written by experts in their fields. We urge you to read them as they may save you a lot of time.

The four sections provide information about the schools and colleges which may be able to help you. Details of what each section contains appear in the Contents.

Each section is divided into two. The first part is the Listings, which provide descriptions of schools and colleges. The second comprises the Directory, which gives basic information about every institution which falls within its section. Both sections are presented geographically by county.

At the back is the Index of all institutions which appear in the book. The letter D preceding each page number indicates where a school or college appears in the Directory. A second figure shows where it may be found among the Listings.

There are many ways to use this book to best advantage. If you seek a school or college in a certain area, look first at the appropriate Directory. It will give you the basic information about all the schools or colleges which may be able to help you.

After you have selected those which may be suitable, look and see if they have taken a Listing. Those that do will have a ★ next to the Directory entry and a separate page number in the Index. This will provide you with much more information about them before you make a direct approach.

If you know of a school, but are not sure where it is located, turn to the Index. From it you will find the information you want.

If you would like to know more about a school or college, use the free reply-paid enquiry cards at the back of the book. We will contact the institution and ask them to send their information to you direct.

Hopefully when you have used this book you will have found a selection of suitable schools or colleges - and even options you had not been previously aware of.

The future shape of GCE AS and A levels

Information supplied by the DfEE

The new AS

The Secretary of State has endorsed the School Curriculum and Assessment Authority's recommendation for the development of a reformulated AS qualification representing the level of achievement expected after one year's study at advanced level. The new AS (the Advanced Subsidiary) will replace the current Advanced Supplementary qualification. The new exam is designed to

- provide a firm foundation for progression to A level;
- offer a worthwhile exit point for students who embark on an A level course but do not wish to continue; and
- meet the needs of students who wish to broaden their main studies (whether A level of GNVQ).

In the new model, the AS will form the first half of the full A level course in terms of syllabus content and time, representing the first two and a half term's work of a traditional A level course. It could also be offered as a one year intensive course or be spread over several years.

The full A level will therefore be made up of two parts: the AS and what might be called the A2 (the second part). It will be possible for students to take the AS examination and then choose whether or not to go on to A level. Alternatively, the AS and the 'A2' could be taken together at the end of the course, thus preserving the traditional linear approach.

For those who go on to sit the full A level, the AS will contribute 40% towards the A level mark (in the same way as a lower weighting is given to modules completed early in an undergraduate course). For students who do not go on to the full A level, the intention is that the AS should carry half the credit of a full A level.

Modular A levels

The Secretary of State has endorsed a number of measures designed to make modular A levels more manageable and more comparable with traditional linear schemes:

- there will be a common timetable of two examination sittings a year in January and June;
- linear and modular forms of A level will be based on single content syllabuses;

- there will be a standard pattern of either four or six modules in all subjects (two or three modules for the AS); and
- resits will be limited to one per module, with the better result counting, except in the case of final modules which will represent 30% of the total marks.

Subject cores

The Secretary of State has welcomed the development of new A level and AS subject cores and endorsed them as the basis for developing new syllabuses. The cores now draw explicit attention to the coverage of key skills. In addition, SCAA has taken the opportunity to address the specific concerns about the coverage of particular subjects raised by last year's SCAA/OFSTED report on examination standards over time. SCAA built in a final review stage in April 1997 to allow for representations for any minor revisions or fine-tuning which may be needed once the boards have started work on developing the new syllabuses.

Syllabus development

The Secretary of State has welcomed the action which SCAA has already taken to reduce the number of AS and A level syllabuses currently available by agreeing with the boards that the number of new syllabuses should not exceed two per board in large entry subjects, and that the boards should share provision in smaller entry subjects.

Exceptional ability

The Secretary of State has welcomed the thrust of Sir Ron Dearing's recommendations for meeting the needs of the most able young people, and in particular the steps the boards have taken to ensure that special papers will continue to be available in most subjects, as well as the further work SCAA intends to undertake on other forms of additional achievement, including the potential role of higher education in certificating achievement above grade A at A level through extension units or modules which build on the subject cores.

Standards and comparability

The Secretary of State has endorsed SCAA's proposals to:

- report on all subjects which are governed by subject criteria at GCSE and subject cores at AS/A level on a five-yearly cycle, with publication of an annual report;
- continue to develop a methodology to reduce differences in standards between subjects; and

- in the meantime publish information about the relative difficulty of different subjects.

Implementation timetable

The Secretary of State has endorsed SCAA's recommendation that the new courses should be introduced from September 1998 on the basis that SCAA agree a timetable with the boards that will enable final approved syllabuses to be delivered to schools and colleges by Christmas 1997, with exemplar material and draft syllabuses available before then.

See also pages 172-173.

A levels: the traditions of academia or the development of our next generation?

Some Heads give their views. First, David Prichard MA, *Headmaster of Wycliffe College, advances the cause of the LADS*

A levels are recognised internationally as a passport to British universities. Some people fear that any tinkering will devalue this gold standard of scholarship. The expansion in the number of universities has caused concern in their faculties that standards have indeed fallen. However, a university experience is now seen by some as an essential road to employment rather than a haven for intellectual development.

Others appreciate that not even a degree will guarantee a job. The student of the '90s is shrewd enough to notice the drift of employment prospects in our global village; the influence of technology; the need for language and the requirement to master fresh knowledge frequently.

The current A level system fails to address such issues. It is folly to truncate swathes of knowledge at 16 when many still remain immature. It is unreasonable to expect all students to select but three or four subjects and so deny them exposure to a wealth of wisdom which should be their birthright.

The recent move to modular A levels is but a tinkering. Already 18 is early enough to sit an A level and in several subjects lack of maturity mitigates against a high grade taken in a module earlier in a Sixth Form course.

Nationally we must recognise that we can ill afford to put 16-year-olds onto an already overcrowded job market. Further years of some education in school is highly desirable. Maturity invariably produces greater understanding and development of latent talent.

At Wycliffe, the significant increase in British students interested in Sports Studies, Media Studies, Theatre Studies, Business Studies *etc*, indicates that previous experience of traditional subjects has little appeal. Most foreign students have a more sharply focused vision of fluent English allied to skills which will advance their prospects in law, medicine or accountancy.

The recent advent of the Diploma of Achievement validated by Oxford and Cambridge is a brilliant concept and provides scope for development of core skills.

The future of A levels should be dependent not so much on the traditions of academia but the development of our next generation. We should be more concerned about a majority than a minority. What are their needs if they are to be able to live fulfilled lives? At one stage a classical education was considered essential. Is it high achievement in a limited field or a broader achievement offering greater scope for employment and personal fulfilment?

The answer is of course both intellectual fulfilment, research capability, the honing of superior talent on the one hand and, for the marginally less gifted in that direction, the opportunity to craft the skills they do have. The backing of a Level A Diploma (LADs) would satisfy all. Some might select to study but three plus As; others six half As; others to gain say ten certificates in a wider range of topics. Subsequently, some might take a one to three year gap; others might find immediate employment and use their golden key to a university later in life when 'resting'.

Perhaps great proficiency in oracy, international relations, the universe and creation, multifaith societies, inter-personal skills, literature and culture, mind and body might better equip our youth to face the challenges of the next century and the chances of creating a wiser society of mankind.

The British have an enviable reputation for creativity and design even if we have often failed to capitalise on such skills. It is vital we equip all our students not only with paper which reflects their academic attainments but also those skills essential for survival in a radically changing employment market.

Tomorrow A levels may be as closely in touch with gold standards as the pound sterling. We are no longer looking at a system designed for the new elite few but at a programme to enhance the intellect and effectiveness of a majority in our nation. Perhaps the fact that Wycliffe College recognises this has resulted in a 33% increase in numbers with even more students advancing to universities.

Andrew Gillespie MA, *Director of Studies, d'Overbroeck's, argues that A levels should stand proudly alongside Vocational Courses and not bend towards them*

"A levels are part of an antiquated educational system which has failed to change with the needs of its customers - in this case the students, their future employers and society in general. What we need is more vocational, more accessible and more relevant educational programmes". So goes one view of the A level system.

It is, however, a view which is fundamentally flawed since it fails to understand the whole basis on which A levels are founded: to develop academic skills and measure their attainment. It is true to say that A levels do not prepare students for specific jobs, nor were they intended to. However, by developing individuals' analytical and evaluative skills they provide students with the intellectual discipline required for effective decision-making in all areas of life. A level students may not be trained in a particular task but they should be able to think through problems, weigh up various factors, reach a balanced decision and express their ideas effectively.

A levels are also attacked on the grounds of relevance and whilst the addition of more modern subjects such as Business Studies and Communications Studies should be welcomed, because it gives students greater choice, this should not hide the fact that A levels do not necessarily have to be relevant. A levels should seek to build core skills in which students are learning how to learn; the content is of less importance than the process.

The danger is that in reaction to recent criticism A levels will be made more practical, more accessible and more modern at the expense of their academic qualities. Whilst there is no doubt that vocational skills have been under-rewarded for far too long and that we should welcome developments such as NVQs, we should not seek to mix different types of courses.

A levels should stand proudly alongside vocational courses and not bend towards them. Our efforts should not be spent trying to merge A levels with something else but should be directed towards ensuring they maintain an appropriate degree of academic rigour to prepare students for university and their careers and be valued as an indicator of their intellectual standard.

Having said this, it may well be argued that under the existing A level system students are made to specialise too early. By broadening students' studies we may be able to provide them with more flexibility later on. The problem is that if we simply increase the number of subjects studied at A level there is a danger that we will create a hurdle that only the most academically gifted will overcome. AS levels were regarded as a solution to this by allowing students to study more subjects without the same amount of subject content.

Unfortunately, as candidate entry figures show, this system seems to lack appeal to both students and teachers and perhaps we should look more closely at the reasons behind this. The future, therefore, may lie in the re-examination of this system or a combination of A, AO and AS levels to achieve a wider coverage of subjects without devaluing the A level currency.

These ideas are presently being examined by the Schools Curriculum Assessment Authority and are likely to lead to a new examination framework for A level by 1998.

J N D Gray BA, *Headmaster of Pocklington School, says that A levels should be retained for their ability to challenge and motivate the brightest*

The system of A levels, as a means of educating, predominantly in 'academic' subjects, has been with us for over 40 years. When introduced it served a small minority who were able to pursue their interests and aptitudes in Higher Education. Nowadays A levels are studied by vastly greater numbers and, in order to cater for the tastes and aptitudes of these students, many subjects of a practical and vocational nature, as well as those of a more conventionally 'academic' order, can be followed.

The benefits of the A level system are that subjects which appeal to the taste or ability of students can be studied in depth and with great rigour. This serves not only as an excellent preparation for the advanced knowledge required in a university education, but also affords the opportunity to the motivated individual of particularised in-depth study, which prepares them for the resourcefulness, initiative and self-discipline required in Higher Education.

Nowadays the diversity of choice enables students to study subjects which contrast or complement each other, thereby allowing options for the future to be kept open. Equally, the more practically-orientated subjects allow students not ideally suited to the three A level route to follow their own strengths in depth: the best aspects of A level, the need for analytical rigour and detailed knowledge, are retained, while time is made available for the crucial applied and practical aspects of courses for which the same aspects have equal significance if different application.

AS levels were introduced to ensure the breadth which educationalists and politicians suspected was missing from a Sixth Form offering A levels alone. They have been a success only in a limited way, perhaps because the universities have been lukewarm in their response, and perhaps because they did not offer a radical enough alternative. The Dearing proposals for a reformed AS are therefore very welcome.

Good schools, however, operate A levels within a Sixth Form system which includes a host of other non-examinable subjects through a General Studies programme. Community service, games, extra curricular activities, cultural events, responsibility within the school and work experience outside, all add up to a healthy, well balanced, demanding education which does much more than teach young people to pass examinations; it also prepares them vitally for the challenges to be met beyond school. Variety and a broadening of horizons are essential components of Sixth Form education.

Alternatives such as GNVQs, the Scottish Highers and the International Baccalaureat all have their merits but A levels, within a well structured Sixth Form education, should be retained for their ability to challenge and motivate the brightest and to offer a very thorough and well based grounding to many others who are not obvious 'high flyers'.

Delivering what the examiner wants

James Burnett, *Principal of Abbey Tutorial College and Chairman of CIFE, outlines the role of the tutorial college*

"Why should I choose an independent sixth form college rather than a school?" is a question that tutorial college principals are often asked. The simple answer is that there is no simple answer. What suits one 16-year-old may not suit another, and an environment that allows one student to expand his or her horizons may have a different effect on others. What is certain is that tutorial colleges (the 'crammers' of old) broaden the spectrum of education available to students and their parents. For those wishing to change school after GCSE, independent sixth form colleges offer a greater flexibility in terms of subject choice and course length, fewer rules and more freedom to develop an enthusiasm for learning, less demands on their time outside the classroom, and more emphasis on academic matters. Small class sizes (usually a maximum of eight) and excellent tutor-student ratios, with help available outside lessons, mean that individual weaknesses can be dealt with effectively and quickly, and potential problems can be rectified easily, allowing the student to develop confidence and self-belief early on in the course.

Extra-curricular activities will generally form a smaller part of the tutorial college day than in the school but the range of activities on offer will, in many cases, be comparable or greater than in the schools. The key word here is choice - students can choose whether to participate in sport, drama or social activities. The student has to take more responsibility for his or her own daily routine within a framework of academic discipline and so, arguably, is better prepared for the demands of university life.

The colleges within the independent sector would list, high - possibly highest - in their priorities, the need to achieve good university places for their students. Increasingly there is an awareness that the choice of university is crucial, and one which will have repercussions throughout the working life. In addition to offering examination-oriented teaching, independent sixth form colleges provide specialised and expert advice on university applications, work experience and choice of suitable courses and institutions; and independent sixth form colleges have been particularly successful placing students on the most prestigious and demanding of university courses such as Medicine and Law.

Tutorial colleges have long been associated with 'cramming'. The evolution of the A level over the last few years has seen a greater emphasis on understanding and less on simple recall of factual information, and our teaching methods have had to develop in order to ensure that our students continue to achieve the excellent results that they do. Where independent sixth form colleges have always led the field is in the way the teaching is at all times directed towards examination success and university placement.

Much is made of the need for 'examination technique' nowadays, but there is no magic solution to examination success. The only way to achieve this is for the student to go into the examination room feeling confident that they have been fully and expertly prepared and that they are not only aware of what the examiner wants from them but are also able to deliver it clearly and concisely. Many independent sixth form colleges offer highly focused revision and retake courses alongside their two year A level programmes, ranging from one-week courses at Easter to a complete A level in a year or less, often with start dates in January as well as September. These are particularly useful for students who feel that, for whatever reason, the first year of their sixth form at school has not been effective - perhaps because of illness or simply because of lack of hard work.

The number of independent sixth form colleges has grown rapidly over the last 30 years. CIFE, the Conference for Independent Further Education, was founded in 1973 in order to promote the highest possible standards of education and welfare within the sector. The 31 member colleges adhere to a strict code of conduct governing the provision and standards of teaching, safety and pastoral care. The colleges undergo regular inspections and all examination results are rigorously audited. The member colleges cover a broad spectrum of education, from London-based science specialists to residential establishments in Shropshire, from co-educational day schools in Cambridge to a girls' boarding school in Berkshire. The one thing we all have in common is a desire to provide a flexible, stimulating and confidence-building environment which adapts to the students, rather than imposing a rigid structure on them.

The British Accreditation Council for Independent Further and Higher Education

by Robin Laidlaw, *Chief Executive, BAC*

Independent (private) colleges are not required by law even to be registered, let alone inspected! Many thousands of students, however, study in independent colleges. How then should a student go about choosing an independent college?

Since its establishment in 1984, the British Accreditation Council for Independent Further and Higher Education - the BAC for short - has set and monitored standards in independent colleges in Britain. By the beginning of the 1995 academic year, BAC had accredited 95 independent colleges, enrolling more than 40,000 students.

A student, whether from Britain or overseas, deciding to study at a BAC-accredited institution can be assured that it has been inspected by a team of experienced and qualified inspectors. The criteria used by them are laid down by the BAC Council which includes representatives of the chief bodies responsible for the maintenance of educational standards in the UK - universities, colleges, national validating bodies, and public and professional examining boards and also those, such as the British Council, with a particular concern for overseas students.

Institutions seeking BAC accreditation must satisfy the BAC under all the following headings:

> Premises and Learning Resources;
> Administration and Staffing;
> Quality control;
> Welfare arrangements; and
> Teaching and Learning.

The BAC also requests information concerning the financial affairs and legal status of institutions seeking accreditation. Once accredited, each institution is required to submit to the BAC an annual report on developments at the institution and is fully re-inspected every five years.

Scrutiny of applications for, and decisions on, accreditation are the responsibility of the Accreditation and Recognition Committee (ARC) which meets four times a year. The ARC consists of Council members and others with experience in further and higher education institutions or inspection experience. The Committee is also responsible for the initial appointment of inspectors and their deployment on individual inspections. The Chief

Inspector to the BAC, a former Registrar with the Council for National Academic Awards (CNAA) advises the ARC on all aspects of the BAC's inspection activities. More than 60 inspectors have so far been used on inspection work.

Students deciding to study at an independent further education institution accredited by the BAC can do so confident that its standards have been independently assessed and are regularly monitored.

The decision to establish the BAC stemmed from the announcement of the Department of Education and Science that it was withdrawing from the inspection and recognition of independent establishments of further education from April 1982. Discussions between responsible parties led to the formation in 1984 of the BAC, a company limited by guarantee and registered as a charity. The need to ensure that the BAC should provide an independent and objective assessment of standards in the independent sector is recognised by the requirement that Council members be nominated by recognised educational and other relevant bodies with no direct involvement or financial interest in the independent sector of education.

Over the years, the BAC has co-operated closely with the British Council's Recognition Scheme for English Language Schools and with the Council for the Accreditation of Correspondence Colleges. In 1990, the three organisations produced the first *Directory of Accredited Independent Colleges in Britain*. It contained the names of almost 350 colleges. In his introduction to the brochure, the Secretary of State for Education and Science welcomed the work of the three accrediting bodies. "The voluntary system of accreditation they have established", he noted, "is the only public guarantee of standards in independent institutions of further and higher education in the UK".

An essential service is being provided by the BAC. More and more individuals and organisations, including government departments, need to establish in an objective way the bona fides of an independent college. The BAC is able to provide an objective and independent assessment of an institution and to do so on a continuing basis.

Significant changes are currently underway in Further and Higher Education in Britain. It is vital that appropriate educational standards are maintained *and are seen to be maintained.* Anyone thinking of studying at an independent college, should look for the BAC logo and make sure that the college chosen is accredited.

Finding the Fees

by Anne Feek, *Managing Director,*
School Fees Insurance Agency

For parents wanting the best education for their children there is one inescapable truth. The earlier the planning begins the better. Advice from an independent financial adviser, with expertise in tax efficient school fees planning, should be sought as early as possible by parents who want to educate their children at an independent school.

The reason for early planning is quite simple. Currently starting at around £1000 as a day pupil at preparatory level, termly fees can rise to more than £4000 for a boarding school. After that, because maintenance grants are means tested and those with high incomes are unlikely to qualify for support, the costs of university or further specialist training can prove equally expensive. Looked at in real terms, the first 20 years or so of a child's life can be frighteningly expensive for the parents.

But having taken the decision to pursue an education in the independent sector for their children, the question for most parents is not whether they can afford it, but how. The options fall mainly between three main methods:

funding from capital;

funding from regular savings through specialist plans;

immediate fees plans.

For those with capital, there is a variety of options including educational trusts, bonds, PEPs and unit trusts. Although they differ in style, where a predicted level of outgoings is to be met, the watch-word is generally 'the safer the better'. Of these, educational trusts are specifically designed to meet termly fees.

If the benefits under an educational trust plan are guaranteed, the investor knows exactly what he or she is getting since the level of benefits to be provided is fixed when the investment is made and relates to the rates prevailing at the time. They have the greatest appeal for the more conservative investor - often grandparents - or for those with less than three years to run before fees are required. Generally, the plans remain extremely flexible in that benefits can be varied, postponed, brought forward or even transferred to another child.

When there are more than three years before fees are required, some educational trust plans provide greater potential for growth. With these the investment, linked to the value of units in chosen funds, will follow the fortunes of those funds up to the time when fees are required. However, investors must realise that the value of the investment can go down as well as up. It is worth noting that investment in these sorts of plans can be both from capital or by monthly payments.

The performance of the chosen funds can then be tracked by the investor, who may decide at any point in the plan's life to convert all or part of the investment to a guaranteed basis. This can be either when fees are required, or earlier if the investment conditions dictate.

A further choice for those with lump sums at their disposal are 'composition schemes' - a system of discounting fees through advanced payments - offered by some schools in the independent sector. Since there is no standard scheme or discount rate that can be quoted, it is a matter for discussing with schools direct.

Nevertheless parents should always take independent advice on this option. Amongst their considerations should be the 'return' in terms of savings on fees, how the school intends to invest the money, what the financial track record is or whether the money can be returned as a result of changes in circumstance (*eg* parent relocation, change of child's educational requirement). In general terms, however, composition schemes are of most value in the short term, particularly where there is a period of less than a year before fees are required.

For those providing school fees from regular savings, there are many choices as well as the monthly version of the educational trust plan already described. These include the familiar assortment of unit trusts, TESSAs and PEPs, although the last are subject to a fixed ceiling for contributions which may well be insufficient to meet projected needs.

Unitised with-profit maximum investment plans have tended to replace the traditional with-profit endowment plans. Careful structuring will ensure the benefits are available for fees at the right time and when not in the end used for school fees, there are no tax implications. There is also the advantage of life assurance cover which can secure school fees in the event of the policy holder's death.

Where Inheritance Tax is an important consideration the policies can be written in Trust. If both parents contribute to the premiums, it is usually advisable to arrange policies on a 'joint life' basis to ensure that benefits are paid in the event of either death. Once again it is important to remember that planning such investment calls for expert help.

The third route to education funding is for those who need to meet fees from what may appear to be inadequate resources. This situation can arise for many reasons: changes of career or of educational needs, or quite simply a peak of expenditure as more than one child needs school fees at the same time.

These are circumstances which loans of various sorts are designed to cover. The role of the school fees specialist is not to act as lender but to conduct a 'financial health check'. Careful examination can lead to a re-structuring of commitments with the aim of making outgoings more manageable.

A mortgage may be used to provide immediate fees, or the property can be used as security to draw loans on a termly basis up to a certain amount. Unsecured loans (typically up to £20,000) can also be arranged either by means of a straightforward capital and interest repayment spread over 10 to 15 years or interest only along with a regular premium policy to repay the total loan plus interest.

Although most investors would agree that loans should be a last, rather than a first, resort there are times when a loan might just save the day.

And, whilst planning as far ahead as possible will obviously permit maximum choice in terms of investment type, even the most careful plans can be subject to change. The creation of even a small financial cushion just a few years ahead of need can provide a safety net strong enough to see parents - and their children - through.

For anyone seeking a good return on their investment, surely that is reason enough for giving at least equal consideration to financial planning as to choosing an independent school.

Display Listings of Independent Tutorial and Sixth Form Colleges

Kent

Rochester Tutors Independent College

BAC CIFE

*New Road House,
3 New Road,
Rochester, Kent ME1 1BD
Tel: 01634 828115 Fax: 01634 405667*

Co-Principals: B. Pain, BSc(Hons) and
S. de Belder, BA(Hons)

Registered with the DfEE, CIFE and BAC

Accredited by BAC

Courses offered: Full range of A, AS and GCSE courses, Oxbridge entry, Art Pre-Foundation, Secretarial Studies and English as a Foreign Language.

No of students: Maximum 150, with equal numbers of male and female.

Age range: 14 and above

Nature of tuition: Small groups, one-to-one.

Average size of class or group: 5

Teacher/student ratio: 1:5

Range of fees as at 1.1.97:

Tuition: Full time £6900 per year
Accommodation: £3150 per year

Arrangements for accommodation: Supervised fully residential on site, self-catering/unsupervised hostel, local family approved by institution.

Facilities: The College has light and spacious classrooms, three fully equipped science laboratories, an up-to-date computing room, a language laboratory, two well-stocked libraries, a careers library, a comfortable student common room, a student refectory and a large examination hall. Extra-curricular activities include sailing, drama, photography, theatre trips and quiz nights.

Subject specialities and academic track record: Over 95% of students achieve the grades needed for higher education. The College has exceptionally strong Mathematics, Science and Art departments which consistently produce outstanding examination results.

Examinations offered (including Boards): All mainstream Examining Boards are available for GCSE, AS and A level subjects.

Destination/career prospects of leavers: The vast majority of students go on to higher education; other career prospects are developed on an individual basis with a qualified careers adviser.

London

Ashbourne Independent Sixth Form College

*17 Old Court Place,
London W8 4PL
Tel: 0171 937 3858 Fax: 0171 937 2207*

Head: Mr M.J. Hatchard-Kirby, MSc, BApSc

No of students: 150

Age range: 16-19

Nature of tuition: small groups.

Average size of class or group: 10 maximum

Range of fees as at 1.1.97: Tuition: £8325-£10,500

Established in 1981 Ashbourne is now regarded as one of the best schools of its type in the UK. Wonderfully situated near Kensington Gardens and Hyde Park, the School is a few minutes away from the excellent museums of Natural History, Science and Geology and the Victoria and Albert Museum.

The atmosphere is adult, friendly and informal and unencumbered by petty restrictions. Working in very small groups which never exceed ten, the College has helped students of all abilities achieve their academic goals. Ashbourne recognizes the importance of communication, individual attention and motivation, and has been particularly successful with those students who need a closely supervised, structure approach to work. A wide-ranging curriculum includes Media Studies and Psychology and each two year student's programme includes thinking skills, trips abroad and participation in an award programme for the Cambridge Diploma of Achievement. Each student is assigned to a senior member of staff and is instructed and monitored in the art of Time Management. At Ashbourne students are encouraged to work hard and the College stays open until 8.00 pm during the week and all day Saturday. The College aims to offer the opportunity for change; many an academic career has been revitalized because of the individual attention offered by small groups, the insistence to aiming high and working hard.

All abbreviations are explained in the Glossary at the back of this Guide.

Specialists in consultancy, design, production and publication of:

Prospectuses - Newsletters - Videos
Magazines - Exhibitions - School Histories
Marketing - Research

For a prompt quotation with no obligation please telephone, fax or write to:

John Catt Educational Ltd
Great Glemham,
Saxmundham,
Suffolk IP17 2DH

Tel: 01728 663666   Fax: 01728 663415

Davies, Laing and Dick

BAC CIFE

*10 Pembridge Square
London W2 4ED
Tel: 0171 727 2797 Fax: 0171 792 0730*

Principal: Ms Elizabeth Rickards, BA, MA, PGCE

Member of CIFE, BAC, ICG

Accredited by BAC

Courses offered: We offer two and one year A levels, as well as short retake courses for A level and GCSE students.

No. of students enrolled: Male: 170 Female: 135

Age range: 16-19

Nature of tuition: Lectures, classes, small groups, one-to-one.

Average size of class or group: 5.6

Teacher/student ratio: 1 : 6

Range of fees as at 1.1.97:

Tuition: £535-£2730 per term
Accommodation: £56-£150 per week

Arrangements for accommodation: Self catering/ unsupervised hostel, local family approved by institution.

Established in 1931, DLD is one of the oldest independent sixth form colleges in London. We specialise in retake examinations, though most of our students come to us at 16, preferring the atmosphere of college life.

Don't forget to make use of the Reader Enquiry Cards at the back of the Guide if you want more information about the Schools or Colleges listed.

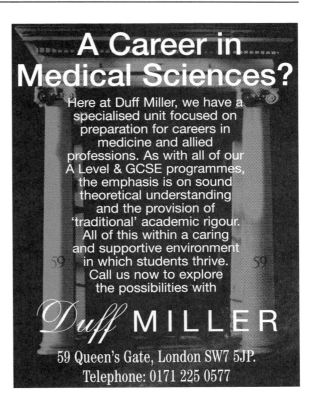

A Career in Medical Sciences?

Here at Duff Miller, we have a specialised unit focused on preparation for careers in medicine and allied professions. As with all of our A Level & GCSE programmes, the emphasis is on sound theoretical understanding and the provision of 'traditional' academic rigour. All of this within a caring and supportive environment in which students thrive. Call us now to explore the possibilities with

Duff MILLER

59 Queen's Gate, London SW7 5JP.
Telephone: 0171 225 0577

What's so special about Lansdowne?

We offer an alternative to sixth form college. An alternative to intensive, high-pressure 'education'. Well prepared, confident, motivated and happy students do exceedingly well at exam time and later in life.
Stressed, worried students don't.
It really is that simple.
Lansdowne offers a wide choice of subjects in our superbly appointed purpose built college, including modern languages, film studies, photography, psychology, theatre studies, and intensive programmes for medical and other retake students.

Call us on 0171 616 4400.
You'll be glad you did.

LANSDOWNE
COLLEGE

Oxford

Abacus College

*Threeways House,
George Street,
Oxford OX1 2BJ*
Tel: 01865 240111 Fax: 01865 247259
E-mail: abacus@dial.pipex.com

Principal: Mrs Laraine Brown, BA, DipEd

Accredited by BAC

Courses offered: One year, two year and five term A level, one term retakes, one year and two year GCSE, English for speakers of other languages, study skills. University foundation courses.

No of students: Male 60 Female 40

Age range: 15-19+

Nature of tuition: Classes, small groups and one-to-one.

Average size of class or group: 6

Teacher/student ratio: 1:3

Range of fees as at 1.1.97:

Tuition: One term £970; one year £2750; two year £2307

Accommodation: £60-£95 per week

Arrangements for accommodation: Self catering/unsupervised hostel, local family approved by institution.

Central Oxford location. Well equipped with own laboratory, library, computer facilities and classrooms. College regards students as adults within a carefully monitored academic environment.

Collingham Oxford

*31 St Giles, Oxford,
Oxfordshire OX1 3LF*
Tel: 01865 728280
Fax: 01865 240126
e-mail: 106035.1714@compuserve.com.uk

Head: A.J. Shepherd, MA(EdMan), BSc, MIBiol, CBiol, CertEd

Member of BAC, ABLS, CIFE

Accredited by BAC, ABLS

Courses offered: A level, GCSE retakes, 1 year and 2 year courses. University foundation courses. EFL courses.

No of students: Male 25 Female 25

Age range: 13-22

Nature of tuition: Small groups, one-to-one.

Average size of class or group: 3

Teacher/student ratio: 1:3

Range of fees as at 1.1.97: Tuition:

A level: November retakes £990
          January retakes £1500
          Others £990 per term

GCSE: Retakes £570 per subject per term

Accommodation: From £95 per week

Arrangements for accommodation: Self catering/unsupervised hostel or local family approved by institution.

Collingham Oxford is located in the centre of Oxford. It is a small, friendly college giving individual attention to students.

John Catt Educational Limited

Great Glemham, Saxmundham,
Suffolk IP17 2DH
Tel: 01728 663666 Fax: 01728 663415

*We specialise in
consultancy, design
and production of
educational publications*

D'Overbroeck's College

1 Park Town,
Oxford OX2 6SN
Tel: 01865 310000 Fax: 01865 552296
E-mail: doverb@rmplc.co.uk

Principals: S. Cohen, BSc
R.M. Knowles, MA, DPhil

Accredited by BAC and ISJC

Courses offered: GCSE and A level. Unusual flexibility in the range and combinations of subjects offered.

No. of students: Male 130 Female 120

Age range: 14-19 (Entry at 13 from September 1998)

Nature of tuition: highly interactive teaching; small groups, on average 5-6 students, with the option of individual tuition where it is deemed necessary.

Range of fees as at 1.12.96:
from £2400 per term (day);
£3600 per term (boarding)

The College provides a unique opportunity to study in a stimulating atmosphere, which is supportive and academically ambitious but less institutionalised than a traditional public school. Students speak readily of the excellence of the teaching, the refreshing rapport with their teachers and of the positive, encouraging and profoundly motivating environment.

Specialists in consultancy, design, production and publication of:

Prospectuses - Newsletters - Videos
Magazines - Exhibitions - School Histories
Marketing - Research

For a prompt quotation with no obligation please telephone, fax or write to:

John Catt Educational Ltd
Great Glemham,
Saxmundham,
Suffolk IP17 2DH

Tel: 01728 663666   Fax: 01728 663415

Modes Study Centre (Science Specialists)

(Founded 1978)

73/75 George Street, Oxford OX1 2BQ
Tel: 01865 245172/249349 Fax: 01865 722443

Principal: Stephen C.R. Moore, MA(Oxon), DPhil(Oxon).

Member of CIFE

Accredited by BAC

Courses offered: A level courses for both 'first time' and 'retake' students in Sciences, Maths, Economics and Geography.

No. of students enrolled as at 1.1.97:

Male: 52 Female: 41

Nature of tuition: Lectures/small groups/free individual tuition where necessary.

Average size of group: 8

Student/teacher ratio: 6:1

Range of fees (inc. VAT) as at 1.1.97:
£791 to £1150 per subject per term.

Accommodation is available with local families approved by the Centre at about £85 per week.

Consistently excellent examination results (87% grades A and B in year to June 1996, 181 entries) enable students to gain admission for the most competitive university courses. The majority (over 150 in the last three years) go on to Medical School or to study Veterinary Science, Dentistry or Pharmacy.

A full range of guides to UK Schools
is also published by
John Catt Educational Ltd.

Oxford Tutorial College

12 King Edward Street, Oxford OX1 4HT
Tel: 01865 793333 Fax: 01865 793233 E-mail: info@oxtutor.co.uk

Principal: Ralph Dennison, BA, PGCE
Member of CIFE, BAC
Accredited by BAC

Courses offered: A level and GCSE courses over one or two years; re-take courses over one term or one year. Oxbridge entrance; holiday and revision courses.

No. of students enrolled as at 1.1.97:
Male 57 Female 49

Age range: 16-25

Nature of tuition: tuition is a combination of small groups and one-to-one tutorials.

Average size of class: 4

Teacher/student ratio: 1:3

Range of Fees (incl VAT) as at 1.1.97:
Tuition: £880 per subject for an eleven-week term
Accommodation: £1045-£1320 for an eleven-week term (half-board)

Arrangements for accommodation:
    Local family approved by institution
    Self catering/supervised hostel

Average amount required by a student to cover educational 'extras' is £100 per annum

Subject specialities and academic track record: the college has built a solid reputation for maximising students' academic performance and enhancing grades. Careful progress monitoring helps keep pass rates high, normally above 80%.

Examinations offered including Boards: the college is a centre for all examining boards; students are entered for the board which seems most suitable, offering the best chances of success.

Destination/career prospects of leavers: the majority of students go on to a good UK university, some continue in higher education overseas and a few embark directly on a career.

Details of courses: courses are available in all A level and GCSE subjects, with flexible starting dates, although most students begin in September or January. Individual tutorials are an essential part of each student's course, a weekly tutorial being held in addition to four small group seminars. This allows for specific attention to each student's study needs and guidance with individual areas of difficulty. In some cases, a course of entirely one-to-one tuition is arranged. Subject teaching is supported by seminars in 'Study Skills', to emphasise the work habits and techniques essential to success. Residential Easter revision courses are held each year.

Academic and student facilities: the college is in central Oxford, well-placed for bookshops, libraries and transportation. As well as seminar and tutorial rooms there is a private study area with text books

and reference materials, computer room and student common room. Past exam papers, syllabuses and examiners' reports are available for student use; there is a photocopier available in the resources room. The art studio and science laboratories are situated close to the main college premises.

Each student is allocated a personal tutor on enrolment. Regular academic counselling sessions are held with the personal tutor, who also offers advice on higher education options.

Entry requirements and procedures: in order to enrol at the college, students complete a registration form with details of previous schooling and examinations taken. Most attend an interview to discuss their proposed courses with the Director of Studies. Before embarking on an A level course, a student will normally be required to have passed at least four GCSE examinations or their equivalent overseas. In all cases, the college seeks an academic reference from each student's previous school. Once the registration form has been submitted and approved, a certificate of studentship is issued as required.

Aims and objectives of the institution: the college aims to instil a well-organised and responsible approach to academic work by emphasising sound study methods, encouraging students' contribution to the learning process and fostering a close working relationship with academic staff. It stresses the need to be fully aware of the specific requirements of examinations and to use the resources and time available to optimum effect. Students are taught to adopt an intelligent, strategic approach to their work and to develop creative, yet pragmatic thinking skills. The ultimate objective is examination success and the development of a self-motivated work ethic, in preparation for higher education.

Specialists in consultancy, design, production and publication of:

- **Prospectuses**
- **Newsletters**
- **Videos**
- **Magazines**
- **Exhibitions**
- **School Histories**
- **Marketing**
- **Research**

Our experience and quality of craftsmanship enable us to offer a service which we believe is unequalled by any other organisation.

For a prompt quotation with no obligation please telephone, fax or write to:

John Catt Educational Ltd

Great Glemham,
Saxmundham,
Suffolk IP17 2DH

Tel: 01728 663666 Fax: 01728 663415

Sussex

Bellerbys College

44 Cromwell Road, Hove,
East Sussex BN3 3ER
Tel: 01273 723911 Fax: 01273 328445

Arbury Road, Cambridge CB4 2JF
Tel: 01223 517037 Fax: 01223 517038

Principal: L. Denholm, MA, MEd, DipRSA

Courses offered: GCSE, A Level, University Foundation, Business Diploma, Law Degree.

No of students: Male 273 (Hove) 74 (Cambridge) Female 175 (Hove) 38 (Cambridge)

Age range: 15-20+

Nature of tuition: Small groups and one to one (if requested).

Average size of class or group: 10 students

Teacher/student ratio: 1:8

Range of fees per academic year as at 1.1.97:
Tuition: £8150-£9150
Accommodation: £3350 for Homestay

Arrangements for accommodation:
Supervised hostel - single rooms in Cambridge, singles/twins/triples in Hove, some with private facilities. Local family approved by institution.

Details of individual courses:
GCSE courses for 3 or 4 terms. Entry in January, September.
A Level courses for 3, 5 or 6 terms. Entry in January, April, September.
Foundation courses for 3 terms leading to guaranteed university entry on successful completion. Entry in January, April, September.
Business Diploma course for 3, 5 or 6 terms. Entry in January, April, September.
Law Degree course for 3 or 9 terms. Entry in January, September.
Specialist English Language courses also available.

Educational extras: £100 - £550 per annum depending on course (lab fees £50 per subject per term).

Subject specialities: The aim of the Colleges is to prepare international and British students for entry to British university in a friendly and informal atmosphere.

Examinations offered: GCE A Level boards: London, AEB, Oxford, Oxford and Cambridge, Cambridge and JMB English. GCSE boards: London and East Anglia, Southern and Midland and IGCE. The Business Diploma course is validated by the Oxford Delegacy of Local Examinations. The Colleges offer the external LLB of the University of London and the first year of De Montfort University's internal Law Degree.

Destination/career prospects of leavers: Each year over 90% of the College's applicants are placed on honours degree courses such as Law, Medicine, Engineering, Pharmacy and Business at top UK universities.

Academic and student facilities: Bellerbys College Hove is located in Hove, adjacent to Brighton on England's mild south coast. The campus comprises six large houses in a residential area close to the town centre and seafront. There are over 40 classrooms, well equipped laboratories for each science subject, a central library, computer rooms, careers resource centre, student common rooms and restaurant.

Bellerbys College Cambridge has two campuses approximately 3km apart. The newly refurbished (1996) Manor Campus is self-contained with full residential amenities. Well appointed classrooms and laboratories, together with the residence and restaurant occupy buildings on either side of an attractive central courtyard. The Clarendon campus is housed in impressive Victorian premises close to the city centre. Study facilities include lecture and seminar rooms, library, computer room and common room with drink/snack facilities.

Both colleges are just one hour by train from London and within easy reach of London's international airports.

Yorkshire

Harrogate Tutorial College

2 The Oval,
Harrogate,
North Yorkshire HG2 9BA
Tel: 01423 501041
Fax: 01423 531110
E-mail: study@htcuk.u-net.com
Internet: www.harrogate.com/htcuk/

Principal: Mr K.W. Pollard, BSc, DipMath, DipEd

Accredited by BAC. British Council Recognised. Member of CIFE and ARELS.

DFEE Registered Independent School.

Courses offered: wide range of GCE A-level and GCSE. One-year and two-year courses. Intensive September - January A-level retake courses (London/AEB). Easter and summer revision courses. EFL throughout the year.

Summer School: English language and activity holidays.

No. of students enrolled as at 1.1.97:

Male: 40 Female: 40

Age range: 15+

Nature of tuition: Classes/small groups/one-to-one.

Average size of class or group: 4

Teacher/student ratio: 1:3

Range of fees (VAT exempt) as at 1.1.97:
Tuition: 3 x GCE A- level or 5 x GCSE 1-year: £6750; 16-weeks £1500 per subject (includes exam fees). Individual subjects pro rata.

Arrangements for accommodation: with host families, £77 per week, half-board weekdays, full board weekends; £60 per week, weekly boarding.

High quality education in a college close to the town centre. Emphasis on academic success in an informal social atmosphere. Help and advice with university applications.

YOUTH FOR BRITAIN

Volunteering by 16-25 year olds

YOUTH FOR BRITAIN has detailed information about 700 organisations with over 250,000 annual placements for young volunteers throughout the UK and in more than 200 countries abroad

- Qualification and interview details
- Application and start dates; length of projects
- Benefits and costs to volunteers
- Projects for disabled volunteers
- And a mass of other information

Your own requirements instantly matched against those of volunteer organisations. To find the right volunteering opportunity for you, contact:

**Youth For Britain,
Higher Orchard, Sandford Orcas,
Dorset DT9 4RP**

Telephone and Fax: 01963 220036

Youth For Britain is a UK registered charity no 1038253

Wales

WAL

New College

(Founded 1980)

*Bute Terrace,
Cardiff CF1 2TE
Tel: 01222 463355 Fax: 01222 489616
Internet: http://www.new-coll-cf.ac.uk*

Principal: Mr W. Hoole, BSc(Hons), CChem, MPS, PhC

Courses offered:
2-year A levels,
1-year Revision A levels,
1-year Foundation - Law/Engineering/Business,
2-year Advanced GNVQ - Business.

No. of students enrolled as at 1.10.96:
Male 101 Female 60

Nature of tuition: seminar

Average size of group: 1:8

Range of fees (incl VAT) as at 1.9.96:
£2575 per term (2 year courses).
£3455 per term for Intensive Revision Course (one year courses).

The College has its own student Hostel to accommodate 60 students under the care of a resident House tutor. Accommodation costs approx £4000/annum.

New College has a large city centre site and its facilities include nine laboratories, large Computer Suite, Art Room, Professional Drama Studio, Common Room, Dining Room and Library.

Pass rate is approximately 95% (approximately 80% at A, B, C).

Directory of Independent Tutorial and Sixth Form Colleges

Bristol

Bristol

CLIFTON TUTORS
31 Pembroke Road, Bristol BS8 3BE
Tel: 0117 9738376/973 0524
Principal: W P Shaw BA
Type: Co-educational Day B7-19 G7-19

MANDER PORTMAN WOODWARD
10 Elmdale Road, Bristol BS8 1SL
Tel: 0117 9255688
Principal: Ms F A Eldridge
Type: Co-educational Day B15-21 G15-21
No of Pupils: B40 G30
Fees: DAY £810-£2990

Berkshire

Reading

PADWORTH COLLEGE
Reading, Berkshire RG7 4NR
Tel: 01734 832644/5
Principal: Dr S Villazon MA, PhD, FRSA
Type: Girls Boarding & Day G14-19
No of Pupils: G125
Fees: FB £11262-£11262
DAY £5631

Cambridgeshire

Cambridge

ABBEY TUTORIAL
4 Trumpington Street, Cambridge CB2 1QA
Tel: 01223 328686
Principal: Joanne Wilcox MA(Oxon), PGCE
Type: Co-educational Day B18-20 G18-20
No of Pupils: B10 G10

CAMBRIDGE ARTS & SCIENCES
13-14 Round Church Street, Cambridge CB5 8AD
Tel: 01223 314431
Principal: Miss E Armstrong BA(Hons)
Type: Co-educational Boarding & Day B15-19 G15-19
No of Pupils: B6 G9 VIth150
Fees: FB £7000-£12500
DAY £4000-£9000

CAMBRIDGE CENTRE FOR SIXTH FORM STUDIES
1 Salisbury Villas, Cambridge CB1 2JF
Tel: 01223 316890
Principals: Dr A M Dawson MA & P C Redhead MA
Type: Co-educational Day & Boarding B14-19 G14-19
No of Pupils: B16 G10 VIth158
Fees: FB £8927-£13,210
DAY £5510-£8550

CAMBRIDGE SEMINARS TUTORIAL COLLEGE
4 Hawthorn Way, Cambridge CB4 1AX
Tel: 01223 313464
Principal: Dr D Stephenson MA, DPhil
Type: Co-educational Day

ST ANDREW'S PRIVATE TUTORIAL CENTRE
2A Free School Lane, Cambridge CB2 3QA
Tel: 01223 360040/364652
Principal: M J Martin BA, PGCE, MSc
Type: Co-educational Day
Fees: DAY £7650

Devon

Exeter

EXETER TUTORIAL COLLEGE
44/46 Magdalen Road, Exeter, Devon EX2 4TE
Tel: 01392 278101
Principal: K D Jack BA, DipEd
Type: Co-educational Day

Plymouth

PLYMOUTH TUTORIAL COLLEGE (EGAS)
11 Seaton Avenue, Plymouth, Devon PL4 6QJ
Tel: 01752 261229
Principals: B A E Stoyel FCollP, CertEd & M M Stoyel BSc
Type: Co-educational Day

Hampshire

Southampton

WESSEX TUTORS
44 Shirley Road, Southampton, Hampshire SO1 3EU
Tel: 01703 334719
Principal: Mrs J E White BA(London)
Type: Co-educational Day B14-21 G14-21
No of Pupils: B20 G20
Fees: DAY £8225

Winchester

WESSEX TUTORS
14/18 Parchment Street, Winchester, Hampshire SO23 8AZ
Tel: 01962 853964
Principal: Mrs E Backhouse MA(Cantab)
Type: Co-educational Day B15-99 G15-99
No of Pupils: B45 G45
Fees: DAY £960-£1920

Hereford & Worcester

Malvern

THE ABBEY COLLEGE
Wells Road, Malvern, Hereford & Worcester WR14 4JF
Tel: 01684 892300
Principal: L James DipAD, ATC
Type: Co-educational Boarding & Day B12-19 G12-19
No of Pupils: B80 G40
Fees: FB £11,400 WB £8400
DAY £5550

Hertfordshire

St Albans

ST ALBANS TUTORS
30 Beaconsfield Road, St Albans, Hertfordshire AL1 3RB
Tel: 01727 842348
Principal: Mrs Hilary Beskeen BA(Hons)
Type: Co-educational Day

Kent

Broadstairs

PARKER-RODES EDUCATIONAL PROGRAMMES
10 Ranelagh Gardens, Broadstairs, Kent CT10 2T
Tel: 01843 602933
Principal: Miss M Rodes LèsL
Type: Co-educational Day

Rochester

★ **ROCHESTER TUTORS INDEPENDENT COLLEGE**
New Road House, Rochester, Kent ME1 1BD
Tel: 01634 828115
Principals: B Pain BSc (Hons) & Simon De Belder BA (Hons)
Type: Co-educational Day & Boarding B14-50 G14-50
No of Pupils: B75 G75
Fees: FB £10,050 DAY £6900

Tonbridge

THE OLD VICARAGE
Marden, Tonbridge, Kent TN12 9AG
Tel: 01622 832200
Principal: Mrs P G Stevens LRAM(S&D)
Type: Girls Day & Boarding G16-50
No of Pupils: G10
Fees: FB £6900 DAY £3975

Leicestershire

Leicester

IRWIN COLLEGE
164 London Road, Leicester LE2 1ND
Tel: 0116 2552648
Principal: A J Elliott BA, MPhil, TEFL
Type: Co-educational Day & Boarding B14-24 G14-24
No of Pupils: B50 G36
Fees: FB £10,500-£11,850 DAY £5840-£5840

Market Harborough

BROOKE HOUSE SIXTH FORM COLLEGE
Leicester Road, Market Harborough, Leicestershire LE16 7AU
Tel: 01858 462452
Principal: Mrs F Colyer MA
Type: Co-educational Day

London

ABBEY TUTORIAL COLLEGE
28a Hereford Road, London W2 5AJ
Tel: 0171 229 5928
Principal: J Burnett BSc
Type: Co-educational Day B18-20 G18-20
No of Pupils: B45 G45
Fees: DAY £1700-£8000

ALBANY COLLEGE
23-24 Queens Road, London NW4 2TL
Tel: 0181 202 9748/5965
Principal: R J Arthy MPhil, MRIC
Type: Co-educational Day B13-18 G13-18
No of Pupils: B110 G80
Fees: DAY £5000-£7200

★ **ASHBOURNE INDEPENDENT SIXTH FORM COLLEGE**
17 Old Court Place, London W8 4PL
Tel: 0171 937 3858
Principal: Mr M J Hatchard-Kirby MSc, BApSc
Type: Co-educational Day B16-19 G16-19
No of pupils: 150
Fees: DAY £8325-£10,500

BLOOMSBURY COLLEGE
52A Walham Grove, London SW6 1QR
Tel: 0171 381 0213
Principal: S Howse BSc, MSc
Type: Co-educational Day B14-19 G14-19
No of Pupils: B25 G20
Fees: DAY £4500-£6500

COLLINGHAM
23 Collingham Gardens, London SW5 0HL
Tel: 0171 244 7414
Principals: G Hattee MA(Oxon),DipEd
& Mrs G Green MSc
Type: Co-educational Day B14-19 G14-19
No of Pupils: B126 G120
Fees: DAY £2940-£7560

DAVID GAME TUTORIAL COLLEGE
86 Old Brompton Road, London SW7 3LQ
Tel: 0171 584 9097/7580
Principal: D T P Game MA, MPhil
Type: Co-educational Day

DAVIES'S COLLEGE
25 Old Gloucester Street, London WC1N 3AF
Tel: 0171 430 1622
Principal: Andrew Williams BA, MSc
Type: Co-educational Day B15-50 G15-50
No of Pupils: B75 G85
Fees: DAY £4950-£5670

★ **DAVIES, LAING & DICK**
10 Pembridge Square, London W2 4ED
Tel: 0171 727 2797
Principal: Ms Elizabeth Rickards BA, MA, PGCE
Type: Co-educational Day B16-19 G16-19
No of Pupils: B170 G135
Fees: DAY £1605-£8190

DUFF MILLER
59 Queen's Gate, London SW7 5JP
Tel: 0171 225 0577
Principal: C Denning Bsc, PGCE
Type: Co-educational Day B13-18 G13-18
Fees: DAY £4950-£5775

EALING TUTORIAL COLLEGE
28a New Broadway, London W5 2AX
Tel: 0181 579 6668
Principal: Mrs G Watt
Type: Co-educational Day B16-19 G16-19
No of Pupils: B24 G20
Fees: DAY £1600-£8250

FINE ARTS COLLEGE
85 Belsize Park Gardens, London NW3 4NJ
Tel: 0171 586 0312
Principals: Candida Cochrane CFA(Oxon)
& Nicholas Cochrane CFA(Oxon)
Type: Co-educational Boarding & Day B15-20 G15-20
No of Pupils: B40 G60
Fees: DAY £2295-£8985

HURON UNIVERSITY USA IN LONDON
58 Prince's Gate, London SW7 2PG
Tel: 0171 584 9696
Principal: Ms Fay Poosti
Type: Co-educational Day B17-60 G17-60

LANSDOWNE INDEPENDENT SIXTH FORM COLLEGE
7-9 Palace Gate, London W8 5LS
Tel: 0171 6164400
Principal: P Templeton BSc(Econ)
Type: Co-educational Day B16-19 G16-19
No of Pupils: B118 G122
Fees: DAY £5925

MANDER PORTMAN WOODWARD
24 Elvaston Place, London SW7 5NL
Tel: 0171 584 8555
Principals: Miss Fiona Dowding MA & Dr Nigel Stout MA, DPhil
Type: Co-educational Day B14-19 G14-19
Fees: DAY £8661

MANDER PORTMAN WOODWARD
108 Cromwell Road, London SW7 4ES
Tel: 0171 835 1355
Principals: Dr Nigel Stout MA, DPhil
& Miss Fiona Dowding MA
Type: Co-educational Day B15-18 G15-18
No of Pupils: B193 G136
Fees: DAY £8190-£8289

MORLEY COLLEGE
61 Westminster Bridge Road, London SE1 7HT
Tel: 0171 928 8501
Type: Co-educational Day

THE TUITION CENTRE
8 Accommodation Road, London NW11 8ED
Tel: 0181 201 8020
Principal: B Canetti BA(Hons), MSc
Type: Co-educational Day B14-20 G14-20
No of Pupils: B40 G35
Fees: DAY £1450-£6800

WESTMINSTER INDEPENDENT SIXTH FORM COLLEGE
82 Old Brompton Road, London SW7 3LQ
Tel: 0171 584 1288
Principal: Mrs Jane Darwin MA, BLit
Type: Co-educational Day

Greater Manchester

Manchester

ABBEY INDEPENDENT COLLEGE
6 - 12 Fountain Street, Manchester M2 2AA
Tel: 0161 839 7332
Principal: Dominic Jordan BA(Cantab)
Type: Co-educational Day B16-20 G16-20
No of Pupils: B75 G75
Fees: DAY £1575-£6250

EDUCARE COLLEGE
Santaidd, Manchester M19 1DR
Tel: 0161 442 0858
Principal: Dr E J Stewart MSc, PhD
Type: Co-educational Day & Boarding B16-50 G16-50
No of Pupils: B33 G16
Fees: DAY £1345

Middlesex

Harrow

GREENHILL COLLEGE
Lowlands Road, Harrow, Middlesex HA1 3AQ
Tel: 0181 422 2388
Type: Co-educational Day

West Midlands

Birmingham

ABBEY TUTORIAL COLLEGE
10 St Paul's Square, Birmingham, West Midlands B3 1QU
Tel: 0121 236 7474
Principal: K Burn
Type: Co-educational Day

MANDER PORTMAN WOODWARD (B'HAM)
38 Highfield Road, Birmingham, West Midlands B15 3ED
Tel: 0121 454 9637
Principal: Keith Munnings BSc, PGCE
Type: Co-educational Day B14-20 G14-20
No of Pupils: B10 G10 VIth80
Fees: DAY £5850

Northamptonshire

Northampton

BOSWORTH TUTORIAL COLLEGE
9-12 St George's Avenue, Northampton NN2 6JA
Tel: 01604 719988
Principal: M A V Broadway BSc, PGCE
Type: Co-educational Day & Boarding B14-20 G14-20
No of Pupils: B51 G42
Fees: FB £10,700 DAY £5840

Oxfordshire

Oxford

★ **ABACUS COLLEGE, OXFORD**
Threeways House, Oxford OX1 2BJ
Tel: 01865 240111
Principal: Mrs Laraine Brown BA, DipEd
Type: Co-educational Day B15-19 G15-19
No of Pupils: B60 G40
Fees: DAY £2750

CHERWELL TUTORS
Greyfriars, Oxford OX1 1LD
Tel: 01865 242670
Principal: P J Gordon BA, CertEd
Type: Co-educational Day

★ **COLLINGHAM OXFORD**
31 St Giles, Oxford OX1 3LF
Tel: 01865 728280
Principal: Mr A J Shephard MA(Ed Man), BSc, CBiol, MIBiol, CertEd
Type: Co-educational Day & Boarding B13-22 G13-22
No of Pupils: B25 G25
Fees: DAY £2970

★ **D'OVERBROECK'S COLLEGE**
1 Park Town, Oxford OX2 6SN
Tel: 01865 310000
Principals: S Cohen BSc & R M Knowles MA, DPhil
Type: Co-educational Day & Boarding B14-19 G14-19
No of pupils: B130 G120
Fees: FB £10,800 DAY £7200

EDWARD GREENE'S TUTORIAL ESTABLISHMENT
45 Pembroke Street, Oxford OX1 1BP
Tel: 01865 248308
Principal: E P C Greene MA
Type: Co-educational Day

★ **MODES STUDY CENTRE (SCIENCE SPECIALISTS)**
73/75 George Street, Oxford OX1 2BQ
Tel: 01865 245172/249349
Principal: S C R Moore MA(Oxon), DPhil(Oxon)
Type: Co-educational Boarding & Day B16+ G16+
No of Pupils: B52 G41
Fees: DAY £2373-£3450 per subject

★ **OXFORD TUTORIAL COLLEGE**
12 King Edward Street, Oxford OX1 4HT
Tel: 01865 793333
Principal: Ralph Dennison BA, PGCE
Type: Co-educational Day B16-25 G16-25
No of Pupils: B57 G49
Fees: FB £5775-£6600 DAY £2640 per subject

ST CLARE'S, OXFORD
139 Banbury Road, Oxford OX2 7AL
Tel: 01865 552031
Head: Mrs M Skarland BA, PGCE(Manchester)
Type: Co-educational Boarding & Day B16-20 G16-20
No of Pupils: B72 G107
Fees: FB £12,820 DAY £8020

Surrey

Croydon

CAMBRIDGE TUTORS COLLEGE
Water Tower Hill, Croydon, Surrey CR0 5SX
Tel: 0181 688 5284/7363
Principal: D N Wilson BA, MLitt, MIL, FCollP, FRSA
Type: Co-educational Day & Boarding B16-19 G16-19
No of Pupils: VIth199
Fees: FB £10,390 DAY £8050

Dorking

HURTWOOD HOUSE
Dorking, Surrey RH5 6NU
Tel: 01483 277416
Principal: K R B Jackson MA, FRSA
Type: Co-educational Day

Sussex

Brighton

BARTHOLOMEWS TUTORIAL COLLEGE
22-23 Prince Albert St, Brighton, East Sussex BN1 1HF
Tel: 01273 205965/205141
Principal: W A Duncombe BSc
Type: Co-educational Boarding & Day B16-19 G16-19
No of Pupils: VIth40 FB4 WB3
Fees: FB £12,500 DAY £10,000

Hastings

MERCELLES
St Peters, Hastings, East Sussex TN35 4BP
Tel: 01424 813330/812002
Principal: Miss S A Mercel
Type: Co-educational Day

YSV COLLEGE
St Peters, Hastings, East Sussex TN35 4BP
Tel: 01424 813330/812002
Principal: Miss S A Mercel BA(Hons), MIBiol, MRSH
Type: Co-educational Day

Hove

★ **BELLERBYS COLLEGE**
44 Cromwell Road, Hove, East Sussex BN3 3ER
Tel: 01273 723911
Principal: L Denholm MA, MEd, DipRSA
Type: Co-educational Day B15-20 G15-20
No of Pupils: B273 G175
Fees: DAY £8150-£9150

St Leonards-on-Sea

SHELAGAR TUTORIAL CENTRE
1 Avon Court, St Leonards-on-Sea, East Sussex TN38 0SY
Tel: 01424 435501
Principal: P Shelton-Agar DipAM
Type: Co-educational Day

Yorkshire

Doncaster

ST MARY'S COLLEGE
83 Thorne Road, Doncaster, South Yorkshire DN1 2ES
Tel: 01302 811999
Principal: Mrs Anabel Donald MA, MLitt(Oxon), DipHE(Lond)
Type: Co-educational Day B16-20 G16-20
No of Pupils: B10 G16
Fees: DAY £4785

Harrogate

★ **HARROGATE TUTORIAL COLLEGE**
2 The Oval, Harrogate, North Yorkshire HG2 9BA
Tel: 01423 501041
Principal: K W Pollard BSc, DipEd, DipMaths
Type: Co-educational Day B15-25 G15-25
No of Pupils: B40 G40
Fees: DAY £6750

Scotland

City of Edinburgh

BASIL PATERSON COLLEGE - ACADEMIC
Dugdale-McAdam House, Edinburgh EH3 6QE
Tel: 0131 556 7695
Principal: R R Mackenzie MA
Type: Co-educational Day & Boarding B16-99 G16-99
No of Pupils: B24 G19
Fees: DAY £1464-£5858

EDINBURGH TUTORIAL COLLEGE & AMERICAN SCHOOL
29 Chester Street, Edinburgh EH3 7EN
Tel: 0131 225 9888
Principal: Sandy Morris BSc(Hons), MInstP
Type: Co-educational Day & Boarding B16-18 G16-18
No of Pupils: B13 G12
Fees: FB £7930 DAY £4935

WALLACE TUTORIAL COLLEGE
17 Dublin Street, Edinburgh EH1 3PG
Tel: 0131 220 3634
Principal: S A Skotzen BSc
Type: Co-educational Day

Wales

Cardiff

Cardiff

★ **NEW COLLEGE**
Bute Terrace, Cardiff CF1 2TE
Tel: 01222 463355
Principal: Mr W Hoole BSc(Hons), CChem, MPS, PhC
Type: Co-educational Day
No of pupils: B101 G60
Fees: £7725-£10,365

Display Listings of Independent Schools offering Sixth Form entry

Berkshire

Downe House School

*Cold Ash,
Thatcham,
Berkshire RG18 9JJ
Tel: 01635 200286 Fax: 01635 202026*

Head: Mrs E. McKendrick, BA (Liverpool) (as from September 1997)

Member of GSA, ISIS, BSA, ISJC, ISBA

Courses offered: 25 A levels available including Economics, Politics, Theatre Studies, Classical Civilisation, History of Art, Business Studies, Computer Studies. All students take General Studies A level and wide ranging General Course.

No of students: Female: 631

Age range: 11-18

Nature of tuition: Residential Girls' Independent Boarding School. Classes and small groups.

Average size of class or group: 2-12

Range of fees as at 1.1.97:

Day: £3000 per term; Boarding: £4140 per term

Arrangements for accommodation: Fully residential on campus.

Set in 100 acre estate near Newbury, Berkshire. Students achieve exemplary A levels. New Science Block, Sixth Form Centre, indoor pool, facilities for the Arts.

Heathfield School, Ascot

*London Road,
Ascot,
Berkshire SL5 8BQ
Tel: 01344 882955
Fax: 01344 890689*

Head Mistress: Mrs J.M. Benammar, BA, M ès Lettres

Member of GSA, SHA, ISIS, GBGSA, BSA

Accredited by ISJC

Courses offered: 21 subjects to GCSE: English, Mathematics, French and one Science compulsory;

Sciences taught as three separate GCSEs. 24 subjects offered at A level.

No of students: 215 Female

Age range: 11-18

Nature of tuition: Classes, small groups, and one-to-one.

Average size of class or group: 5 in Sixth Form (16 in Junior).

All go on to Higher Education, 100% pass rate at

A level in 1995, 40th in the *Financial Times* top 1000 in 1996.
Teacher/student ratio: 1:7
Range of fees as at 1.9.96: £4375 per term
Arrangements for accommodation: fully residential.
Original Georgian house set in 38 acres has been extended to include new Science block, Art studio, Sports Hall and UVI accommodation. London 30 miles. Heathrow 15 miles.
Heathfield School is a registered charity, and exists to provide a high quality education for girls.

St Joseph's Convent School

Upper Redlands Road,
Reading,
Berkshire RG1 5JT
Tel: 01734 661000

Head: Veronica Brookes, BEd(Hons)
Member of GSA. Accredited by GSA.
Courses offered: 22 subjects offered at A level, many offered at AS. All subjects taught by subject specialists. Centre of excellence for Music and Drama.
No of students: Female 350
Age range: 11-18
Nature of tuition: Classes, small groups, one-to-one.
Average size of class or group: 8
Teacher/student ratio: 1:10
Range of fees as at September 1996:
Tuition: £1355 per term
The School was founded in 1894 by Roman Catholic Sisters and welcomes girls of all denominations. Housed in purpose built building. Sixth Form block.
St Joseph's Convent School Reading Trust is a Charity (No 277077) which exists to advance education.

Cheshire

Stockport Grammar School

Buxton Road,
Stockport,
Cheshire SK2 7AF
Tel: 0161 456 9000

Head: Ian Mellor, MA
Member of HMC, GBA
Courses offered: Advanced Level.
No of students: Male 505 Female 495
Age range: 11-18
Nature of tuition: Classes, small groups, one-to-one.
Average size of class or group: 10
Teacher/student ratio: 1: 10
Range of fees as at 1.1.97:
Tuition: £1362 per term
A traditional academic grammar school, preparing its Sixth Formers for university, with a national reputation for excellent public examination results and wide-ranging sporting and extra-curricular opportunities.
Stockport Grammar School, a registered charity, exists for the education of children.

Cornwall

Truro High School for Girls

Falmouth Road,
Truro,
Cornwall TR1 2HU
Tel: 01872 72830 Fax: 01872 79393

Head: Mr J. Graham-Brown, BA(Hons), MPhil
Member of GSA, SHA

Courses offered: English, Mathematics, Biology, Chemistry, Physics, Art, Computer Studies, Food, Business Studies, French, Geography, German, History, Latin, Music, Religious Studies, Textiles, Photography, Greek, Theatre Studies, Spanish, Italian.

No of students: Female 440 Male 3

Age range: Girls 3-18, Boys 3-5

Nature of tuition: Classes, small groups and one-to-one.

Average size of class or group: 12

Teacher/student ratio: 1:10

Range of fees per term as at 1.1.97:

Tuition: from £899-£1460

Accommodation: Weekly boarding £1170, Full boarding £1205

Arrangements for accommodation: Fully residential on campus.

Truro High School is an independent girls' school set in an area of outstanding natural beauty but also has the benefit of the amenities of the city of Truro.

Truro High School for Girls is a registered charity which exists to give education to children.

Specialists in consultancy, design, production and publication of:

- Prospectuses
- Newsletters
- Videos
- Magazines
- Exhibitions
- School Histories
- Marketing
- Research

Our experience and quality of craftsmanship enable us to offer a service which we believe is unequalled by any other organisation.

For a prompt quotation with no obligation please telephone, fax or write to:

John Catt Educational Ltd

Great Glemham,
Saxmundham,
Suffolk IP17 2DH

Tel: 01728 663666 Fax: 01728 663415

Derbyshire

Ockbrook School

*The Settlement,
Ockbrook, Derby DE7 3RJ
Tel: 01332 673532 Fax: 01332 665184*

Head: Denise P. Bolland BA, MSc

Member of GSA, GBGSA

Accredited by GSA

Courses offered: Full range of A level and AS level courses. All Sixth Form students also complete the Diploma of Achievement (OCEAC), together with courses in IT and PE. Our Sixth are fully involved in the life and running of the school.

No of students: Male 70 Female 390

Age range: 3-18 years

Nature of tuition: Tutor groups, classes, small groups, one-to-one.

Average size of class or group: 7

Teacher/student ratio: 1: 5

Range of fees as at 1.1.97:

Tuition: £3978 per annum
Accommodation: £3414 per annum

Arrangements for accommodation: Fully residential on campus.

Subject specialities and academic track record: 1996 - Top of Derbyshire League Table for GCSE performance. A level pass rate 100%. GCSE pass rate 95%.

Examinations offered: A levels: Art and Design, Biology, Social Biology, Business Studies, Drama, English Literature, Geography, History, Home Economics, Mathematics, Modern Languages, Music, PE, Physics, Chemistry, Religious Studies. Full range of AS levels. Diploma of Achievement and short courses, *eg* French for Business, Photography and Spanish. Some students study for the LLAM Award.

Destination/career prospects of leavers: With one or two exceptions, all our Sixth Formers proceed to higher education. A small number embark upon management training courses.

Academic and student facilities: Our Sixth Form students are accommodated in newly refurbished Upper and Lower Sixth Form centres.

Ockbrook lies mid-way between Derby and Nottingham, off the A52 (junction 25, M1). Easy access to Derby, Nottingham and Loughborough.

Ockbrook School, a registered charity, exists to provide a quality education for pupils aged 3-18 years.

Gloucestershire

Wycliffe College

*Bath Road,
Stonehouse,
Gloucestershire GL10 2JQ
Tel: 01453 822432 Fax: 01453 827634
Internet: http://www.campus.bt.com/
CampusWorld/orgs/org 1656/index.html*

Headmaster: D.C.M. Prichard, MA, FRSA
Member of HMC, ISIS, ISJC
Accredited by DFEE

Courses offered: A levels in all principal subjects plus A level Theatre Studies, Business Studies, Sports Studies. One-year Sixth Form Development Course leading to Certificate in Further Studies.

No of students: Male 260 Female 131

Age range: 13-18

Nature of tuition: Classes, small groups and one-to-one personal tutorials.

Average size of class: 10
Teacher/student ratio: 1:9

Range of fees per term (incl VAT) as at 1.1.97:
Tuition: £2850-£3000
Accommodation: £1200-£1250

Arrangements for accommodation: Fully residential on campus with en-suite study bedrooms for most Sixth Formers. New £1m Dining Hall with tuck shop, café and dance floor. Personal Tutor System.

Numerous awards for academic and sport, music, art, drama and technology. 90%+ proceed to university. 96% pass rate at A level 1996.
90 activities on offer annually. Two miles east M5(J13), two hours from London by road and rail.

Wycliffe College Incorporated is a registered charity and exists for education.

Hampshire

Bedales School

*Petersfield,
Hampshire GU32 2DG
Tel: 01730 263286*

Head: Mrs A.A. Willcocks, MA Cambridge (New Hall), BMus Birmingham

Member of HMC, SHA, SHMIS

Courses offered: Unusually broad curriculum to GCSE - all standard Arts, Humanities and Science at A-Level subjects, as well as Economics, Design and Theatre Studies and Modern Languages.

No of students: Male 200 Female 200 (approx)

Age range: 8-18

Nature of tuition: Lectures, classes, small groups, one-to-one.

Average size of class or group: 15

Teacher/student ratio: 1:10

Range of fees as at 1.1.97:
Day: £3189 Boarding: £4332

Arrangements for accommodation: Fully residential on campus.

Fully co-educational Junior and Senior School set in beautiful Hampshire countryside. High academic standards, and the place of music, arts and crafts is central.

Bedales School is a charitable trust for the purpose of educating children.

North Foreland Lodge

*Sherfield-on-Loddon,
Hook,
Hampshire RG27 0HT
Tel: 01256 882431*

Head: Miss S.R. Cameron, BA

Member of GSA, BSA, SHA, GBGSA

Courses offered: A wide range of A levels in over 20 subjects. A/S level courses and a broad variety of general subjects are also available.

No of students: Female 120

Age range: 11-18

Nature of tuition: Classes, small groups, one-to-one.

Average size of class or group: 5 in Sixth Form (12 in rest of school)

Teacher/student ratio: 1:8

Range of fees as at 1.1.97:

Tuition and accommodation: Day £2350 per term; Boarding £3850 per term

Arrangements for accommodation: Fully residential on campus.

The School is well equipped and is set in 90 acres of scenic parkland. The M3 (J6) and the M4 (J11) are about 10 minutes drive by car.

North Foreland Lodge is a Charitable Trust for the secondary education of girls.

John Catt Educational Limited

Great Glemham, Saxmundham,
Suffolk IP17 2DH
Tel: 01728 663666 Fax: 01728 663415

We specialise in consultancy, design and production of educational publications

St Swithun's School

*Alresford Road,
Winchester,
Hants SO21 1HA
Tel: 01962 861316*

Head: Dr Helen Harvey

Member of GSA

Courses offered: A free choice of 23 A Levels. The General Studies Course provides breadth and girls are encouraged to continue a modern foreign language. All girls go on to Further Education and there is a significant entry to Oxbridge.

No of students: 115 Girls in the Sixth Form

Age range: 16-18

Nature of tuition: Small classes with less formal teaching.

Range of fees as at 1.1.97:
£2330 per term for Day Pupils
£3860 per term for Weekly/Full Boarding

Arrangements for accommodation: Boarding or day pupils.

Purpose-built study facilities are provided for both boarders and day girls. The atmosphere of independence and self-motivation helps to prepare girls for university life.

The School (a registered charity) exists to provide education to girls aged 11 to 18 years.

Hereford & Worcester

Malvern College

*Malvern,
Worcestershire WR14 3DF
Tel: 01684 892333 Fax: 01684 572398
E-mail: inquiry@malcol.worcs.sch.uk*

Head: Hugh C.K. Carson, BA

Member of HMC

Courses offered: More than 20 A level courses, AS courses and the International Baccalaureate.

No of students: Male 428 (223 in Sixth Form) Female 181 (96 in Sixth Form)

Nature of tuition: Classes, small groups.

Average size of class or group: 10-12

Teacher/student ratio: 1: 9

Range of fees as at 1.1.97:
Tuition: £3090 per term
Accommodation: £1160 per term

Arrangements for accommodation:
Fully residential on campus.

Fully co-educational from 3-18, day and boarding school. Beautiful rural setting close to M5 and 40 minutes from Birmingham Airport. New extensively equipped Technology Centre.

Malvern College, a registered charity, exists to provide a quality all round education for pupils aged 3 to 18.

Hertfordshire

Haberdashers' Aske's School for Girls

*Aldenham Road,
Elstree, Hertfordshire WD6 3BT
Tel: 0181 953 4261*

Head Mistress: Mrs P A Penney, BA, FRSA, FIMgt

Member of GSA

Courses offered: A level Art, Classical Civilisation, Economics, English, Geography, History, Latin, Mathematics, Further Mathematics, French, German, Spanish, Music, Religious Studies, Biology, Physics, Chemistry, Technology. Many AS levels.

No of students: 240 Girls in Sixth Form (1145 total)

Age range: 4-18

Nature of tuition: classes and small groups

Average size of class or group: 10-12 in Sixth Form

Range of fees as at 1.1.97: £4410 per annum

Highly academic girls' school with excellent facilities, adjacent to Haberdashers' Boys with whom there are shared activities and a joint transport service (83 routes).

The School is part of the Robert Aske Charity and exists to provide education for girls. Registered Charity No. 313996.

Don't forget to make use of the Reader Enquiry Cards at the back of the Guide if you want more information about the Schools or Colleges listed.

St Edmund's College

*Old Hall Green, Ware,
Hertfordshire SG11 1DS
Tel: 01920 821504*

Head: D.J.J. McEwen, MA(Oxon), FRSA

Member of HMC

Courses offered: A levels and AS levels in 20 subjects; GNVQ Advanced Level Business; GNVQ Advanced Level Art & Design.

No of students: Male 80 Female 60

Age range: 16-19

Nature of tuition: Classes, small groups.

Average size of class or group: 9

Teacher/student ratio: 1: 6

Range of fees as at 1.1.97:

Boarding: £3440 per term

Arrangements for accommodation: Fully residential on campus in twin or single study bedrooms.

400 acre campus in rural Hertfordshire just north of the M25 half-way between Cambridge and Central London. England's oldest Catholic school first founded in 1568.

St Edmund's College, a registered charity, exists to provide Catholic education for children.

Kent

Bedgebury School

*Goudhurst, Cranbrook,
Kent TN17 2SH
Tel: 01580 211221/211954 Fax: 01580 212252*

Headmistress: Mrs L.J. Griffin, BA, BPhil
Member of GSA, ISIS, GBGSA

Courses offered: Exceptionally wide range of 25 A and AS levels including Art, Theatre Studies, Communications, Business Studies and Computing, Interior Design and Product Design. Specialist centre for Art, Ceramics and Jewellery. Sixth Form vocational courses include City & Guilds Fashion, City & Guilds Professional Cook's course, RSA Secretarial, BTEC Business and Finance (Equestrian) and BHSAI Teacher's Certificate offered in our BHS Approved Grade 5 Riding Centre with 50 horses, two indoor schools and cross country course. Access to 1000 acres of forest riding, superb outdoor pursuits with 15 stage assault course, abseiling and climbing wall. Watersports on our 22 acre lake. All Sixth Form take 3-day Personal Leadership course.

No of students in Sixth Form: 97

Age range: 16-19

Nature of tuition: Classes, small groups.

Teacher/student ratio: 1:8 (Sixth Form 1:6)

Range of fees per term (VAT zero rated) as at 1.1.97:
Day £547 to £2332, Boarding £2475 to £3767

Entry: Open entry Sixth Form but proven willingness to work essential.

Details from The Registrar 01580 211954.

Girls' boarding school set in 250 acres of Weald of Kent countryside. New Sixth Form boarding house added in 1991. Easy access London, Gatwick, Heathrow, Channel ports and tunnel.

Bedgebury School is a registered charity providing a widely based Christian education.

Cranbrook School

*Waterloo Road,
Cranbrook, Kent TN17 3JD
Tel: 01580 712163 Fax: 01580 715365*

Head: Mr P A Close, MA, FRSA

Member of STABIS. Grant maintained - DFE

Courses offered: Five year course leading to nine or more GCSEs, followed by three A levels and/or AS levels. 98% pass rate at A level.

No. of students in Sixth Form:
Male: 155 Female: 116

Age range: 13-18

Nature of tuition: Classes

Average size of class: 16 (12 in Sixth Form)

Teacher/student ratio: 1:14

Arrangements for accommodation: Fully residential on campus.

Range of fees at 1.9.96: Tuition: nil

Accommodation: £5100 per annum

Cranbrook is a Grant Maintained Grammar School in the Kentish Weald within one hour of London. High academic standards - excellent drama, music, sporting facilities.

Cranbrook School (GM), a registered charity, existing to promote education in Cranbrook.

Farringtons & Stratford House

*Perry Street,
Chislehurst,
Kent BR7 6LR
Tel: 0181 467 0256 Fax: 0181 467 5442*

Head: Mrs B.J. Stock, BA Hons

Member of GSA, GBSA, BSA

Courses offered: Full range of A, A/S and GCSE courses. A London Chamber of Commerce and Industry "Foreign Languages at work" Commercial French course also available as a one year option with A level. RSA, Pitmans and LCCI keyboard courses and CLAIT.

No of female students: 85

Age range: 16-18 in Sixth Form.

Nature of tuition: Classes, small groups, one-to-one.

Average size of group: 6-8

Teacher/student ratio: 1:5

Range of fees (incl VAT) as at 1.1.97:

Tuition and Accommodation: From £1735 to £3426 per term (depending on whether day or full boarding places)

Arrangements for accommodation: Fully residential on campus for boarders. Day girls accepted.

Set in 25 acres, 12 miles from Central London, near M25 and international airports. New Sports Hall, new Technology Centre, Swimming Pool, Computer Rooms, Careers and FE Service. 94% university entry in 1996. Sixth Form entry: 5+ A*-C GCSEs. Excellent music and drama facilities. Duke of Edinburgh Award Scheme, Young Enterprise.

Registered Charity No. 307916. Farringtons & Stratford House exists solely to provide a high quality, caring education for girls.

Specialists in consultancy, design, production and publication of:

**Prospectuses - Newsletters - Videos
Magazines - Exhibitions - School Histories
Marketing - Research**

For a prompt quotation with no obligation please telephone, fax or write to:

John Catt Educational Ltd

Great Glemham,
Saxmundham,
Suffolk IP17 2DH

Tel: 01728 663666 Fax: 01728 663415

Lancashire

Leicestershire

Arnold School

*Lytham Road,
Blackpool,
Lancashire FY4 1JG
Tel: 01253 346391 Fax: 01253 407245*

Head: Mr W T Gillen, MA

Member of HMC

Accredited by DfE

Courses offered: A full range of subjects in the arts, sciences and modern languages offered to GCSE and A level. Also GNVQ Business and Finance.

No of students: Male 411 Female 402

Age range: 11-18

Nature of tuition: Lectures, classes, small groups and one-to-one

Average size of class or group: 20

Teacher/student ratio: 1:10

Range of fees as at 1.9.96:

Tuition: £3900 per year

A thriving co-educational independent school located one mile from Blackpool airport, and two miles from the centre. One mile from the M55.

Arnold School is a Charitable Trust for the education of pupils aged 3-18 years.

Leicester Grammar School

*8 Peacock Lane,
Leicester LE1 5PX
Tel: 0116 291 0500*

Head: J.B. Sugden, MA(Cantab), MPhil, FRSA

Member of HMC

Courses offered: A levels: Art, Biology, Chemistry, DT, Economics, English, French, General Studies, Geography, German, Greek, History, Latin, Mathematics (Pure, Applied, Statistics), Further Maths, Music, Physics, Physical Education, Religious Studies, Theatre Studies. Various AS levels.

No of students: Male 325 Female 287

Age range: 10-18

Nature of tuition: Classes/small groups.

Average size of class or group: Sixth Form 8; GCSE 14; Lower School 24

Teacher/student ratio: 1:11

Range of fees as at 1.1.97:
Tuition: £4320 per annum

Academic, co-educational, city-centre Sixth Form; average A levels BBB; top co-educational school nationally on A levels 1993; extensive sporting, musical, dramatic, artistic opportunities; compulsory IT and foreign language in LVI; prefectorial responsibilities.

Leicester Grammar School Trust, a registered charity, exists to provide high quality education for local boys and girls.

All abbreviations are explained in the Glossary at the back of this Guide.

Loughborough Grammar School

*6 Burton Walks,
Loughborough,
Leicestershire LE11 2DU
Tel: 01509 233233 Fax: 01509 210486*

Head: Mr D.N. Ireland, MA

Member of HMC

Courses offered: Most A level subjects on offer, plus a number of A/S and GCSE as well.

No of students: 940 - 270 Sixth Form, Boys only

Age range: 10-18

Nature of tuition: Classes, small groups.

Average size of class or group: 9.4

Teacher/student ratio: 1:13

Range of fees as at 1.1.97:

Tuition: Day £4662 per annum
Weekly Boarding/Tuition £7551 per annum
Termly Boarding/Tuition £8586 per annum

Accommodation: Full boarding, weekly boarding and day boy.

Arrangements for accommodation: fully residential on campus.

Top academic results, most boys going on to university, over 20 each year to Oxford and Cambridge. Situated in attractive grounds alongside sister school 11-18, and co-educational Prep School. Excellent facilities, sport, drama, music with close co-operation with girls High School at Sixth Form level, extensive clubs and societies, big emphasis on outdoor pursuits.

Loughborough Grammar School is a Registered Charity which exists to provide high quality education for boys aged 10-18 years.

London

Alleyn's School

*Townley Road,
Dulwich, London SE22 8SU
Tel: 0181 693 3422*

Head: C.H.R. Niven, MA, DipEd, Dr de l'Univ(Lille)

Member of HMC

Courses offered: A Levels: Maths, Further Maths, Physics, Chemistry, Biology, Design & Technology, Computing, French, German, Latin, Greek, Classical Civilisation, History, Geography, Religious Studies, Economics, Business Studies, English, Theatre Studies, Art & Design, Music, Spanish.

No of students: Male 452 Female 472

No of students in Sixth Form: 258

Age range: 11-18

Nature of tuition: Classes, small groups, one-to-one.

Average size of class or group: 10

Teacher/student ratio: 1:10

Range of fees as at 1.1.97: Tuition: £1965

Warm and friendly atmosphere, set in 26 acres. Good transport links including own coaches. High academic standards with excellent facilities for sport and a strong reputation for the performing arts.

An independent co-educational school believing in personal achievement and a well rounded education. Registered Charity No. 1057971.

**A full range of guides to UK Schools
is also published by
John Catt Educational Ltd.**

Blackheath High School GPDST

Vanbrugh Park, London SE3 7AG
Tel: 0181 853 2929 Fax: 0181 853 3663

Head: Miss R.K. Musgrave, MA (Oxon)
Member of GSA

Courses offered: Art, Biology, Business Studies, Chemistry, Classics, Drama, Economics, English, French, Geography, German, Greek (Ancient), IT, Latin, Mathematics, Media Studies, Music, PE, Physics, RE, Science, Technology.

No of students: 616 (70 in Sixth Form)

Age range: 4-18

Range of fees as at 1.1.97:
Senior School £1640 per term
Junior School £1288 per term

Blackheath High School, founded in 1880, is a successful and expanding academic school which offers a broad and stimulating curriculum in a warm and friendly environment. Admission, which is by examination and interview, is competitive and bursaries, scholarships and Government Assisted Places are available. The School is a member of the GPDST and GSA.

Middle School girls (11-14) enjoy a real breadth of studies and at GCSE level a wide variety of subjects is offered, including the separate sciences and Ancient Greek. After A level, almost all pupils proceed to higher education; many achieve success in joining highly competitive professions.

Pastoral and careers education is strong and full use is made of the many facilities which London affords. The sense of community is striking.

The School is housed in a spacious and elegant new home comprising both purpose-built and historic buildings, just off the A2 near Docklands, Greenwich and the Blackwall Tunnel. Pupils do, in fact, come from a wide area stretching from Kent to north of the River Thames. Public transport is excellent and the School is easily accessible by train, bus or private car.

All departments have enjoyed recent major investments in property and pupils are offered really excellent facilities in convenient and attractive buildings.

Visitors are always welcome and the Headmistress likes to discuss each girl's particular needs individually with pupils and parents.

The Girls' Public Day School Trust, a registered charity, No. 1026057, exists to provide an excellent education for girls at a modest cost to parents.

Channing School

Highgate, London N6 5HF
Tel: 0181 340 2328 Fax: 0181 341 5698

Head: Mrs I.R. Raphael, MA (Cantab)
Member of GSA
Accredited by DFEE

Courses offered: 17 academic A levels, including Art and Music, plus AS where demand can be accommodated. A broad General Studies course includes lectures at Highgate School.

No of students: Female 35 per year

Age range: 16-18

Nature of tuition: Classes, small groups.

Average size of class or group: 7

Teacher/student ratio: 1:7

Range of fees as at 1.1.97: Tuition: £1960 per term

Five Assisted Places available for Sixth Form entry.

Set in the heart of Highgate, Channing offers a Sixth Form course tailored to each individual student. Excellent A level results, appropriate university placements, wide-ranging careers.

City of London School for Girls

*Barbican,
London EC2Y 8BB
Tel: 0171 628 0841 Fax: 0171 638 3212*

Headmistress: Dr Burne, BA, PhD, FRSA
Member of GSA

Courses offered: 27 courses are offered at A level; five at A/S level; and there is a range of general studies.

No of female students: 161

Age range: 16-18

Nature of tuition: Classes, small groups.

Average size of class or group: 10

Teacher/student ratio: approximately 1:11 (throughout whole school, 7-18 years)

Range of fees per term (incl VAT) as at 1.9.96: £1809

Details of courses: Girls take three or more A level subjects, chosen from 27 courses including Sciences, Arts, Humanities, Modern Languages and Classics. They also take a General Studies programme which includes public speaking, a lecture series, recreational activities, community service, Information Technology and a Modern Language.

Subject specialities and academic track record: The School has a high academic standard across the Curriculum with a 96.8% pass rate at A and A/S level in 1996, with 62% of passes being at Grade A or B.

Examinations offered (including boards): Most subjects taken use the University of London A level Examination Board. Other Boards used are Oxford, Oxford & Cambridge, AEB.

Destination/career prospects of leavers: Nearly all leavers go on to University; others attend Art colleges, other specialist colleges, or Medical Schools. 14 girls went to Oxbridge in 1996.

Academic and student facilities: Sixth Form life focuses on the impressive new Sixth Form suite which includes a Common Room with refreshment facilities, well equipped Lecture Theatre and study room. The new Lakeside Library and Careers Department are also extensively used. Other facilities include a new Design Technology Centre, computer room, laboratories, art and music rooms, tennis courts, large gymnasium, refurbished indoor swimming pool and assembly hall with modern stage lighting. A recording studio opened in 1993. The School is now on a RM Network.

The School benefits academically and culturally from its location in the Barbican within easy reach of art galleries, museums and other institutions.

Dulwich College

London SE21 7LD
Tel: 0181 693 3601
Fax: 0181 693 6319

Head Master: G.G. Able, MA, MA

Member of HMC, GBA, BSA, ISIS

Courses offered: A levels and AS levels in total of 24 subjects.

No of students: 1380 Male

Age range: 7-18

Nature of tuition: classes and small groups

Average size of class or group: 10 post-GCSE

Teacher/student ratio: 1:11.5

Range of fees as at 1.9.96:

Tuition: £2106 per term

Accommodation: £2106 per term (full); £1936 per term (weekly)

Arrangements for accommodation: fully residential.

Elegant Victorian buildings; impressive modern facilities; leafy suburb, central London five miles. 95% leavers to university; 1996: 27 to Oxford and Cambridge.

Dulwich College is a registered charity, and exists to provide education for children.

Details of Examinations offered by Schools and Colleges appear at the back of the Guide.

Specialists in consultancy, design, production and publication of:

- **Prospectuses**
- **Newsletters**
- **Videos**
- **Magazines**
- **Exhibitions**
- **School Histories**
- **Marketing**
- **Research**

Our experience and quality of craftsmanship enable us to offer a service which we believe is unequalled by any other organisation.

For a prompt quotation with no obligation please telephone, fax or write to:

John Catt Educational Ltd

Great Glemham,
Saxmundham,
Suffolk IP17 2DH

Tel: 01728 663666 Fax: 01728 663415

Francis Holland School

Clarence Gate,
Ivor Place, London NW1 6XR
Tel: 0171 723 0176 Fax: 0171 706 1522

Head: Mrs Pamela Parsonson, MA(Oxon)
Member of GSA, GBSA
Accredited by GSA
Courses offered: 20 A Level courses include Classical Civilisation, Economics, History of Art, Politics, Latin, Greek, Italian and other traditional subjects with 12 offered at AS Level.
No of students: Female 380 (99 in Sixth Form)
Age range: 11-18
Nature of tuition: Classes, small groups.
Average size of class or group: 18 (pre GCSE) and 8 (Sixth Form)

Teacher/student ratio: 1:10.5
Range of fees as at 1.1.97:
Tuition: £5295 per annum

The School, founded in 1878, is near Regent's Park and easily accessible by bus or train (Baker St). The fine building incorporates good provision for Sixth Formers already, and a new Sixth Form Centre was built during 1995.

The Francis Holland (Church of England) Schools Trust Ltd exists to provide high quality education for girls and religious instruction in accordance with the principles of the Church of England and is itself a Charitable Trust (312745).

Francis Holland School

39 Graham Terrace,
London SW1W 8JF
Tel: 0171 730 2971

Head: Mrs Jennifer Anderson, MA (Cantab), MA (London)
From September 1997: Miss Stephanie Pattenden, BA (Durham)
Member of GSA, GBGSA
Courses offered: 18 A level courses include Classical Civilisation, Economics, History of Art, Latin, Music and other traditional subjects. General Studies offered at AS level.
No of students: Female 365 (50 in Sixth Form)
Age range: 4-18
Nature of tuition: Classes, small groups.

Average size of class or group: 8 in Sixth Form
Teacher/student ratio: 1: 9.4
Range of fees as at 1.1.97: Tuition: £6330 per annum

The School, founded in 1881, is on a central site near Sloane Square and is easily accessible by bus or underground. It is very convenient for museums and the Houses of Parliament.

The school is a registered charity which exists to provide high quality education for girls and religious instruction in accordance with the principles of the Church of England. It is a Charitable Trust.

The Godolphin and Latymer School

*Iffley Road,
Hammersmith,
London W6 0PG
Tel: 0181 741 1936 Fax: 0181 746 3352*

Headmistress: Miss Margaret Rudland, BSc

Independent Girls' School

Member of GSA; Accredited by ISJC

Courses offered: 25 subjects to Advanced Level, 14 subjects to Advanced Supplementary Level, and a full General Studies programme.

No of students: 700   Age range: 11-18

Nature of tuition: classes

Average size of class: 6-12 at Sixth Form level

Teacher/student ratio: 1:10 (throughout the school)

Range of fees (incl VAT) as at 1.1.97: £1875 per term

The School stands on a four-acre site, including playing fields, served by excellent public transport. An academic Sixth Form, with most going on to Higher Education.

The object of the Godolphin and Latymer School, a registered charity, is the provision and conduct of a day school for girls.

James Allen's Girls' School

*East Dulwich Grove,
London SE22 8TE
Tel: 0181 693 1181
Fax: 0181 693 7842*

Headmistress: Mrs Marion Gibbs, BA, MLitt

Member of GSA, GBGSA

Courses offered: 26 A level subjects (including Politics, Philosophy, Ancient Greek, Theatre Studies, History of Art, Design and Technology, Italian, Russian). Wide range of AS and General Studies courses. All girls continue with a modern foreign language for the first year.

No of female students: 207

Age range: 16-18

Nature of tuition: Classes, small groups.

Average size of class or group: 9

Range of fees per term (incl VAT) as at 1.1.97:
Tuition: £2050

Dulwich Village, Inner London, twenty-two acres of grounds. Excellent sport facilities, theatre. Sixth form part of school, but has own identity. Academic, very strong Arts and Sciences.

The School has charitable status (No 312750) and exists for the education of children.

**Don't forget to make use of the Reader Enquiry Cards at the back of the Guide
if you want more information about the Schools or Colleges listed.**

John Catt Educational Limited
Great Glemham, Saxmundham,
Suffolk IP17 2DH
Tel: 01728 663666 Fax: 01728 663415

*We specialise in
consultancy, design
and production of
educational publications*

Latymer Upper School

*King Street,
Hammersmith,
London W6 9LR
Tel: 0181 741 1851 Fax: 0181 748 5212*

Head: C. Diggory, BSc, CMath, FIMA, FRSA

Member of HMC, GBA. Accredited by HMC.

Courses offered: A levels in the traditional subjects, Oxbridge, A/S, and General Studies Courses with Games in a strong and diverse extra-curricular provision.

No of students: Male 940; 280 in Sixth Form (including 35 girls from 1996)

Age range: 7-18

Nature of tuition: Small groups.

Average size of class or group: 8

Range of fees as at 1.1.97:

Tuition: £6180. Some scholarships available.

Latymer's Sixth Form would suit hard working and able students seeking excellent tuition and top results. The School is well placed for public transport.

The School has charitable status and provides quality education.

Don't forget to make use of the Reader Enquiry Cards at the back of the Guide if you want more information about the Schools or Colleges listed.

Lycée Français Charles de Gaulle

*35 Cromwell Road,
London SW7 2DG
Tel: 0171 584 6322 Fax: 0171 823 7684*

Proviseur: Henri-Laurent Brusa, Agrégé de l'Université; PhD (English Literature) - La Sorbonne University

Recognised by DfEE

Courses offered: GCSE; GCE A level (Arts and Sciences: seven Modern Languages taught); French Baccalauréat.

No. of pupils: Male 1400 Female 1500

Age range: 4-19

Nature of tuition: Classes.

Average size of class: 10 at A level

Teacher/student ratio: 1:8 for A level/GCSE

Range of fees (incl VAT) as at 1.1.97:

Tuition: Primary £615 per term;
Secondary £1118 per term

The Lycée is a bicultural school with pupils of many nationalities. Most sixth-formers enter University. Pupils with GCSEs are accepted into the school on A level courses.

Specialists in consultancy, design, production and publication of:

**Prospectuses - Newsletters - Videos
Magazines - Exhibitions - School Histories
Marketing - Research**

For a prompt quotation with no obligation please telephone, fax or write to:

John Catt Educational Ltd

Great Glemham,
Saxmundham,
Suffolk IP17 2DH
Tel: 01728 663666   Fax: 01728 663415

Mill Hill School

The Ridgeway,
Mill Hill Village,
London NW7 1QS
Tel: 0181 959 1176 Fax: 0181 906 2614

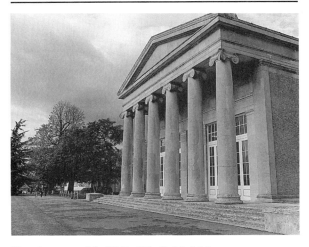

Headmaster: Mr W.R. Winfield, MA
Member of HMC, ISIS, SHA
No of pupils enrolled as at 1.1.97:
Pre-prep (Grimsdell): 120 pupils
Junior (Belmont): 350 pupils
Senior (Mill Hill): 535 pupils
(including Sixth Form: 220 pupils)
Age range: 4-18. Boarders from 11
Teacher/student ratio: 1: 10
Range of fees per annum as at 1.1.97:
Boarding: £12,045
Day: (13-18) £7815, (7-13) £6105
Religious affiliation: Non-denominational

The Mill Hill School Foundation offers education to boys and girls aged three to 18 in its three schools. Founded in 1807, the schools occupy a magnificent 120-acre parkland site only 10 miles from central London and within easy reach of Heathrow airport and motorway, bus and rail links. Boarding for boys and girls starts at the age of 11. The 200 or so boarders form the heart of a vibrant, open and cosmopolitan community, where the contribution of every child is valued.

Curriculum: Boys and girls enter the Senior School at 13 and take GCSEs three years later. Pupils study a wide range of subjects in the first year so that GCSE choices are based on experience. The 'core' subjects are separately setted; the pace and level of teaching therefore suited to individuals' abilities.

All pupils in their first year visit a European city for four days as part of the School's *European Initiative*. Further opportunities exist for up to half those studying French, German and Spanish to spend two or three weeks on exchange. Other pupils take an integrated programme of field work for one week at the School's Field Study Centre in Dentdale, Cumbria.

In the Sixth Form pupils take three or four A levels. Suitable candidates are prepared for entry to Oxford or Cambridge including STEP and S level. Around 90% of Sixth Formers go on to Higher Education; in 1996, the A level pass rate was 92% and 90% for GCSE.

Entry requirements, procedures and scholarships:
13+ entry is by interview, Entrance Scholarship or Common Entrance Examination or own assessment.

16+ entry: Girls and boys can join the Sixth Form where provisional acceptance is dependent on GCSE forecasts, interviews and the previous school's testimonial.

Government Assisted Places are available for 13 year olds and Sixth Formers. The School offers up to 12 academic and music scholarships annually. Further information on registration can be obtained from the Registrar who arranges visits and interviews for all potential pupils and their parents throughout school-time during the week.

Academic facilities: Teachers have their own specialist classrooms. The teacher/pupil ratio of 1:10 means that set sizes are favourable: Lower School sets average 18, Sixth Form sets average 12. The central library, stocked with 15,000 books and five computer terminals, provides excellent facilities for general reading and study, and Departments have their own resource-bases.

The School has over 100 Apple Macintosh computers together with colour printers, scanners and much up-to-date software. These are available to all pupils and are utilised by all departments.

The Music School has 10 teaching and practice rooms, and a Recital Hall and a computerised recording studio. Almost any instrument may be learned and vocal theory and practice studied. The Choir and Orchestra, Chamber Orchestra, Wind Band and Jazz Group perform in concerts throughout the year. Drama is also a high profile activity which involves most pupils at some time in their career.

Extra-curricular activities include a Community Service Group, the Duke of Edinburgh Award

Scheme and a Combined (Army and Navy) Cadet Force. A wide range of societies cater for a variety of interests.

Sports, games and leisure facilities: The School is situated in the Green Belt on the edge of London with 120 acres of parkland. The generous playing fields are matched by a Sports Hall, providing indoor facilities, two swimming pools, tennis and squash courts, Eton Fives courts, an all-weather pitch and an indoor range.

Mill Hill is proud of its strong tradition in its sports. Boys take rugby, hockey and cricket; girls, hockey and netball as their major sports. Competitive excellence is highly valued and the coaching skills are exceptional. In recent years Mill Hill teams have toured Australia, Barbados, South Africa and several European countries. It equally encourages individual sports; regardless of physical prowess boys and girls develop worthwhile skills leading to social participation in later life.

Pastoral care: New pupils are allocated to one of nine Houses, four of which are boarding. The Housemaster/Housemistress is the first link between parents and the School in any matter relating to welfare and progress. Each pupil also has an academic Tutor and close links with parents are maintained through regular meetings and full reports. The School flexi-boarding arrangements enable boarders to go home each weekend if parents wish, alternatively pupils can be fully occupied at Mill Hill. Further parental contact is encouraged through various cultural and social clubs. Links with the outside world are actively maintained, notably through very thorough careers advice and work experience programmes.

In 1995 the Foundation opened Grimsdell, the Mill Hill Pre-Preparatory School, which accepts up to 120 boys and girls in a superbly refurbished house within the School grounds. The Head, Mrs Pauline Mills, and her staff of 15 teachers and assistants provide a modern, integrated learning and activity programme which leads naturally to entry into Belmont, the Junior School (Master, Mr John Hawkins), from which it is expected pupils will pass to Mill Hill, although some may be prepared for entry to other senior schools.

In 1996 a five-year development plan was started involving the three schools of the Foundation to ensure the successful introduction of co-education and a general upgrading of many of the academic, pastoral and extra-curricular facilities in preparation for the educational challenges of the millennium.

The Mount School

Milespit Hill,
Mill Hill,
London NW7 2RX
Tel: 0181 959 3403 Fax: 0181 959 1503

Principal: Mrs Margaret Pond, BSc(Lond), MIBiol

Member of ISA, ISIS, Association of Heads of Independent Schools, Association of Headmistresses

Accredited by Department of Education

Courses offered: English, Maths, three Sciences, History, French, Classical Studies, History of Art, Geography, Business Studies, Economics, Music, Theatre Studies, Music, Spanish, RE, Sociology, Politics, Latin, Italian - flexibility of choice.

No of students: Female 335

Age range: 5-18 (50 in Sixth Form)

Nature of tuition: Classes, small groups.

Average size of class or group: 20 to GCSE; A level average 10

Teacher/student ratio: 1:11

Range of fees as at 1.1.97:
Tuition: £1065-£1250 per term

Arrangements for accommodation: accommodation advice only.

The School is near Mill Hill East Station on Green Belt. Caring, supportive environment. Overseas pupils have English tuition if necessary. Minority Studies encouraged. Careful careers guidance.

The Mount School, a charitable company, exists to promote the advancement of education of girls.

Details of Examinations offered by Schools and Colleges appear at the back of the Guide.

Queen's College, London

W1

(Founded 1848)

*Harley Street,
London W1N 2BT
Tel: 0171 636 2446 (Registrar) Fax: 0171 436 7607*

Patron: HM The Queen Mother
Principal: The Hon Lady Goodhart, MA (Oxon)
Member of GSA, GBGSA
Type: Independent Girls' Day School

Courses offered: The curriculum is designed to meet the needs of the individual. We offer a wide range of A level subjects including Computing, and aim to provide almost any combination, including cross-curricular options. In their first year Sixth Form girls also follow a General Studies course. We prepare girls for entry to Oxford and Cambridge and other Universities and Colleges of Art and Music. Applicants should have five good GCSE grades for entry into the Sixth Form.

Those wishing to apply for scholarships to the Sixth Form should contact the registrar by 1st November of the year before entry.

Age range: 11-18

No of pupils enrolled as at 1.9.96: 386
101 Girls in Senior College (Sixth Form)

Range of fees per annum (incl VAT) as at 1.9.96:
Tuition: £6105

Academic and Leisure facilities include new science and computer laboratories, excellent playing fields in Regent's Park and many and varied visits and outings to museums, art galleries, theatres and other places of interest as well as educational trips abroad.

Queen's College London was the pioneer institution for the academic education of women, providing the first ever qualifications. Started in 1848 by Professor F.D. Maurice, the Christian Socialist, it received the first charter for female education in 1853.

A registered charity, its aim is to promote self motivation and independence of mind within an academic framework.

St Dunstan's College

SE6

*Stanstead Road,
Catford,
London SE6 4TY
Tel: 0181 690 1274
Fax: 0181 314 0242*

Headmaster: J.D. Moore, MA
Member of HMC

Courses offered: A wide range of A level subjects, including Latin, Further Maths, Business Studies, Economics, Theatre Studies, Physical Education, Politics, German and Spanish, supported by a full General Studies programme.

No of students: Male 155 Female 26

Age range: 16-18 (also pupils of 4-16)

Nature of tuition: Classes, small groups.

Average size of class or group: 7.5

Teacher/student ratio: 1:11 in whole school

Range of fees as at 1.1.97:

Tuition: £1790 per term to include lunches

The College is well served by public transport and its own coach services, with many excellent extra-curricular opportunities including a range of sports, drama, music, CCF, Community Service.

St Dunstan's College, a registered charity, exists to provide high quality education for local boys and girls.

Specialists in consultancy, design, production and publication of:

**Prospectuses - Newsletters - Videos
Magazines - Exhibitions - School Histories
Marketing - Research**

For a prompt quotation with no obligation please telephone, fax or write to:

John Catt Educational Ltd

Great Glemham,
Saxmundham,
Suffolk IP17 2DH

Tel: 01728 663666 Fax: 01728 663415

St James Independent School for Girls

19 Pembridge Villas,
London W11 3EP
Tel: 0171 229 2253
Fax: 0171 792 1002

Principal: Mrs Laura Hyde, CertEd
Member of ISA Accredited by ISJC

Courses offered: A levels in English, Mathematics, Further Mathematics, Physics, Chemistry, Biology, History, Law, Economics, Religious Studies, Greek, Latin, Sanskrit, French, Classical Civilisation, Art & Design and Music.
AS Mathematics.
Oxbridge entrance.

No of students: 28-30 Age range: 16-18

Nature of tuition: Small groups, some combined with St James Independent School for Boys.

Average size of class or group: 5-10

Range of fees as at 1.1.97: Tuition: £1665 per term
Sports: Lacrosse, athletics, netball, volleyball, gymnastics, cross-country running, 'The St James Challengers' (adventure training club) and Duke of Edinburgh Award Scheme.

Non-examination subjects: Philosophy, Current Affairs, Singing, Music, Dressmaking, Rhetoric/Debating, Law & Government, Computer Skills, School Orchestra and Drama.

Senior Independent School in Central London with Sixth Forms. The School aims to develop a strong, self-disciplined balance in its pupils which draws on a clear knowledge and understanding of fine principles of human conduct. At Sixth Form level, students are prepared to meet life in society with dignity, generosity and clarity of purpose. Students engage in a vigorous and stimulating programme in a friendly and harmonious environment. Sixth Form study rooms and common room are provided. Unlike the rest of the School, Sixth Form students are not required to wear uniform.

The Independent Educational Association Ltd is a registered charity, the purpose of which is to make the education at St James available to as many children as possible.

St James Independent School for Boys

Pope's Villa, Cross Deep,
Twickenham, Middlesex TW1 4QG
Tel: 0181 892 2002
Fax: 0181 892 4442

Principal: Nicholas Debenham, MA(Cantab)
Member of ISA
Accredited by ISJC

Courses offered: A Levels in English, Mathematics, Further Maths, Physics, Chemistry, Biology, History, Medieval History, Law, Economics, Greek, Latin, Sanskrit, French, Classical Civilisation, Art and Music.

No of students: Male 30-40 in Sixth Form

Age range: 10-18

Nature of tuition: Small groups.

Average size of class or group: 5-6

Range of fees as at 1.1.97:

Tuition: £1665 per term

Secondary Independent School in Twickenham with Sixth Forms. Small enthusiastic groups for A Level. Full school programme includes non-A-Level tuition.

The Independent Educational Association Ltd, a registered Charity, aims to make the education of St James available to as many children as possible.

Specialists in consultancy, design, production and publication of:

Prospectuses - Newsletters - Videos
Magazines - Exhibitions - School Histories
Marketing - Research

For a prompt quotation with no obligation please telephone, fax or write to:

John Catt Educational Ltd

Great Glemham,
Saxmundham,
Suffolk IP17 2DH

Tel: 01728 663666   Fax: 01728 663415

Virgo Fidelis Convent

*Central Hill,
Upper Norwood,
London SE19 1RS
Tel: 0181 670 6917*

Head: Sister Madeleine, BA, DipEd

Member of ISIS

Accredited by ISAI

Courses offered: 14 courses offered in major Arts subjects, the Classics, French, English, History, Art, Music. The Sciences are taught separately. Tuition is in very small groups: from three (or less) to six.

No of students: 150

Age range: 11-18

Nature of tuition: By trained teacher graduate specialists.

Average size of class or group: Lower Sixth: 7; Upper Sixth: 8

Teacher/student ratio: 1:3

Range of fees as at 1.1.97: Tuition: £1425 per term

The School is in a beautiful rural setting. It is ecumenical in outlook, cultivates Christian values with high academic standards. Organises exchanges with French schools.

The Congregation of Our Lady of Fidelity, a registered charity, exists mainly for pupils whose family circumstances render it impossible to meet the standard fee and who desire an independent school and would benefit from it.

YOUTH FOR BRITAIN
Volunteering by 16-25 year olds

YOUTH FOR BRITAIN has detailed information about 700 organisations with over 250,000 annual placements for young volunteers throughout the UK and in more than 200 countries abroad

- Qualification and interview details • Application and start dates; length of projects •
- Benefits and costs to volunteers • Projects for disabled volunteers •
- And a mass of other information

*Your own requirements instantly matched against those of volunteer organisations.
To find the right volunteering opportunity for you, contact:*

**Youth For Britain,
Higher Orchard, Sandford Orcas, Dorset DT9 4RP**

Telephone and Fax: 01963 220036

Youth For Britain is a UK registered charity no 1038253

Middlesex

Halliford School

Russell Road, Shepperton, Middlesex TW17 9HX
Tel: 01932 223593 Fax: 01932 229781

Principal: J.R. Crook, CertEd(Lond), BA(Wales)
Member of SHMIS, GBA
Accredited by DfEE, ISJC
No of students: Male 284
Age range: 11-19
Nature of tuition: Classes, small groups.
Average size of class or group: 7 (in Sixth Form)
Teacher/student ratio: 1:11.8
Range of fees as at 1.1.97: Tuition: £860-£1560
Subject specialities and academic track record: The results of public examinations have improved steadily over the past ten years and promise to continue to do so. In 1996 the pass rate at A level was 91.9%.

Examinations offered: 20 A level and 12 AS level subjects are available in a variety of combinations. They are: Art, Biology, Business Studies, Chemistry, Computing, Design & Technology, Economics, English Literature, French, Geography, German, Government & Politics, History, Latin, Mathematics, Further Mathematics, Music, Physics, Psychology, and Theatre Studies. Extra help is readily available for students who aspire to 'Oxbridge' entry.

Destination/career prospects of leavers: 90% of Upper Sixth students attained university places in 1996. Our interest in our students extends beyond A level. Help and advice are at hand before *and after* the results are published.

Academic and student facilities: Specialist accommodation has recently been built for Science, Information Technology, Art, Music, Design & Technology and Theatre Studies. There are on-site playing fields, an open-air heated swimming pool, a multi-gym and a Sixth Form Centre for relaxation and private study.

Halliford enjoys a delightful location on the banks of the Thames. Recently it has expanded its Sixth Form to include girls and also has Sixth Form teaching arrangements with St David's School for Girls, Ashford.

Halliford School is a Registered Charity which exists for the purpose of providing a high quality education.

St David's School

*Church Road,
Ashford,
Middlesex TW15 3DZ
Tel: 01784 252494 Fax: 01784 248652*

Head: Mrs J.G. Osborne, BA(Hons), DipEd

Member of GSA, GBSA

Courses offered: A levels and/or AS levels in Maths, English, French, German, Geography, History, Physics, Chemistry, Biology, Theatre Studies, Business Studies, Psychology, Computing, Economics, Government & Politics, Art, Design & Technology, Latin.

No of students: Male 50-60 (consortium) Female 45-50

Age range: 16-18

Nature of tuition: Classes, small groups, one-to-one.

Average size of class or group: 5-10

Teacher/student ratio: 1: 5 or 1: 10

Range of fees as at 1.1.97:

Day £1650 per term
Weekly Boarding £2820 per term
Full Boarding £2995 per term

Arrangements for accommodation: Full or weekly boarding available. Fully residential on campus.

Independent girls' school 5-18 (250 in Senior School). Sixth Form consortium with Halliford Boys' School. On main Waterloo to Windsor rail line. Just off M25 and A30. Peaceful and picturesque 30 acres setting.

The Most Honourable and Loyal Society of Ancient Britons, a registered charity, aims to provide education for girls to the age of 18 in the buildings and land of the Society at Ashford, Middlesex.

Northamptonshire

Quinton House School

*Upton Hall,
Upton,
Northampton NN5 4UX
Tel: 01604 752050 Fax: 01604 581707*

Head: Mr G.H. Griffiths, BA, DASE, FRGS

Member of ISAI

Accredited by DfE

Courses offered: Full range of courses to AS and A level including Modern Languages, Sciences, Mathematics, General Studies, Psychology and other subjects to meet pupils needs wherever possible.

No of students: Male 165 (12 in Sixth)
Female 160 (15 in Sixth)

Age range: 3-18

Nature of tuition: Small groups and one-to-one.

Average size of class or group: 1-5

Teacher/student ratio: 1: 2

Range of fees as at 1.1.97:

Tuition: £1287 per term (£3861 pa)

Arrangements for accommodation: advice only.

Set in beautiful parkland on the edge of Northampton, Quinton House School offers sound traditional education in a friendly atmosphere encouraging confidence and personal responsibility.

Oxfordshire

D'Overbroeck's College

1 Park Town,
Oxford OX2 6SN
Tel: 01865 310000 Fax: 01865 552296
E-mail: doverb@rmplc.co.uk

Principals: S. Cohen, BSc
R.M. Knowles, MA, DPhil

Accredited by BAC and ISJC

Courses offered: GCSE and A level. Unusual flexibility in the range and combinations of subjects offered.

No. of students: Male 130 Female 120

Age range: 14-19 (Entry at 13 from September 1998)

Nature of tuition: highly interactive teaching; small groups, on average 5-6 students, with the option of individual tuition where it is deemed necessary.

Range of fees as at 1.12.96:

from £2400 per term (day);
£3600 per term (boarding)

The College provides a unique opportunity to study in a stimulating atmosphere, which is supportive and academically ambitious but less institutionalised than a traditional public school. Students speak readily of the excellence of the teaching, the refreshing rapport with their teachers and of the positive, encouraging and profoundly motivating environment.

A full range of guides to UK Schools is also published by John Catt Educational Ltd.

St Mary's School, Wantage

Wantage, Oxfordshire OX12 8BZ
Tel: 01235 763571 Fax: 01235 760467

Head: Mrs S. Bodinham, BSc, AKC, AdvDipEd
Member of GSA, BSA, GBGSA

Accredited by DfEE

Courses offered: wide and flexible options are offered. A level subjects include History of Art, Theatre Studies, Classical Civilisation, Economics, Business Studies and Politics. AS level or Mature GCSE subjects can be combined with A levels, as can parts of the Office Technology and Administration Course. Girls can also choose from a wide selection of extra courses in practical subjects, languages and sports activities, *etc*. All girls follow Personal Development and Ethics courses.

1, 2 and 3 year courses available. Direct A level entry or Foundation Course for those who have not reached the required A level entry.

Entry requirements: Five GCSE passes (including English Language).

No of students: Female 225

Age range: 11-18

Nature of tuition: Small groups

Average size of class or group: 6

Teacher/student ratio: 1:6
Range of fees as at 1.1.97: Boarding: £3850 per term
Arrangements for accommodation: Fully residential on campus.
The School is situated on a continuous site in a small market town at the foot of the Downs, with easy access to the M4 and airports.
This Church of England school, a registered charity, exists to provide full boarding education for girls aged 11-18.

Shropshire

Moreton Hall

Weston Rhyn,
Oswestry,
Shropshire SY11 3EW
Tel: 01691 773671 Fax: 01691 778552

Head: Jonathan Forster, BA, FRSA
Independent Girls' Boarding and Day School
Age range: 10-18. Boarders from 10
No. of pupils enrolled as at 1.1.97: 280
Senior: 190; Sixth Form: 90
Fees per annum:
Day: £8100; Boarding: £11,700
Religious denomination: Church of England
Member of SHA, GSA, GBGSA, ISCO, ISIS
Details of courses: All A level courses, including Russian, Greek, Spanish and Theatre Studies.
Subject specialities and academic track record: Choices 50-50 Arts - Science. Specialist subjects, History of Art, Russian, Theatre Studies. Sixth form encouraged to take Modern Languages, Information Technology, Spoken English plus A levels. GNVQ Leisure & Tourism.
Examinations offered including Boards: A levels: Physics, Latin, Spanish, French, Chemistry, Home Economics, Italian, Biology, Music, English Literature, Statistics, History, Social and Environmental Biology, Art and Design, Business Studies, History of Art, Geography, German, Russian, Mathematics. GNVQ: Leisure & Tourism. AS levels: Physics, Biology, Music. Boards include Oxford, NEAB, AEB, LEAC.
Destination/career prospects of leavers: Over 90% take degree courses. Media, Business Studies, Science, Medicine, Law.
Academic and student facilities: New IT Centre. All Sixth form in study bedrooms. Upper Sixth in separate Hall of residence. Sixth form bar, Leisure Centre, Midland Bank, Students Union (Fax, photocopier), Seminar rooms, tutor system, Careers advice six days per week. Opportunity to work in

Wychwood School

74 Banbury Road,
Oxford OX2 6JR
Tel: 01865 557976 Fax: 01865 556806

Principal: Mrs M.L. Duffill, CertEd
Member of GSA
Accredited by GSA
Courses offered: All standard A level courses offered. Minority subjects *eg* Classical Civilisation, Economics are offered if three or more girls are interested.
No of students: Female 33 (in the Sixth Form)
Age range: 16-18
Nature of tuition: Classes, small groups and one-to-one.
Average size of class or group: 6
Teacher/student ratio: 1:4
Financial Times League Table of 1000 top schools, Wychwood placed 199.
Range of fees as at 1.9.96:
Day £1510, Full Boarding £2395,
Weekly Boarding £2310
Arrangements for accommodation: Fully residential on campus.
Six Assisted Places available in Sixth Form.
Wychwood is situated in the City of Oxford. This enables students to use all the art, music and cultural facilities of this university town.
Wychwood School is a Charitable Trust set up for educational purposes.

Travel Centre or Midland Bank training centre. Own farm run by Sixth form.

Energetic, enterprising. 100 acre grounds, 17 miles from Shrewsbury. Links with Shrewsbury School. Art, Music, Drama, Sport. Outstanding academic results to match.

Moreton Hall Educational Trust Ltd, a registered charity, exists to provide high quality education for girls.

Oswestry School

*Upper Brook Street,
Oswestry,
Shropshire SY11 2TL
Tel: 01691 655711 Fax: 01691 671194*

Head: P.K. Smith, MA(Cantab), MEd, FRGS
Member of SHMIS, SHA, IAPS, ISIS
Accredited by ISJC

Courses offered: A levels in all principal subjects plus A level Latin, Greek, Music, Sports Studies, Business Studies. One year Sixth Form Development course leading to Diploma of Achievement plus Leadership and Interview training.

Age range: 9-18

Nature of tuition: Lectures, classes, small groups, one-to-one.

Average size of class or group: 12

Teacher/student ratio: 1:8

Range of fees as at 1.9.96:

Tuition: £1698 per term inclusive (up to age 11); £1850 per term inclusive (from age 11)

Scholarships available (academic, music, art, sport).

Arrangements for accommodation: Fully residential on campus. Separate self-contained Sixth Form Boarding Houses for boys and girls.

Founded in 1407. Attractive site overlooking Shropshire plain but within walking distance of market town. Easy access to Birmingham and Manchester airports.

Oswestry School is a non-denominational foundation and registered charity existing to provide young men and women the best possible education and preparation for life.

Somerset

Bruton School for Girls

*Sunny Hill,
Bruton,
Somerset BA10 0NT
Tel: 01749 812277 Fax: 01749 812537*

Headmistress: Mrs J.M. Wade, MSc

No of students: 540; Sixth Form 94

Age range: 8-18

Sixth Form fees per annum:

Day: £4011, Boarding: £7761

Scholarships: Details of the Government Assisted Places, Academic and Music Scholarships which are available may be obtained from the Registrar.

Sixth Form Entry requirements: Five GCSE grades of C or above. Offers are based on forecast GCSE grades, report from the present school and interview.

We offer A level courses in recognised principal subjects as well as Business Studies, Design Technology and Theatre Studies. These are complemented by AS subjects, a General Studies course, a wide range of extra-curricular activities and comprehensive careers advice. Our A level results are excellent and our pupils proceed to a wide variety of university courses.

We can offer Scholarships, Bursaries and Government Assisted Places for pupils entering the School at this stage. Further details can be obtained from the Registrar.

Bruton School for Girls Charitable Trust exists to provide education for girls.

All abbreviations are explained in the Glossary at the back of this Guide.

Sidcot School

*Winscombe,
North Somerset BS25 1PD
Tel: 01934 843102 Fax: 01934 844181*

Principal: Dr Christopher Greenfield, MA, MEd
Member of GBA, SHMIS
Accredited by ISJC
Courses offered: Wide range of GCSE, GNVQ, A Level and AS Level courses.
No of students in Sixth Form: Male 63 Female 62
Age range: 9-18 (in whole school of 410)
Nature of tuition: Lectures, classes, small groups, individual tuition/independent study facilities also available.
Average size of class or group: 15; 9 at A Level
Teacher/student ratio: 1:10
Range of fees as at 1.1.97:
Tuition: £1975 per term - 3 terms per year
Accommodation: £1335
Arrangements for accommodation: Fully residential on campus.
In rural North Somerset, Sidcot offers a supportive environment for boarders and day scholars of both sexes. Individuality is combined with excellent examination success.
Sidcot School Charitable Trust exists to provide education for boys and girls up to University level.

Specialists in consultancy, design, production and publication of:

- **Prospectuses**
- **Newsletters**
- **Videos**
- **Magazines**
- **Exhibitions**
- **School Histories**
- **Marketing**
- **Research**

Our experience and quality of craftsmanship enable us to offer a service which we believe is unequalled by any other organisation.

For a prompt quotation with no obligation please telephone, fax or write to:

John Catt Educational Ltd

Great Glemham,
Saxmundham,
Suffolk IP17 2DH

Tel: 01728 663666 Fax: 01728 663415

Surrey

Caterham School

*Harestone Valley Road,
Caterham, Surrey CR3 6YA
Tel: 01883 343028 Fax: 01883 347795*

Headmaster: Mr R.A.E. Davey, MA (Dublin)
Member of HMC Accredited by DfE

Courses offered: A levels and some A/S courses. All students take three or four A level subjects or the equivalent.

No of students: Male 500 Female 200
(Sixth Form 210)

Age range: 11-18

Nature of tuition: classes

Average size of class: 10

Teacher/student ratio: 1:10

Range of fees per term (incl VAT) as at 1.9.96:
Tuition: Day £2030; Boarding £3710-£3910
Scholarships and Assisted Places available.

Arrangements for accommodation: Fully residential on campus.

Details of individual courses: A level subjects: English Literature, French, German, Latin, Greek, Spanish, Classical Civilisation, History, Religious Studies, Mathematics, Further Mathematics, Physics, Chemistry, Biology, Human Biology, Geography, Economics, Business Studies, Music, Art, CDT. Some of these subjects are available as AS courses. The subjects may be taken in many combinations timetabled to meet demand.

Subject specialities and academic record: 98% pass rate at A level. 82% of grades A, B, C.

Examinations offered: A levels and some AS primarily of the University of London Board. RSA - Information Technology.

Destination/career prospects: Almost all students go on to Further Education (98% in 1996).

Academic and student facilities: The academic

departments of the School are well resourced and additionally there are two networked IT rooms and a modern staffed library. Caterham offers a wide range of sporting activities (principal games: Rugby, Netball, Hockey and Cricket). Music at the School is expressed through choirs and orchestras. There is a lively Drama department and 25 clubs and societies.

Situated on an eighty-acre wooded valley site in the North Downs. The School is a day and boarding school for boys and girls from 11-18.

Recently the School's facilities have been enhanced by a £3 million development plan. This included:

1. A new teaching block of 24 classrooms allowing to teach in faculties.
2. A new sports centre opened by Sebastian Coe on 7th November 1996.
3. An Astroturf pitch.
4. A new girls boarding house.

Caterham School is a registered charitable trust which aims to provide a high quality all-round education in a caring Christian context.

King Edward's School, Witley

Godalming,
Surrey GU8 5SG
Tel: 01428 682572 Fax: 01428 682850

Head Master: R.J. Fox, MA, CMath, FIMA
Member of HMC

Courses offered: A level Biology, Chemistry, Physics, Maths, English, French, German, Economics, Business Studies, Classics, Religious Studies, Art, History, Geography, CDT, Theatre Studies.

No of students in Sixth Form: Male 82 Female 64

Age range: 16-18 (Sixth Form)

Nature of tuition: Small groups.

Average size of class or group: 12 (depending on subject)

Teacher/student ratio: 1:8

Range of fees as at 1.1.97: £3150 per term

Arrangements for accommodation: Fully residential.

Set in 100 acres on the Surrey/Sussex/Hants border. One hour from Heathrow and Gatwick, and 50 minutes by rail from Waterloo. Superb modern facilities.

King Edward's School, Witley, a registered charity, provides a structured education with superb facilities and offers substantial bursaries for families with boarding need.

Looking for a school ?

John Catt publish a range of guides covering British independent and maintained schools together with helpful advice and editorials for parents seeking preparatory, secondary or further education for their children.

• *Which School ?* •

comprehensive guide to day, boarding, preparatory or secondary independent schools in the UK

Which School? in East Anglia • Which School? for A Levels
Which School? The Midlands & Wales
Which School? The South-West • Education after Sixteen
Which School? The North • Guide to Boarding Schools
Which London School? • Which School? for Special Needs
Schools in Scotland • Maintained Secondary Schools

Published by

John Catt Educational Ltd

Great Glemham, Saxmundham,
Suffolk IP17 2DH
Tel: 01728 663666 Fax: 01728 663415

Specialists in consultancy, design, production and publication of:

Prospectuses - Newsletters - Videos
Magazines - Exhibitions - School Histories
Marketing - Research

For a prompt quotation with no obligation please telephone, fax or write to:

John Catt Educational Ltd

Great Glemham,
Saxmundham,
Suffolk IP17 2DH

Tel: 01728 663666 Fax: 01728 663415

Prior's Field

*Godalming,
Surrey GU7 2RH
Tel: 01483 810551
Fax: 01483 810180*

Headmistress: Mrs J.M. McCallum, BA
Member of GSA, GBGSA
Courses offered: GCSE, GCSE retakes, A level, A/S level, Oxbridge entry. Secretarial Studies, RSA, Pitmans.
No of students: Female: Total 230 Sixth Form 40
Age range: 11-18
Nature of tuition: Classes, small groups.
Average size of Sixth Form class or group: 5
Teacher/student ratio: 1:4.8 (Sixth Form)
Range of fees (incl VAT) as at 1.9.96:
Tuition: £2289; Accommodation: £1140
Arrangements for accommodation: Fully residential on campus.
Academic Scholarships.

Prior's Field Sixth Form has grown by more than 100% in the last ten years. The students live in Huxley House, designed to provide accommodation similar to a university hall of residence with a kitchen, large common room and IT facilities. Each Sixth Former has a single study bedroom.

The School is situated half a mile from the A3 and from Charterhouse, three miles from Guildford. Transfer to Heathrow and Gatwick is arranged and a bus service to London is operated for weekly boarders.

Academic standards are high and most girls proceed from the School into higher education. The School is extremely successful on a regional level at public speaking, Young Enterprise Business, and tennis. Sixth Formers often participate in the Duke of Edinburgh Award Scheme. Theatre Studies, Business Studies and Media Studies at A level have been introduced in recent years and many girls continue into journalism, Drama and Art school. Oxbridge entrants receive special tuition.

A levels are taught in small groups and fieldwork in the United Kingdom and Europe and visits to London lectures and theatres are encouraged. Sixth Form students often take the responsibility for younger pupils on an informal basis for recreational activity.

Prior's Field School Trust is a registered charity. Its aim is to provide a sound academic education for girls in a friendly environment. Scholarships at Sixth Form level are competed for by examination (or portfolio for Art and Photography) in the Autumn term prior to entry.

John Catt Educational Limited

Great Glemham, Saxmundham,
Suffolk IP17 2DH
Tel: 01728 663666 Fax: 01728 663415

*We specialise in
consultancy, design
and production of
educational publications*

The Royal School

*Farnham Lane,
Haslemere,
Surrey GU27 1HQ
Tel: 01428 605805 Fax: 01428 607451*

Head: Mr Colin Brooks, BA(Hons), AdDipEd, CertEd, FRGS, FRMetS

Member of GSA, GBGSA

Courses offered: A levels, AS levels, Extra GCSEs, Advanced Information Technology, variety of language courses; BHSAI course.

No of students: Female 65

Age range: 16-18

Nature of tuition: Small groups.

Average size of class or group: 6

Teacher/student ratio: 1: 6

Range of fees as at 1.1.97:

Tuition: £2019 per term
Accommodation: £1150 per term

Arrangements for accommodation: Fully residential on campus.

Details of courses: A levels: Art, Design Technology, Economics & Business, English Literature, Geography, History, Mathematics, Further Mathematics, Media Studies, French, German, Spanish, Music, Psychology, Religious Studies, Biology, Chemistry, Physics, General Studies; most subjects can be taken at AS level by negotiation. Range of extra GCSEs: Drama, Statistics, Psychology, PE, Languages. Advanced I.T. course. Variety of language courses. BHSAI (British Horse Society Assistant Instructors) course.

Subject specialities and academic track record:
1995: 93% A-E, 70% A-C, 93% go on to degree courses
1996: 97% A-E, 87% A-C, 90% go on to degree courses

Examinations offered including Boards: A level Boards include ULEAC, AEB, NEAB, Cambridge. Cambridge Advanced IT Certificate. British Horse Society Assistant Instructors Certificate.

Destination/career prospects of leavers: Almost all girls proceed to degree courses at well-established universities. 1996 - 55% Arts courses, 17% Social Science courses and 28% to Science courses.

Academic and student facilities: Each study/bedroom is equipped for independent research using the most up-to-date technology. Joint ventures with other schools and a stimulating extra-curricular programme of visits and lectures ensure breadth and a challenging intellectual dimension alongside excellent A level teaching.

The Royal School occupies a superb site in an area of outstanding natural beauty in Surrey, convenient for the main airports and London.

The Royal School is a Registered Charity providing high quality education for girls.

Specialists in consultancy, design, production and publication of:

- Prospectuses
- Videos
- Exhibitions
- Marketing
- Newsletters
- Magazines
- School Histories
- Research

Our experience and quality of craftsmanship enable us to offer a service which we believe is unequalled by any other organisation.

For a prompt quotation with no obligation please telephone, fax or write to:

John Catt Educational Ltd

Great Glemham,
Saxmundham, Suffolk IP17 2DH
Tel: 01728 663666   Fax: 01728 663415

St Catherine's School

*Bramley, Guildford,
Surrey GU5 0DF
Tel: 01483 893363 Fax: 01483 893003*

Principal: Mrs C.M. Oulton, MA (Oxon)
No of students:
Junior: 185; Senior: 376; Sixth Form: 103

Age range: 4-18

Middle and Senior fees per annum as at 1.1.97:
Day: £6300, Boarding: £10,350

Quality is the key to St Catherine's. There are about 450 girls in the Senior School, of whom about one quarter are full or weekly boarders. Nearly half of the Sixth Form board, attracted by the superb facilities and wide range of activities available for older girls. The purpose-built Centenary Building offers a high level of comfort and good study conditions. Almost every girl goes on to university, and there is a regular Oxbridge entry. 21 subjects are offered at A level; General Studies is taken in the Lower Sixth as an AS level, and many other subjects are also offered at AS level to ensure girls the widest possible choice of study.

St Catherine's success rate at GCSE and A level is outstanding, due in part to the fine quality of the teaching, and to the individual attention received by every girl; maximum numbers for a Sixth Form group are 12, but in fact many subjects are taught in much smaller groups, where individual difficulties can be discussed and resolved. Art, music, sport and drama are fostered, and Sixth Formers have recently achieved success in lacrosse at county and national level (the Head of PE at St Catherine's is an all-England lacrosse coach, and another member of the PE department coaches the Junior England netball team). Seven girls currently play in County lacrosse teams, and Sixth Formers also play netball and squash at County level. A tour of Australia is currently being organised for senior netball and lacrosse players; 25 girls will be involved during the summer holidays in 1997.

Music is an important feature of school life, with several choirs, an orchestra and two concert bands practising each week and performing in concerts and recitals. St Catherine's senior choir has sung recently in Italy and the Czech Republic; the choir also joins the choir of Cranleigh School (its brother school) in local and charity concerts, and each year the Choral Society gives a major performance. Inter-House and inter-School debates are organised. There is a popular 'Play in a Day' group and Young Enterprise flourishes, at school and regional level. Work experience is an important feature of life in the Lower Sixth, and girls this year have travelled as far as Brussels, Vienna and New York to broaden their horizons. Visits to Sixth Form Study days, conferences and museums are encouraged, and girls are given guidance on careers and options for study at university throughout the Sixth Form.

St Catherine's is fortunately located at the heart of the attractive Surrey village of Bramley. The fine original school buildings are complemented by new classrooms and laboratories, and a new Creative Arts workshop was opened in June 1996. A state-of-the-art drama studio, built on the site of the old art rooms is now used by all the girls.
St Catherine's is set in extensive grounds, with an indoor swimming pool, gymnasium, floodlit netball and tennis courts and lacrosse pitches on site. Guildford, with its excellent facilities, and main-line station, is three miles away. Access to Gatwick and Heathrow is easy via the A3 and M25, and travel arrangements are made for overseas boarders. Girls also attend from a wide catchment area in the South East; many use the daily coach service to and from Farnham and Woking.

St Catherine's places great emphasis on providing a fully supportive and friendly boarding and day atmosphere, and a network of house mistresses and personal tutors provide pastoral support. Girls are encouraged and expected to work hard to achieve their full potential both in the classroom and out of it. High standards of behaviour are expected, and good manners are fostered.

The Corporation of Cranleigh and Bramley Schools is a registered charity (No 312039). Teaching at St Catherine's, as detailed in its 'Object' is in accordance with the principles of the Church of England, and the School has its own attractive Chapel in the grounds.

West Sussex

Farlington School

*Strood Park,
Horsham,
West Sussex RH12 3PN
Tel: 01403 254967/263068 Fax: 01403 272258*

WSX

Age range: 4-18

Nature of tuition: Classes, small groups, one-to-one.

Average size of class or group: 14

Teacher/student ratio: 1: 7

Range of fees as at 1.1.97:

Tuition: £885-£2030 per term
Accommodation: £1260 per term

Arrangements for accommodation: Fully residential on campus in boarding house.

No uniform required in Sixth Form.

Situated in 34 acres of parkland on Surrey-Sussex border, 20 minutes from Gatwick Airport. A level pass rate 98.5% in 1996. National Schools Riding Association Champions for fifth year.

Farlington School exists for the purpose of educating girls.

Head: Mrs P.M. Mawer, BA

Member of GSA, BSA

Accredited by ISJC

Courses offered: Broadly-based academic curriculum. Wide range of subjects offered at GCSE; 18 subjects at A level, including Sociology and Theatre Studies. General Studies AS studied by all Sixth Formers.

No of students: Female 350 (50 in Sixth Form)

Wiltshire

The International School of Choueifat UK

*Ashwicke Hall,
Marshfield,
Wiltshire SN14 8AG
Tel: 01225 891841 Fax: 01225 891011
Email: isc-uk@cityscape.co.uk
Internet: http://www.sabis.com/school-network*

Director: Mr Salah Ayche

Courses offered: English Language and Literature, Arabic Language and Literature, French, Mathematics, Further Maths (Pure & Applied), Physics, Chemistry, Biology, History, Economics, Statistics, Art.

No of students: Male 100 Female 20

Age range: 9-18

Nature of tuition: Classes

Average size of class or group: 12

Teacher/student ratio: 1:7

Range of fees as at 1.9.96: £3100-£3300 per term (This is exclusively a boarding school)

Arrangements for accommodation: Fully residential on campus.

Situated in 150 acres of woodlands in the heart of lush Wiltshire. Offers courses leading to IGCSE and A-Levels, SAT I, SAT II and Advanced Placement. Also offers intensive courses to students with academic problems or students wishing to transfer from the national curriculum to the English or American systems.

Yorkshire

Pocklington School

(Founded 1514)

*West Green, Pocklington,
York YO4 2NJ
Tel: 01759 303125 Fax: 01759 306366*

Headmaster: J.N.D. Gray, BA

Member of HMC. Accredited by HMI.

Courses offered: Full range of A level subjects, including Design and Technology, Latin and Greek, Theatre Studies.

No of students: Male 460 Female 301

Age range: 7-18

Nature of tuition: Classes.

Average size of class: 20 up to GCSE; Sets for A level

Teacher/student ratio: 1:12

Range of fees per term (incl VAT) as at 1.9.96:
Tuition: 7+: £1009; 8-18: £1703
Accommodation (11 to 18): £1265

Arrangements for Boarding: Fully residential on campus.

Set in 70 acres on the edge of a market town; noted for high academic achievement, music, sport, art and design; lively and friendly boarding community.

Pocklington School is a registered charity and exists to provide education for young people.

Details of Examinations offered by Schools and Colleges appear at the back of the Guide.

Sheffield High School GPDST

*10 Rutland Park,
Sheffield S10 2PE
Tel: 0114 266 0324 Fax: 0114 267 8520*

Head: Margaret Houston, BA, PGCE

Member, Girls' Public Day School Trust

Courses offered: 26 subjects at A and AS level, Careers, Information Technology, Young Enterprise, Understanding Industry, PE, Work Experience, Community Service and extra-curricular courses.

No of students: 563 Girls (117 in Sixth Form)

Age range: 11-18

Nature of tuition: Classes, small groups and (where appropriate) one-to-one.

Average size of class or group: 10

Teacher/student ratio: 1:13

Range of fees as at 1.1.97:

Tuition: £1380 per term all inclusive - no extras.

The Sixth Form encourages and achieves very high academic standards and gives excellent careers advice. The Sixth Form Centre provides opportunities for work, relaxation and friendship.

The Girls' Public Day School Trust (Sheffield High School) exists for the education of girls.

St Hilda's School

*Sneaton Castle,
Whitby,
North Yorkshire YO21 3QN
Tel: 01947 600051 Fax: 01947 603490*

Principal: Mrs Mary Blain, BEd, MA

Member of: ISA, ISIS

Accredited by ISJC

Courses offered: 19 GCSEs, 21 A levels. Word Processing/IT Skills.

No. of students: Male 78 Female 146

Age range: 2-18

Nature of tuition: Classes, small groups.

Average size of class: 15

Teacher/student ratio: 1:8

Range of fees at 1.9.96:

Tuition (Day): £940 to £1600 per term
Tuition and Accommodation (Boarding): £2475 to £2950 per term

Arrangements for accommodation: Fully residential on campus.

Small Independent, Christian School set in beautiful countryside. The atmosphere of the School is a well disciplined family environment. High standards of work are expected and good results achieved.

St Hilda's School is a registered charity and exists to provide a sound Christian education to boys and girls of any denomination.

Specialists in consultancy, design, production and publication of:

**Prospectuses - Newsletters - Videos
Magazines - Exhibitions - School Histories
Marketing - Research**

For a prompt quotation with no obligation please telephone, fax or write to:

John Catt Educational Ltd
Great Glemham,
Saxmundham,
Suffolk IP17 2DH

Tel: 01728 663666 Fax: 01728 663415

Northern Ireland

Scotland

Friends' School, Lisburn

*6 Magheralave Road,
Lisburn, Co Antrim,
N Ireland BT28 3BH
Tel: 01846 662156 Fax: 01846 672134
E-mail: libfsl@rmplc.co.uk*

Head Master: J T Green, MA
Member of Governing Bodies Association, Boarding Schools Association
Accredited by DENI (Dept of Education N.I.)
Courses offered: 19 subjects are offered at GCSE and 19 at A level, plus three at A/S. Pupils are also entered successfully each year for Oxford and Cambridge. A wide range of non-examination courses is also available in the Sixth Form.
No of students: Male 457 Female 488
Age range: 11-18
Nature of tuition: classes
Average size of class or group: 20
Teacher/student ratio: 1:16
Range of fees as at 1.1.97:
Tuition: £0 - £2607 p.a. (Children of EC Nationals do not pay tuition fees)
Accommodation: £3328 p.a. (Termly); £3198 p.a. (Weekly)
Arrangements for accommodation: Fully residential.
Friends' School Lisburn, a registered charity, is a co-educational, voluntary, grammar school, founded by the Religious Society of Friends (Quakers) in 1774, which aims to pursue the idea of excellence within a caring, supportive community.

Kilgraston School

*Bridge of Earn,
Perthshire,
Scotland PH2 9BQ
Tel: 01738 812257 Fax: 01738 813410*

Head: Mrs Juliet L Austin, BA(Hons)
Member of GSA, SHA, HAS, ISIS, ISCO, ISBA
Accredited by Scottish Dept of Education
Courses offered: Scottish Examination Board Standard and Higher Grades; GCE A level; EFL. Good SEB grades ensure entry to universities throughout the UK.
No of students: 250 Girls
Age range: 5-18
Nature of tuition: classes
Average size of class or group: 12-16
Teacher/student ratio: 1:8
Range of fees per annum as at 1.1.97:
Tuition: (5-7) £3690; (8-12) £5355; (12-18) £5955
Accommodation: (8-12) £3990; (12-18) £4380
Arrangements for accommodation: fully residential.
Kilgraston, easily accessible in the heart of Scotland, offers academic excellence, superb facilities, modern classrooms, comfortable accommodation, a comprehensive curriculum and an extensive range of outdoor and social activities.
Kilgraston is a charitable trust which provides academic excellence while encouraging students to develop their individual talents and personalities.

Directory of Independent Schools with Sixth Form entry

Bristol

Bristol

BADMINTON SCHOOL
Westbury-on-Trym, Bristol BS9 3BA
Tel: 0117 9623141
Head: Mrs Jan Scarrow BA, PGCE
Type: Girls Boarding & Day G4-18
No of Pupils: G375 VIth90 FB220
Fees: FB £8550-£11,850
DAY £3150-£6600

BRISTOL CATHEDRAL SCHOOL
College Square, Bristol BS1 5TS
Tel: 0117 9291872
Head: K J Riley BA, MEd
Type: Boys Day B10-18 G16-18
No of Pupils: B450 G22
Fees: DAY £4194

BRISTOL GRAMMAR SCHOOL
University Road, Bristol BS8 1SR
Tel: 0117 9736006
Head: C E Martin MA
Type: Co-educational Day B11-18 G11-18
No of Pupils: B677 G366 VIth292
Fees: DAY £3888

CLIFTON COLLEGE
32 College Road, Bristol BS8 3JH
Tel: 0117 9739187
Head: A H Monro MA(Cantab)
Type: Co-educational Boarding & Day B13-18 G13-18
No of Pupils: B470 G160 VIth270 FB390
Fees: FB £12,150 DAY £8430

CLIFTON HIGH SCHOOL
College Road, Bristol BS8 3JD
Tel: 0117 973 0201
Head: Mrs Y G Graham DrsLitt
Type: Girls Day & Boarding B3-11 G3-18
No of Pupils: B95 G644 VIth131 FB16 WB6
Fees: FB £8115-£8535
DAY £840-£4470

COLSTON'S COLLEGIATE SCHOOL
Bristol BS16 1BJ
Tel: 0117 9655207
Head: D G Crawford BA, DLC
Type: Co-educational Boarding & Day B3-18 G3-18
No of Pupils: B339 G115 VIth103 FB55
Fees: FB £8610-£10,590 WB £8610-£10,590
DAY £2655-£5745

COLSTON'S GIRLS' SCHOOL
Cheltenham Road, Bristol BS6 5RD
Tel: 0117 9424328
Head: Mrs J P Franklin BA(Hons)
Type: Girls Day G10-18
No of Pupils: G380 VIth120
Fees: DAY £2616-£3840

QUEEN ELIZABETH'S HOSPITAL
Berkeley Place, Bristol BS8 1JX
Tel: 0117 9291856
Head: Dr R Gliddon BSc, PhD
Type: Boys Day & Boarding B11-18
No of Pupils: B520 VIth130 FB85
Fees: FB £6957 DAY £3915

REDLAND HIGH SCHOOL FOR GIRLS
Redland Court, Bristol BS6 7EF
Tel: 0117 9245796
Head: Mrs C Lear BA(Hons)
Type: Girls Day G3-18
No of Pupils: G818 VIth125
Fees: DAY £2067-£4200

THE RED MAIDS' SCHOOL
Bristol BS9 3AW
Tel: 0117 9622641
Head: Miss S Hampton JP, BSc
Type: Girls Boarding & Day G11-18
No of Pupils: G505 VIth130 FB95
Fees: FB £776-£7776 DAY £3888

WESTWING SCHOOL
Kyneton House, Bristol BS12 2JZ
Tel: 01454 412311
Head: Mrs A Rispin BA, MEd, CDip, AF
Type: Girls Boarding & Day B3-8 G3-18
No of Pupils: B6 G73 VIth7
Fees: FB £7005-£7650
DAY £1890-£3690

Bedfordshire

Bedford

BEDFORD HIGH SCHOOL
Bromham Road, Bedford MK40 2BS
Tel: 01234 360221
Head: Mrs B E Stanley BA
Type: Girls Day & Boarding G7-18
No of Pupils: G714 VIth206
Fees: FB £7767-£9042 WB £7767-£8940
DAY £3474-£4749

BEDFORD MODERN SCHOOL
Manton Lane, Bedford MK41 7NT
Tel: 01234 364331
Head: S Smith MA
Type: Boys Day & Boarding B7-18
No of Pupils: B1182 FB55 WB6
Fees: FB £7560-£9189 WB £6612-£8805
DAY £3210-£4839

BEDFORD SCHOOL
De Parys Avenue, Bedford MK40 2TU
Tel: 01234 340444
Head: Dr I P Evans MA, PhD, CChem, MRSC
Type: Boys Day & Boarding B13-18
No of Pupils: B424 VIth284
Fees: FB £11,670 DAY £7350

DAME ALICE HARPUR SCHOOL
Cardington Road, Bedford MK42 0BX
Tel: 01234 340871
Head: Mrs R Randle BA, MA(Ed)
Type: Girls Day G7-18
No of Pupils: G737 VIth185
Fees: DAY £3387-£4674

Berkshire

Ascot

★ **HEATHFIELD SCHOOL**
London Road, Ascot, Berkshire SL5 8BQ
Tel: 01344 882955
Head: Mrs J M Benammar BA, MèsL
Type: Girls Boarding G11-18
No of Pupils: G215 VIth57 FB215
Fees: FB £13,125

LICENSED VICTUALLERS' SCHOOL
London Road, Ascot, Berkshire SL5 8DR
Tel: 01344 882770
Head: Mr I A Mullins BEd(Hons), MSc, MBIM
Type: Co-educational Boarding & Day B4-18 G4-18
No of Pupils: B375 G228 VIth79 FB98 WB66
Fees: FB £8937-£9930 WB £8937-£9930
DAY £3699-£5610

MARIST CONVENT SENIOR SCHOOL
Kings Road, Ascot, Berkshire SL5 7PS
Tel: 01344 24291
Head: Mrs K Butwilowska JP, BA, Med
Type: Girls Day G11-18
No of Pupils: G293 VIth62
Fees: DAY £3900-£3900

ST GEORGE'S SCHOOL
Ascot, Berkshire SL5 7DZ
Tel: 01344 20273
Head: Mrs A M Griggs BA, TCert
Type: Girls Boarding & Day G11-18
No of Pupils: G214 VIth75
Fees: FB £11,625 DAY £6825

ST MARY'S SCHOOL
St Mary's Road, Ascot, Berkshire SL5 9JF
Tel: 01344 23721/27788
Head: Sister M Frances Orchard IBVM, BA, PGCE
Type: Girls Boarding & Day G11-18
No of Pupils: G241 VIth95 FB326
Fees: FB £11,833 DAY £7101

Crowthorne

WELLINGTON COLLEGE
Crowthorne, Berkshire RG45 7PU
Tel: 01344 771588
Head: C J Driver BA, BEd, MPhil
Type: Boys Boarding & Day B13-18 G16-18
No of Pupils: B744 G51 FB690
Fees: FB £12,270 DAY £8955

Maidenhead

CLAIRES COURT SCHOOL
Ray Mill Road East, Maidenhead, Berkshire SL6 8TE
Tel: 01628 411471
Head: D H Course BA
Type: Boys Day B11-18 G16-18
No of Pupils: B216 VIth52
Fees: DAY £4605-£5325

MAIDENHEAD COLLEGE CLAIRES COURT GIRLS
1 College Avenue, Maidenhead, Berkshire SL6 6AW
Tel: 01628 411480
Head: Mrs A C Pitts CertEd
Type: Girls Day B2-11 G2-18
No of Pupils: B54 G214 VIth52
Fees: DAY £3345-£4965

Reading

BRADFIELD COLLEGE
Reading, Berkshire RG7 6AR
Tel: 01734 744203
Head: Mr P B Smith MA
Type: Boys Boarding B13-18 G16-18
No of Pupils: B500 G120
Fees: FB £4275 DAY £3206

DOUAI SCHOOL
Reading, Berkshire RG7 5TH
Tel: 01734 715200
Head: Dom E Power OSB, MA, PhD
Type: Co-educational Boarding & Day B10-18 G10-18
No of Pupils: B100 G30 VIth70
Fees: FB £10,545 WB £8445
DAY £5535-£6780

LEIGHTON PARK SCHOOL
Shinfield Road, Reading, Berkshire RG2 7DH
Tel: 01734 872065
Head: J H Dunston MA
Type: Co-educational Boarding & Day B11-18 G11-18
No of Pupils: B178 G68 VIth121
Fees: FB £9999-£11,754
DAY £7416-£8820

PANGBOURNE COLLEGE
Reading, Berkshire RG8 8LA
Tel: 01734 842101/2
Head: A B E Hudson MA(Oxon), DipEd(London)
Type: Co-educational Boarding & Day B11-18 G11-18
No of Pupils: B191 G8 VIth159
Fees: FB £8625-£11,880
DAY £6030-£8310

PRESENTATION COLLEGE
63 Bath Road, Reading, Berkshire RG30 2BB
Tel: 01734 572861
Head: Rev Terence Hurley BSc, HDE, FPM
Type: Boys Day B4-18 G16-18
No of Pupils: B350
Fees: DAY £3240-£3600

QUEEN ANNE'S SCHOOL
6 Henley Road, Reading, Berkshire RG4 6DX
Tel: 0118 947 1582
Head: Mrs D Forbes MA(Oxon)
Type: Girls Boarding & Day G11-18
No of Pupils: G320 VIth120
Fees: FB £11,820 DAY £7740

★ ST JOSEPH'S CONVENT SCHOOL
64 Upper Redlands Road, Reading, Berkshire RG1 5JT
Tel: 01734 661000
Head: Mrs V Brookes BEd(Hons)
Type: Girls Day G11-18
No of Pupils: G350 VIth63
Fees: DAY £4065

THE ABBEY SCHOOL
Kendrick Road, Reading, Berkshire RG1 5DZ
Tel: 01734 872256
Head: Miss B C L Sheldon BA, CertEd, ACE
Type: Girls Day B4-7 G4-18
No of Pupils: G830 VIth180
Fees: DAY £3525-£4350

THE ORATORY SCHOOL
Reading, Berkshire RG8 0PJ
Tel: 01491 680207
Head: S W Barrow BA
Type: Boys Boarding & Day B11-18
No of Pupils: B276 VIth138
Fees: FB £9255-£11,760 DAY £6675-£8220

Sonning-on-Thames

READING BLUE COAT SCHOOL
Holme Park, Sonning-on-Thames, Berkshire RG4 6SU
Tel: 0118 9441005
Head: Rev A C E Sanders MA(Oxon), MEd
Type: Boys Day & Boarding B11-18 G16-18
No of Pupils: B545 G45 VIth190 FB25 WB40
Fees: FB £10,050 WB £9735 DAY £5514

Sunningdale

HURST LODGE
Charters Road, Sunningdale, Berkshire SL5 9QG
Tel: 01344 22154
Head: Mrs A Smit
Type: Girls Day & Boarding B2-7 G2-18
No of Pupils: B22 G178
Fees: FB £10,485 DAY £1905-£6195

Thatcham

★ DOWNE HOUSE SCHOOL
Thatcham, Berkshire RG18 9JJ
Tel: 01635 200286
Head: Mrs E McKendrick BA
Type: Girls Boarding & Day G11-18
No of Pupils: G631 VIth168
Fees: FB £12,420 DAY £9000

Windsor

THE BRIGIDINE SCHOOL
King's Road, Windsor, Berkshire SL4 2AX
Tel: 01753 863779
Head: Mrs M B Cairns BSc
Type: Girls Day B3-7 G3-18
No of Pupils: B4 G322 VIth30
Fees: DAY £3210-£4680

Wokingham

BEARWOOD COLLEGE
Wokingham, Berkshire RG41 5BG
Tel: 01734 786915
Head: R J Belcher BSc, PhD, CBiol, MIBiol
Type: Co-educational Boarding & Day B11-19 G11-19
No of Pupils: B142 G6 VIth69
Fees: FB £9450-£10,500
DAY £5265-£5850

LUCKLEY-OAKFIELD SCHOOL
Luckley Road, Wokingham, Berkshire RG40 3EU
Tel: 01734 784175
Head: R C Blake MA(Oxon), MPhil(Soton)
Type: Girls Day & Boarding G11-18
No of Pupils: G180 VIth50 FB45 WB45
Fees: FB £8349 WB £8184
DAY £5175

Buckinghamshire

Buckingham

AKELEY WOOD SCHOOL
Buckingham MK18 5AE
Tel: 01280 814110
Head: J C Lovelock BA, CertEd
Type: Co-educational Day B10-18 G10-18
No of Pupils: B200 G160
Fees: DAY £3795-£4380

STOWE SCHOOL
Buckingham MK18 5EH
Tel: 01280 813164
Head: J G L Nichols MA
Type: Boys Boarding & Day B13-18 G16-18
No of Pupils: B460 G110
Fees: FB £13,500 DAY £9450

Gerrards Cross

HOLY CROSS CONVENT
The Grange, Gerrards Cross, Buckinghamshire SL9 9DW
Tel: 01753 895600
Head: Dr David Walker BA, MEd, Phd
Type: Girls Day & Boarding G4-18
No of Pupils: G435 VIth35
Fees: FB £9000 DAY £3030-£3180

ST MARY'S SCHOOL
Packhorse Road, Gerrards Cross, Buckinghamshire SL9 8JQ
Tel: 01753 883370
Head: Mrs F Balcombe BA(Hons), PGCE
Type: Girls Day G3-18
No of Pupils: G270 VIth33
Fees: DAY £2765-£5295

High Wycombe

PIPERS CORNER SCHOOL
High Wycombe, Buckinghamshire HP15 6LP
Tel: 01494 718255
Head: Mrs V M Stattersfield, MA(Oxon), PGCE
Type: Girls Boarding & Day G4-18
No of Pupils: G290 VIth60
Fees: FB £8004-£9702 WB £7944-£9582
DAY £2805-£5808

WYCOMBE ABBEY SCHOOL
High Wycombe, Buckinghamshire HP11 1PE
Tel: 01494 520381
Head: Mrs J M Goodland BA(Hons), CertEd
Type: Girls Boarding & Day G11-18
No of Pupils: G340 VIth160
Fees: FB £12,780 DAY £9585

Milton Keynes

BURY LAWN SCHOOL
Soskin Drive, Stantonbury Fields, Milton Keynes,
Buckinghamshire MK14 6DP
Tel: 01908 220345/01404 881702
Head: Mrs H W K Kiff BA(Hons), AdvCertEd
Type: Co-educational Day B1-18 G1-18
No of Pupils: B177 G156 VIth17
Fees: DAY £3495-£5010

GYOSEI INTERNATIONAL SCHOOL UK
Japonica Lane, V10 Brickhill Street, Milton Keynes,
Buckinghamshire MK15 9JX
Tel: 01908 690100
Head: K Tagawa
Type: Co-educational Boarding & Day B12-18 G12-18
No of Pupils: B149 G93 FB33
Fees: FB £11,340-£11,500
DAY £6340-£6450

Cambridgeshire

Cambridge

ST MARY'S SCHOOL
Bateman Street, Cambridge CB2 1LY
Tel: 01223 353253
Head: Ms M Conway MA(Oxon)
Type: Girls Day & Boarding G11-18
No of Pupils: G520 VIth110
Fees: WB £3270 DAY £4140

THE LEYS SCHOOL
Cambridge CB2 2AD
Tel: 01223 355327
Head: Rev Dr John C A Barrett MA
Type: Co-educational Boarding & Day B13-18 G13-18
No of Pupils: VIth199
Fees: FB £12,300 DAY £8790

THE PERSE SCHOOL
Hills Road, Cambridge CB2 2QF
Tel: 01223 568300
Head: N P Richardson MA, PGCE
Type: Boys Day B11-18 G16-18
No of Pupils: B534 VIth144
Fees: DAY £4839

THE PERSE SCHOOL FOR GIRLS
Union Road, Cambridge CB2 1HF
Tel: 01223 359589
Head: Miss H S Smith MA(Oxon), PGCE
Type: Girls Day G7-18
No of Pupils: G590 VIth120
Fees: DAY £4200-£4935

Ely

THE KING'S SCHOOL
Ely, Cambridgeshire CB7 4DB
Tel: 01353 662824
Head: R H Youdale MA
Type: Co-educational Day & Boarding B2-18 G2-18
No of Pupils: B411 G276 VIth115
Fees: FB £6705-£12,030 WB £6705-£12,030
DAY £2625-£8055

Huntingdon

KIMBOLTON SCHOOL
Huntingdon, Cambridgeshire PE18 0EA
Tel: 01480 860505
Head: R V Peel BSc
Type: Co-educational Day & Boarding B7-18 G7-18
No of Pupils: B390 G329 FB59
Fees: FB £8595 DAY £4155-£4995

Peterborough

LAXTON SCHOOL
Oundle, Peterborough, Cambridgeshire PE8 4AR
Tel: 01832 273569
Head: R I Briggs MA(Cantab)
Type: Co-educational Day B11-18 G11-18
No of Pupils: B84 G54 VIth68
Fees: DAY £5355

OUNDLE SCHOOL
Peterborough, Cambridgeshire PE8 4EN
Tel: 01832 273536
Head: D B McMurray MA
Type: Co-educational Boarding B11-18 G11-18
No of Pupils: B373 G107 VIth354 FB854
Fees: FB £9825-£12,855

PETERBOROUGH HIGH SCHOOL
Westwood House, Peterborough, Cambridgeshire PE3 6JF
Tel: 01733 343357
Head: Mrs A J V Storey BA
Type: Girls Day & Boarding B4-8 G4-18
No of Pupils: B12 G278
Fees: FB £7380-£7863
DAY £3270-£3915

Wisbech

WISBECH GRAMMAR SCHOOL
Wisbech, Cambridgeshire PE13 1JX
Tel: 01945 583631
Head: R S Repper MA(Oxon), FIMgt
Type: Co-educational Day B11-18 G11-18
No of Pupils: B254 G238 VIth150
Fees: DAY £4650

Cheshire

Alderley Edge

MOUNT CARMEL SCHOOL
Wilmslow Road, Alderley Edge, Cheshire SK9 7QE
Tel: 01625 583028
Head: Mrs K Mills BA
Type: Girls Day G3-18
No of Pupils: B11 G448 VIth78
Fees: DAY £2361-£3765

ST HILARY'S SCHOOL
Alderley Edge, Cheshire SK9 7AG
Tel: 01625 583532
Head: Mrs G M Case BA
Type: Girls Day G3-18
No of Pupils: G206 VIth29
Fees: DAY £2175-£4041

Altrincham

LORETO CONVENT GRAMMAR SCHOOL
Dunham Road, Altrincham, Cheshire WA14 4AH
Tel: 0161 928 3703
Head: Sr Aileen McEvoy
Type: Girls Day G11-18
No of Pupils: G800 VIth180
Fees: DAY £2892

NORTH CESTRIAN GRAMMAR SCHOOL
Dunham Road, Altrincham, Cheshire WA14 4AJ
Tel: 0161 928 1856
Head: D G Vanstone MA
Type: Boys Day B11-18
No of Pupils: B350
Fees: DAY £3630

ST AMBROSE COLLEGE
Altrincham, Cheshire WA15 0HE
Tel: 0161 980 2711
Head: G E Hester
Type: Boys Day B11-18
No of Pupils: B750
Fees: DAY £3300

Cheadle

CHEADLE HULME SCHOOL
Claremont Road, Cheadle, Cheshire SK8 6EF
Tel: 0161 488 3330
Head: D J Wilkinson MA, MLitt, FRSA
Type: Co-educational Day B7-18 G7-18
No of Pupils: B463 G450 VIth239
Fees: DAY £3573-£4086

Chester

ABBEY GATE COLLEGE
Saighton Grange, Chester, Cheshire CH3 6EG
Tel: 01244 332077
Head: E W Mitchell BA, PGCE
Type: Co-educational Day B7-18 G7-18
No of Pupils: B147 G119 VIth76
Fees: DAY £2730-£4221

THE KING'S SCHOOL
Wrexham Road, Chester, Cheshire CH4 7QL
Tel: 01244 680026
Head: A R D Wickson MA
Type: Boys Day B7-18
No of Pupils: B540 VIth140
Fees: DAY £2772-£4230

THE QUEEN'S SCHOOL
City Walls Road, Chester, Cheshire CH1 2NN
Tel: 01244 312078
Head: Miss D M Skilbeck BA
Type: Girls Day G4-18
No of Pupils: B16 G494 VIth130
Fees: DAY £2385-£4320

Macclesfield

THE KING'S SCHOOL
Cumberland Street, Macclesfield, Cheshire SK10 1DA
Tel: 01625 618586
Head: A G Silcock MA
Type: Co-educational Day B7-18 G7-18
No of Pupils: B705 G348 VIth290
Fees: DAY £3450-£4395

Northwich

THE GRANGE SCHOOL
Bradburns Lane, Northwich, Cheshire CW8 1LU
Tel: 01606 74007
Head: E S Marshall MA, LGSM
Type: Co-educational Day B4-18 G4-18
No of Pupils: B557 G526 VIth131
Fees: DAY £2625-£3675

Stockport

★ **STOCKPORT GRAMMAR SCHOOL**
Buxton Road, Stockport, Cheshire SK2 7AF
Tel: 0161 456 9000
Head: I Mellor MA
Type: Co-educational Day B4-18 G4-18
No of Pupils: B505 G495
Fees: DAY £4086

Cornwall

Penryn

TREMOUGH CONVENT SCHOOL
Penryn, Cornwall TR10 9EZ
Tel: 01326 372226
Head: Mrs M Biscoe BA(Hons), CertEd, DipMaths
Type: Girls Day & Boarding B3-11 G3-18
No of Pupils: B18 G198 VIth20
Fees: WB £4743-£4902
DAY £1575-£3087

Penzance

THE BOLITHO SCHOOL
Penzance, Cornwall TR18 4JR
Tel: 01736 63271
Head: I Halford MA(Oxon)
Type: Girls Day & Boarding B2-11 G2-18
No of Pupils: B35 G135
Fees: FB £7281-£7965
DAY £1005-£4206

Truro

THE DUCHY GRAMMAR SCHOOL
Tregeye, Truro, Cornwall TR3 6JH
Tel: 01872 862289
Head: M L Fuller MSc, BSc
Type: Co-educational Day & Boarding B3-18 G3-18
No of Pupils: B63 G31 VIth11 FB13 WB17
Fees: FB £7941-£8865 WB £7644-£8568
DAY £2511-£4752

★ **TRURO HIGH SCHOOL FOR GIRLS**
Falmouth Road, Truro, Cornwall TR1 2HU
Tel: 01872 72830
Head: J Graham-Brown BA(Hons), MPhil
Type: Girls Day & Boarding B3-5 G3-18
No of Pupils: B3 G440 VIth90
Fees: FB £7995 WB £7890 DAY £4380

TRURO SCHOOL
Trennick Lane, Truro, Cornwall TR1 1TH
Tel: 01872 72763
Head: G A G Dodd MA
Type: Co-educational Day & Boarding B3-18 G3-18
No of Pupils: B832 G396 VIth238 FB229
Fees: FB £7770-£8958
DAY £2925-£4812

Cumbria

Barrow-in-Furness

OUR LADY'S, CHETWYNDE SCHOOL
Rating Lane, Barrow-in-Furness, Cumbria LA13 0NY
Tel: 01229 824210
Head: Mrs Margaret Stones
Type: Co-educational Day B3-18 G3-18
No of Pupils: B260 G256
Fees: DAY £2182

Carlisle

AUSTIN FRIARS SCHOOL
Etterby Scaur, Carlisle, Cumbria CA3 9PB
Tel: 01228 28042
Head: Rev D Middleton OSA
Type: Co-educational Boarding & Day B11-18 G11-18
No of Pupils: B181 G122 VIth82
Fees: FB £7956-£8226 DAY £4554

LIME HOUSE SCHOOL
Holm Hill, Carlisle, Cumbria CA5 7BX
Tel: 01228 710225
Head: N A Rice BA, CertEd
Type: Co-educational Boarding & Day B3-19 G3-19
No of Pupils: B134 G100
Fees: FB £4500-£8250 DAY £1350-£3750

Carnforth

CASTERTON SCHOOL
Carnforth, Lancashire LA6 2SG
Tel: 015242 71202
Head: A F Thomas MA(Cantab)
Type: Girls Day & Boarding G8-18
No of Pupils: G256 VIth94
Fees: FB £7050-£9030 DAY £4920-£5664

Sedbergh

SEDBERGH SCHOOL
Sedbergh, Cumbria LA10 5HG
Tel: 01539 620535
Head: C H Hirst MA
Type: Boys Boarding B10-18
No of Pupils: B340 VIth120
Fees: FB £8640-£12,150

St Bees

ST BEES SCHOOL
St Bees, Cumbria CA27 0DS
Tel: 01946 822263
Head: P A Chamberlain BSc
Type: Co-educational Boarding & Day B11-18 G11-18
No of Pupils: B150 G141 VIth86
Fees: FB £7674-£10,491 WB £7068-£9993 DAY £5853-£7210

Windermere

ST ANNE'S
Windermere, Cumbria LA23 1NW
Tel: 01539 446164
Head: R D Hunter MA(Cantab)
Type: Girls Day & Boarding G11-18
No of Pupils: G166 VIth74
Fees: FB £9540 DAY £5700-£6330

Derbyshire

Buxton

TOR SCHOOL
St John's Road, Buxton, Derbyshire SK17 6SJ
Tel: 01298 22745
Head: Mr Curtis
Type: Co-educational Day & Boarding B2-18 G2-18
No of Pupils: B57 G65 VIth9
Fees: FB £7000-£7500 DAY £1700-£2500

Derby

DERBY HIGH SCHOOL
Hillsway, Derby, Derbyshire DE23 7DT
Tel: 01332 514267
Head: Dr G H Goddard FRCS, CChem
Type: Girls Day B3-11 G3-18
Fees: DAY £3075-£4170

★ **OCKBROOK SCHOOL**
The Settlement, Ockbrook, Derby, Derbyshire DE7 3RJ
Tel: 01332 673532
Head: Ms Denise P Bolland BA, MSc, MIMgt
Type: Girls Day & Boarding B3-11 G3-18
No of Pupils: B70 G390
Fees: FB £7392 DAY £3978

Matlock

ST ELPHIN'S SCHOOL
Matlock, Derbyshire DE4 2HA
Tel: 01629 732687
Head: Mrs Valerie Fisher BA
Type: Girls Day & Boarding G2-18
No of Pupils: G225
Fees: FB £9197-£10,197 WB £9197-£10,197 DAY £4839-£5940

Repton

REPTON SCHOOL
The Hall, Repton, Derbyshire DE65 6FH
Tel: 01283 559220
Head: G E Jones MA
Type: Co-educational Boarding & Day B13-18 G13-18
No of Pupils: B228 G135 VIth188
Fees: FB £12,120 DAY £9120

Sheffield

MOUNT ST MARY'S COLLEGE
Spinkhill, Sheffield, Derbyshire S31 9YL
Tel: 01246 433388
Head: P B Fisher MA
Type: Co-educational Boarding & Day B13-19 G13-19
No of Pupils: B305 G165 VIth136 FB186 WB68
Fees: FB £8970 DAY £6063

Devon

Ashburton

SANDS SCHOOL
Greylands, Ashburton, Devon TQ13 7AX
Tel: 01364 653666
Head: Sean Bellamy MA(Cantab), PGCE
Type: Co-educational Day B10-18 G10-18
No of Pupils: B19 G21 VIth10
Fees: DAY £3300

Barnstaple

WEST BUCKLAND SCHOOL
Barnstaple, Devon EX32 0SX
Tel: 01598 760281
Head: M Downward MA(Cantab)
Type: Co-educational Day & Boarding B11-18 G11-18
No of Pupils: B205 G146 VIth120 FB113
Fees: FB £6510-£9450 WB £6510-£9450 DAY £5130

Beaworthy

SHEBBEAR COLLEGE
Beaworthy, Devon EX21 5HJ
Tel: 01409 281228
Head: R J Buley MA
Type: Co-educational Boarding & Day B3-18 G3-18
Fees: FB £5490-£8880 DAY £1500-£4785

Bideford

EDGEHILL COLLEGE
Northdown Road, Bideford, Devon EX39 3LY
Tel: 01237 471701
Head: Mrs E M Burton BSc, AKC
Type: Co-educational Boarding & Day B3-18 G3-18
No of Pupils: B116 G330 VIth80 FB72 WB17
Fees: FB £6870-£9570 WB £6210-£8655 DAY £2535-£5265

GRENVILLE COLLEGE
Belvoir Road, Bideford, Devon EX39 3JR
Tel: 01237 472212
Head: Dr M C V Cane PhD, BSc, MRSC
Type: Co-educational Boarding & Day B2-18 G2-18
No of Pupils: B157 G96 VIth76 FB100
Fees: FB £8190-£10,551 WB £7710-£10,404 DAY £2538-£5175

Exeter

BRAMDEAN GRAMMAR SCHOOL
Richmond Lodge, Homefield Road, Exeter, Devon EX1 2QR
Tel: 01392 273387
Head: D A Connett
Type: Boys Day & Boarding B11-17 G16-17
No of Pupils: B180 WB25
Fees: WB £4092 DAY £627

EXETER SCHOOL
Manston Terrace, Exeter, Devon EX2 4NS
Tel: 01392 273679
Head: N W Gamble BA, MEd
Type: Boys Day & Boarding B11-18 G16-18
No of Pupils: B560 VIth290 FB45
Fees: FB £3750 DAY £3615-£4200

MAGDALEN COURT SCHOOL
Uplands, Exeter, Devon EX1 2LX
Tel: 01392 494919/01626 852257
Head: Mrs J Jenner BEd(Hons), BA
Type: Co-educational Day B3-18 G3-18
No of Pupils: B40 G40 VIth20
Fees: DAY £1800-£3600

ST MARGARET'S EXETER
147 Magdalen Road, Exeter, Devon EX2 4TS
Tel: 01392 273197
Head: Mrs M D'Albertanson MA
Type: Girls Day G5-18
No of Pupils: G450 VIth79
Fees: DAY £2784-£4326

THE MAYNARD SCHOOL
Denmark Road, Exeter, Devon EX1 1SJ
Tel: 01392 273417
Head: Miss F Murdin MA(Oxon)
Type: Girls Day G7-18
No of Pupils: G431 VIth111
Fees: DAY £3570-£4440

Newton Abbot

STOVER SCHOOL
Newton Abbot, Devon TQ12 6QG
Tel: 01626 54505
Head: P E Bujak BA, MA, CEd, ARHists
Type: Girls Day & Boarding G11-18
No of Pupils: B6 G135 VIth31 FB62 WB80
Fees: FB £8475 WB £8250 DAY £4425

Plymouth

PLYMOUTH COLLEGE
Plymouth, Devon PL4 6RN
Tel: 01752 203300
Head: A J Morsley BSc, ARCS, AFIMA, FRSA
Type: Co-educational Boarding & Day B11-18 G11-18
No of Pupils: B349 G49 VIth198
Fees: FB £9585 DAY £4995

ST DUNSTAN'S ABBEY SCHOOL
The Millfields, Plymouth, Devon PL1 3JL
Tel: 01752 201350/1
Head: R A Bye MA, AdvDipEd, CertEd
Type: Girls Day & Boarding G2-18
No of Pupils: G300 VIth40
Fees: FB £7680-£8652 WB £5541-£8652
DAY £2577-£4860

Tavistock

KELLY COLLEGE
Tavistock, Devon PL19 0HZ
Tel: 01822 612010
Head: M Turner MA
Type: Co-educational Day & Boarding B4-18 G4-18
No of Pupils: B160 G160 VIth90
Fees: FB £9720-£11,670 WB £9720-£11,670
DAY £4600-£7335

Teignmouth

TRINITY SCHOOL
Buckeridge Road, Teignmouth, Devon TQ14 8LY
Tel: 01626 774138
Head: C J Ashby BSc(Hons), PGCE
Type: Co-educational Day & Boarding B3-18 G3-18
No of Pupils: B148 G113 VIth23
Fees: FB £8085-£8985 WB £8085-£8985
DAY £2715-£4335

Tiverton

BLUNDELL'S
Tiverton, Devon EX16 4DN
Tel: 01884 252543
Head: J Leigh MA(Cantab)
Type: Co-educational Boarding & Day B11-18 G11-18
No of Pupils: B286 G82 FB235
Fees: FB £9786-£11,145
DAY £5436-£6795

Torquay

STOODLEY KNOWLE SCHOOL
Ansteys Cove Road, Torquay, Devon TQ1 2JB
Tel: 01803 293160
Head: Sr Perpetua
Type: Girls Day & Boarding G2-18
No of Pupils: G185 VIth12 WB70
Fees: WB £4854 DAY £3438

Dorset

Blandford

BRYANSTON SCHOOL
Blandford Forum, Dorset DT11 0PX
Tel: 01258 452411
Head: T D Wheare MA
Type: Co-educational Day & Boarding B13-18 G13-18
No of Pupils: B400 G260
Fees: FB £13,230 DAY £8820

CLAYESMORE SCHOOL
Blandford Forum, Dorset DT11 8LL
Tel: 01747 811217
Head: D J Beeby MA(Cantab)
Type: Co-educational Boarding & Day B13-18 G13-18
No of Pupils: B186 G96 VIth80
Fees: FB £11,640 DAY £8145

CROFT HOUSE SCHOOL
Blandford Forum, Dorset DT11 0QS
Tel: 01258 860295
Head: M Hawkins BA, DEA
Type: Girls Day & Boarding G11-18
No of Pupils: G130
Fees: FB £9360 DAY £6600

MILTON ABBEY SCHOOL
Blandford Forum, Dorset DT11 0BZ
Tel: 01258 880484
Head: W V Hughes-D'Aeth BA, PGCE
Type: Boys Boarding & Day B13-18
No of Pupils: B195 VIth80
Fees: FB £12,090 DAY £7746

Bournemouth

TALBOT HEATH
Rothesay Road, Bournemouth, Dorset BH4 9NJ
Tel: 01202 761881
Head: Mrs C Dipple BA, MèsL, FRSA
Type: Girls Day & Boarding B3-7 G3-18
No of Pupils: B2 G553 VIth95
Fees: FB £7170-£9150
DAY £1650-£5250

WENTWORTH COLLEGE
College Road, Bournemouth, Dorset BH5 2DY
Tel: 01202 423266
Head: Miss S Coe BA(Hons), PGCE, FRGS
Type: Girls Boarding & Day G11-18
No of Pupils: G180 VIth50 FB12 WB12
Fees: FB £9330 WB £9330
DAY £5850

Christchurch

HOMEFIELD SCHOOL (PREP & SENIOR DEPTS)
Salisbury Road, Christchurch, Dorset BH23 7AR
Tel: 01202 476644
Head: A C Partridge DipEd, ACP, FRSA, FRGS
Type: Co-educational Boarding & Day B3-18 G3-18
No of Pupils: B250 G100 VIth6 FB42 WB8
Fees: FB £8859-£10,425
DAY £2875-£4320

Lyme Regis

ALL HALLOWS COLLEGE
Lyme Regis, Dorset DT7 3RA
Tel: 01297 626110
Head: K R Moore MA, FGS, CGeol
Type: Co-educational Boarding & Day B11-18 G11-18
No of Pupils: B110 G40 VIth38 FB180
Fees: FB £10,275 WB £8850
DAY £3900-£5250

Shaftesbury

ST MARY'S SCHOOL
Shaftesbury, Dorset SP7 9LP
Tel: 01747 854005
Head: Sr M Campion Livesey IBVM, MA(Cantab)
Type: Girls Boarding & Day G9-18
No of Pupils: G310 VIth77 FB225
Fees: FB £9540-£9990
DAY £6090-£6420

Sherborne

SHERBORNE SCHOOL
Abbey Road, Sherborne, Dorset DT9 3AP
Tel: 01935 812249
Head: P H Lapping MA(Oxon)
Type: Boys Boarding & Day B13-18
No of Pupils: B320 VIth270 FB600
Fees: FB £13,125 DAY £10,005

SHERBORNE SCHOOL FOR GIRLS
Sherborne, Dorset DT9 3QN
Tel: 01935 812245
Head: Miss J M Taylor BSc, DipEd
Type: Girls Boarding & Day G11-18
No of Pupils: G267 VIth157 WB267
Fees: FB £12,240 DAY £8550

ST ANTONY'S-LEWESTON SCHOOL
Sherborne, Dorset DT9 6EN
Tel: 01963 210691
Head: Miss Brenda King BA, BD
Type: Girls Day & Boarding G11-18
No of Pupils: G270 VIth70 FB180
Fees: FB £10,935 DAY £7140

Wimborne

CANFORD SCHOOL
Wimborne, Dorset BH21 3AD
Tel: 01202 841254
Head: J D Lever MA
Type: Co-educational Boarding & Day B13-18 G13-18
No of Pupils: B242 G21 VIth242 FB348
Fees: FB £12,380 DAY £9285

Durham

Barnard Castle

BARNARD CASTLE SCHOOL
Barnard Castle, County Durham DL12 8UN
Tel: 01833 690222
Head: F S McNamara BA, DipEd
Type: Co-educational Boarding & Day B4-18 G4-18
No of Pupils: B389 G87 VIth148
Fees: FB £6405-£8358 DAY £3441-£4947

Darlington

HURWORTH HOUSE SCHOOL
The Green, Darlington, County Durham DL2 2AD
Tel: 01325 720645
Head: Dr M F Rymer BA, PhD
Type: Boys Day B3-18
No of Pupils: B160
Fees: DAY £2985-£4779

POLAM HALL
Grange Road, Darlington, County Durham DL1 5PA
Tel: 01325 463383
Head: Mrs H C Hamilton BSc
Type: Girls Day & Boarding G4-18
No of Pupils: G356 VIth73
Fees: FB £7404-£9159
DAY £2067-£4479

Durham

DURHAM HIGH SCHOOL FOR GIRLS
Farewell Hall, Durham, County Durham DH1 3TB
Tel: 0191 384 3226
Head: Miss M L Walters
Type: Girls Day G4-18
No of Pupils: G365 VIth62
Fees: DAY £2883-£4854

DURHAM SCHOOL
Durham, County Durham DH1 4SZ
Tel: 0191 384 7977
Head: M A Lang MA, FRSA
Type: Boys Day & Boarding B11-19 G16-19
No of Pupils: B286 G38 VIth137 FB131
Fees: FB £9693-£11,406
DAY £5085-£7419

Stockton-on-Tees

TEESSIDE HIGH SCHOOL
The Avenue, Stockton-on-Tees, Durham TS16 9AT
Tel: 01642 782095
Head: Miss J F Hamilton BSc(Hons)(Lond), AFIMA
Type: Girls Day G3-18
No of Pupils: G470 VIth65
Fees: DAY £2790-£3936

Essex

Brentwood

BRENTWOOD SCHOOL
Ingrave Road, Brentwood, Essex CM15 8AS
Tel: 01277 212271
Head: J A B Kelsall
Type: Co-educational Day & Boarding B7-18 G11-18
No of Pupils: FB60
Fees: FB £9615 DAY £5496

Chelmsford

NEW HALL SCHOOL
Chelmsford, Essex CM3 3HT
Tel: 01245 467588
Head: Sr Anne Marie CRSS, MA(Cantab)
Type: Girls Boarding & Day G11-18
No of Pupils: G420 VIth116
Fees: FB £10,830 WB £10,620
DAY £6930

Chigwell

CHIGWELL SCHOOL
High Road, Chigwell, Essex IG7 6QF
Tel: 0181 501 5700
Head: D Gibbs
Type: Boys Day & Boarding B7-18 G16-18
No of Pupils: B505 VIth195 FB28 WB42
Fees: FB £6711-£9993 WB £6342-£9459
DAY £4275-£6573

Dunmow

FELSTED SCHOOL
Dunmow, Essex CM6 3LL
Tel: 01371 820258
Head: S C Roberts MA
Type: Co-educational Boarding & Day B13-18 G13-18
No of Pupils: B180 G86 VIth180
Fees: FB £12,360 DAY £9030

Halstead

GOSFIELD SCHOOL
Cut Hedge Park, Halstead, Essex CO9 1PF
Tel: 01787 474040
Head: John Shaw MA, MABE
Type: Co-educational Day & Boarding B3-18 G3-18
No of Pupils: B79 G43 VIth12
Fees: FB £7605-£9900 WB £7605-£9900
DAY £2970-£5310

Ilford

ILFORD URSULINE HIGH SCHOOL
Morland Road, Ilford, Essex IG1 4QS
Tel: 0181 554 1995
Head: Miss J Reddington CertEd
Type: Girls Day G4-18
No of Pupils: G315 VIth54
Fees: DAY £3400-£4575

PARK SCHOOL FOR GIRLS
20 Park Avenue, Ilford, Essex IG1 4RS
Tel: 0181 554 2466
Head: Mrs N O'Brien BA
Type: Girls Day G7-18
No of Pupils: G186 VIth19
Fees: DAY £2730-£3630

Saffron Walden

FRIENDS' SCHOOL
Mount Pleasant Road, Saffron Walden, Essex CB11 3EB
Tel: 01799 525351
Head: Mrs Jane Laing BA
Type: Co-educational Day & Boarding B3-18 G3-18
No of Pupils: B155 G151 VIth60 FB87
Fees: FB £6885-£10,614
DAY £2400-£6369

Woodford Green

BANCROFT'S SCHOOL
Whitehall Road, Woodford Green, Essex IG8 0RF
Tel: 0181 505 4821
Head: Dr P R Scott MA, DPhil
Type: Co-educational Day B7-18 G7-18
No of Pupils: B463 G488 VIth232
Fees: DAY £4308-£5694

Gloucestershire

Cheltenham

CHELTENHAM COLLEGE
Bath Road, Cheltenham, Gloucestershire GL53 7LD
Tel: 01242 513540
Head: P D V Wilkes
Type: Boys Day & Boarding B13-18 G16-18
No of Pupils: B485 G84
Fees: FB £12,210 DAY £9225-£12,210

CHELTENHAM LADIES' COLLEGE
Bayshill Road, Cheltenham, Gloucestershire GL50 3EP
Tel: 01242 520691
Head: Mrs A V Tuck MA, PGCE, MIL
Type: Girls Boarding & Day G11-18
No of Pupils: G574 VIth270
Fees: FB £12,900-£13,650
DAY £8190-£8790

DEAN CLOSE SCHOOL
Cheltenham, Gloucestershire GL51 6HE
Tel: 01242 522640
Head: C J Bacon MA, DipEd
Type: Co-educational Boarding & Day B12-18 G12-18
No of Pupils: B253 G209 VIth105 FB309
Fees: FB £12,840 DAY £8955

ST EDWARD'S SCHOOL
Ashley Road, Cheltenham, Gloucestershire GL52 6NT
Tel: 01242 583955
Head: A J Martin MA, DipEd, FCollP
Type: Co-educational Day B2-18 G2-18
No of Pupils: B255 G260 VIth95
Fees: DAY £2100-£5625

Cirencester

RENDCOMB COLLEGE
Cirencester, Gloucestershire GL7 7HA
Tel: 01285 831213
Head: J N Tolputt MA
Type: Co-educational Boarding & Day B11-18 G11-18
No of Pupils: B153 G87 VIth82 FB201
Fees: FB £8400-£10,800
DAY £6450-£8550

Gloucester

SELWYN SCHOOL
Matson House, Gloucester GL4 6DY
Tel: 01452 305663
Head: Miss Leslie Brown BA, MA(Ed), CertEd
Type: Girls Day & Boarding B3-11 G3-18
No of Pupils: B35 G165 FB46 WB12
Fees: FB £6060-£8430
DAY £2047-£4800

THE KING'S SCHOOL
Pitt Street, Gloucester GL1 2BG
Tel: 01452 521251
Head: P R Lacy MA
Type: Co-educational Day & Boarding B4-19 G4-19
No of Pupils: B254 G108 VIth102
Fees: FB £5184-£9326 WB £5184-£9326
DAY £2040-£5982

WYNSTONES SCHOOL
Gloucester GL4 0UF
Tel: 01452 522475
Head: Chairman of the College of Teachers
Type: Co-educational Day & Boarding B4-18 G4-18
No of Pupils: B153 G159
Fees: FB £6339-£6510 DAY £2535-£3576

Lechlade

ST CLOTILDE'S SCHOOL
Lechlade Manor, Lechlade, Gloucestershire GL7 3BB
Tel: 01367 252259
Head: Miss A G Wood BA(Hons), AdDipEd
Type: Girls Boarding & Day B3-8 G3-18
No of Pupils: B15 G123
Fees: WB £8490 DAY £1380-£5070

Stonehouse

★ **WYCLIFFE COLLEGE**
Stonehouse, Gloucestershire GL10 2JQ
Tel: 01453 822432
Head: D C M Prichard MA, FRSA
Type: Co-educational Boarding & Day B13-18 G13-18
No of Pupils: B260 G131
Fees: FB £12,150-£12,750
DAY £8550-£9000

Tetbury

WESTONBIRT SCHOOL
Tetbury, Gloucestershire GL8 8QG
Tel: 01666 880333
Head: Mrs G Hylson-Smith BA, DipCEG
Type: Girls Boarding & Day G11-18
No of Pupils: G160 VIth60 FB200
Fees: FB £11,340 WB £11,340
DAY £7380

Tewkesbury

BREDON SCHOOL
Pull Court, Tewkesbury, Gloucestershire GL20 6AH
Tel: 01684 293156
Head: Mr C E Wheeler BEd, MIMgt
Type: Co-educational Boarding & Day B12-18 G12-18
No of Pupils: B159 G41 VIth65
Fees: FB £8400-£12,540 WB £8220-£12,360
DAY £2610-£7600

Hampshire

Bramdean

BROCKWOOD PARK KRISHNAMURTI EDUCATION CENTRE
Bramdean, Hampshire SO24 0LQ
Tel: 01962 771744
Heads: C Foster & I Peters
Type: Co-educational Boarding B14-19 G14-19
No of Pupils: B33 G22
Fees: FB £8000

Farnborough

FARNBOROUGH HILL
Farnborough Road, Farnborough, Hampshire GU14 8AT
Tel: 01252 545197
Head: Miss R McGeoch MA, MLitt
Type: Girls Day G11-18
No of Pupils: G414 VIth111
Fees: DAY £4782

SALESIAN COLLEGE
Reading Road, Farnborough, Hampshire GU14 6PA
Tel: 01252 542919
Head: Rev Br M Delmer SDB, BEd
Type: Boys Day B11-18
No of Pupils: B466
Fees: DAY £3234

Hook

LORD WANDSWORTH COLLEGE
Long Sutton, Hook, Hampshire RG29 1TB
Tel: 01256 862482
Head: G de W Waller MA, MSc
Type: Boys Day & Boarding B11-18 G16-18
No of Pupils: B322 VIth158
Fees: FB £9456-£9972 WB £9456-£9972
DAY £7380-£7752

★ **NORTH FORELAND LODGE**
Hook, Hampshire RG27 0HT
Tel: 01256 882431
Head: Miss S R Cameron BA
Type: Girls Boarding & Day G11-18
No of Pupils: G120 FB108
Fees: FB £11,550 DAY £7050

New Milton

BALLARD COLLEGE
Fernhill Lane, New Milton, Hampshire BH25 5JL
Tel: 01425 611090
Head: Rev Andrew Folks BA, DipTh
Type: Co-educational Boarding & Day B11-18 G11-18
No of Pupils: VIth20
Fees: FB £8850 WB £8295 DAY £5655

Petersfield

★ **BEDALES SCHOOL**
Church Road, Petersfield, Hampshire GU32 2DG
Tel: 01730 263286
Head: Mrs Alison Willcocks MA, BMus
Type: Co-educational Boarding & Day B8-18 G8-18
No of Pupils: B200 G200 FB346
Fees: FB £12,996 DAY £9567

CHURCHERS COLLEGE
Portsmouth Road, Petersfield, Hampshire GU31 4AS
Tel: 01730 263033
Head: G W Buttle BA, PGCE, MA, FRSA
Type: Co-educational Day B4-18 G4-18
No of Pupils: B341 G221 VIth141
Fees: DAY £2790-£5250

Portsmouth

THE PORTSMOUTH GRAMMAR SCHOOL
High Street, Portsmouth, Hampshire PO1 2LN
Tel: 01705 819125
Head: A C V Evans MA, MPhil, FIL
Type: Co-educational Day B4-18 G4-18
No of Pupils: B677 G274 VIth198
Fees: DAY £3048-£4755

Romsey

EMBLEY PARK SCHOOL
Embley Park, Romsey, Hampshire SO51 6ZE
Tel: 01794 512206
Head: D F Chapman BA(Dunelm), FCollP
Type: Co-educational Boarding & Day B3-18 G3-18
No of Pupils: B243 G129 VIth57
Fees: FB £4785-£10,395
DAY £1470-£5835

STANBRIDGE EARLS SCHOOL
Stanbridge Lane, Romsey, Hampshire SO51 0ZS
Tel: 01794 516777
Head: H Moxon MA, DipEd
Type: Co-educational Boarding & Day B11-18 G11-18
No of Pupils: B151 G40 VIth48
Fees: FB £11,070-£12,120
DAY £8310-£9090

Southampton

KING EDWARD VI SCHOOL
Kellett Road, Southampton, Hampshire SO15 7UQ
Tel: 01703 704561
Head: P B Hamilton
Type: Co-educational Day B11-18 G11-18
No of Pupils: B753 G200
Fees: DAY £5016

ST MARY'S COLLEGE
57 Midanbury Lane, Southampton, Hampshire SO9 4TG
Tel: 01703 671267
Head: Rev Brother Peter
Type: Boys Day B3-18
No of Pupils: B450
Fees: DAY £1095-£3285

THE ATHERLEY SCHOOL
Hill Lane, Southampton, Hampshire SO16 5RG
Tel: 01703 772898
Head: Miss A Burrows
Type: Girls Day B3-11 G3-19
No of Pupils: B69 G365
Fees: DAY £3198-£4482

Southsea

PORTSMOUTH HIGH SCHOOL GPDST
Kent Road, Southsea, Hampshire PO5 3EQ
Tel: 01705 826714
Head: Mrs J M Dawtrey BA
Type: Girls Day G4-18
No of Pupils: G625 VIth90
Fees: DAY £3036-£4140

ST JOHN'S COLLEGE
Grove Road South, Southsea, Hampshire PO5 3QW
Tel: 01705 815118
Head: Mr G Morgan
Type: Co-educational Day & Boarding B4-18 G4-18
No of Pupils: B555 G55 VIth90 FB85
Fees: FB £7140-£8100
DAY £2820-£4050

Winchester

★ **ST SWITHUN'S SCHOOL**
Alresford Road, Winchester, Hampshire SO21 1HA
Tel: 01962 861316
Head: Dr H L Harvey BSc
Type: Girls Boarding & Day G11-18
No of Pupils: G348 VIth115
Fees: FB £11,580 DAY £6990

WINCHESTER COLLEGE
College Street, Winchester, Hampshire SO23 9NA
Tel: 01962 854328
Head: J P Sabben-Clare MA
Type: Boys Boarding & Day B13-18
No of Pupils: B406 VIth284
Fees: FB £13,290 DAY £9966

Hereford & Worcester

Bromsgrove

BROMSGROVE SCHOOL
Bromsgrove, Hereford & Worcester B61 7DU
Tel: 01527 579679
Head: Timothy M Taylor MA, DipEd
Type: Co-educational Day & Boarding B7-18 G7-18
No of Pupils: B511 G344 VIth275
Fees: FB £9105-£10,305 DAY £5895-£6750

Hereford

THE HEREFORD CATHEDRAL SCHOOL
Old Deanery, Hereford HR1 2NG
Tel: 01432 363522
Head: Dr H C Tomlinson BA, FRHistS, FRSA
Type: Co-educational Day & Boarding B3-18 G3-18
No of Pupils: B325 G305 VIth175 FB50
Fees: FB £7980-£7980
DAY £4530-£4530

Kidderminster

HOLY TRINITY SCHOOL
Birmingham Road, Kidderminster,
Hereford & Worcester DY10 2BY
Tel: 01562 822929
Head: Mrs S M Bell MEd
Type: Girls Day B2-11 G2-18
No of Pupils: B21 G259 VIth29
Fees: DAY £2055-£3885

Malvern

LAWNSIDE
Albert Road South, Malvern, Hereford & Worcester WR14 3AJ
Tel: 01684 568168
Head: Miss J A Harvey GNSM, LRAM, PGCE
Type: Girls Boarding & Day G11-18
No of Pupils: G130 FB130
Fees: FB £9585 DAY £5685

★ **MALVERN COLLEGE**
College Road, Malvern, Hereford & Worcester WR14 3DF
Tel: 01684 892333
Head: Hugh C K Carson BA
Type: Co-educational Boarding & Day B13-18 G13-18
No of Pupils: B428 G181 VIth319
Fees: FB £12,750 DAY £9270

MALVERN GIRLS' COLLEGE
15 Avenue Road, Malvern, Hereford & Worcester WR14 3BA
Tel: 01684 892288
Head: Rev P D Newton BA, MPhil, PGCE
Type: Girls Boarding & Day G11-18
No of Pupils: G744 VIth176
Fees: FB £11,700 DAY £7800

ST JAMES'S AND THE ABBEY
185 West Malvern Road, Malvern,
Hereford & Worcester WR14 4DF
Tel: 01684 560851
Head: Miss E M Mullenger BA
Type: Girls Boarding & Day G11-18
No of Pupils: G130 VIth50 FB120 WB28
Fees: FB £10,962 WB £10,962
DAY £7308

Tenbury Wells

SAINT MICHAEL'S COLLEGE
Oldwood Road, Tenbury Wells,
Hereford & Worcester WR15 8PH
Tel: 01584 811300
Head: Stuart Higgins BA, MEd
Type: Co-educational Boarding B14-19 G14-19
No of Pupils: B27 G23 VIth68
Fees: FB £10,545

Worcester

ROYAL GRAMMAR SCHOOL WORCESTER
Worcester WR1 1HP
Tel: 01905 613391
Head: W A Jones MA
Type: Boys Day B7-18
No of Pupils: B706 VIth210 WB10
Fees: DAY £3672-£4590

ST MARY'S CONVENT SCHOOL
Worcester WR5 2HP
Tel: 01905 357786
Head: Mrs M Kilbride
Type: Girls Day B3-8 G3-18
Fees: DAY £2055-£3315

THE ALICE OTTLEY SCHOOL
Upper Tything, Worcester WR1 1HW
Tel: 01905 27061
Head: Miss C Sibbit MA
Type: Girls Day G3-18
No of Pupils: G557 VIth144
Fees: DAY £2355-£5052

THE KING'S SCHOOL
Worcester WR1 2LH
Tel: 01905 23016
Head: Dr J M Moore JP, MA, PhD
Type: Co-educational Day & Boarding B7-18 G7-18
No of Pupils: B486 G254 VIth228
Fees: FB £7230-£9099
DAY £3381-£5250

Hertfordshire

Barnet

ST MARTHA'S SENIOR SCHOOL
Camlet Way, Barnet, Hertfordshire EN5 5PX
Tel: 0181 449 6889
Head: Sr M Cecile Archer BA(Hons), PGCE
Type: Girls Day G11-18
No of Pupils: G354 VIth50
Fees: DAY £3150

Berkhamsted

BERKHAMSTED SCHOOL
Castle Street, Berkhamsted, Hertfordshire HP4 2BB
Tel: 01442 863236
Type: Boys Day & Boarding B7-18 G16-18
No of Pupils: B730 G14
Fees: FB £11,034 DAY £6774

BERKHAMSTED SCHOOL FOR GIRLS
Kings Road, Berkhamsted, Hertfordshire HP4 3BG
Tel: 01442 862168
Head: Dr P Chadwick MA(Cantab), MA(London), PhD(London)
Type: Girls Day & Boarding B3-7 G3-18
No of Pupils: B19 G410 VIth88 FB24 WB21
Fees: FB £9327 WB £9327
DAY £3474-£5487

EGERTON-ROTHESAY SCHOOL
Durrants Lane, Berkhamsted, Hertfordshire HP4 3UJ
Tel: 01442 865275
Head: J R Adkins BSc(Hons), PGCE
Type: Co-educational Day B2-18 G2-18
No of Pupils: B283 G171 VIth21
Fees: DAY £534-£5490

HARESFOOT SENIOR SCHOOL
The Common, Berkhamsted, Hertfordshire HP4 2QF
Tel: 01442 877215
Head: D L Davies MA
Type: Co-educational Day B11-18 G11-18
No of Pupils: B44 G14 VIth3
Fees: DAY £4800-£5850

Bishop's Stortford

BISHOP'S STORTFORD COLLEGE
Maze Green Road, Bishop's Stortford, Hertfordshire CM23 2QZ
Tel: 01279 838575
Head: S G G Benson
Type: Boys Boarding & Day B13-18 G16-18
No of Pupils: B318 G30 FB160
Fees: FB £10,020 DAY £7230

Directory - Independent Schools with Sixth Form entry

Borehamwood

HABERDASHERS' ASKE'S SCHOOL
Butterfly Lane, Borehamwood, Hertfordshire WD6 3AF
Tel: 0181 207 4323
Head: Mr J W R Golding MA
Type: Boys Day B7-18
No of Pupils: B1300
Fees: DAY £5136-£5601

★ **HABERDASHERS' ASKE'S SCHOOL FOR GIRLS**
Aldenham Road, Borehamwood, Hertfordshire WD6 3BT
Tel: 0181 953 4261
Head: Mrs P A Penney BA, FRSA, FIMgt
Type: Girls Day G4-18
No of Pupils: G1145 VIth240
Fees: DAY £4410

Bushey

C K H R IMMANUEL COLLEGE
87/91 Elstree Road, Bushey, Hertfordshire WD2 3RH
Tel: 0181 950 0604
Head: Myrna Jacobs BA(Hons)
Type: Co-educational Day B11-18 G11-18
No of Pupils: B166 G128 VIth29
Fees: DAY £5650

Elstree

ALDENHAM SCHOOL
Elstree, Hertfordshire WD6 3AJ
Tel: 01923 858122
Head: S R Borthwick BSc, CPhys, MInstP
Type: Boys Boarding & Day B11-18 G16-18
No of Pupils: B375 VIth120 FB100
Fees: FB £8316-£11,910
DAY £5196-£8175

Hatfield

QUEENSWOOD SCHOOL
Shepherd's Way, Hatfield, Hertfordshire AL9 6NS
Tel: 01707 652262
Head: Clarissa Farr MA
Type: Girls Boarding & Day G11-18
No of Pupils: G288 VIth102
Fees: FB £10,974-£11,958
DAY £6768-£7374

Hertford

HAILEYBURY
Hertford, Hertfordshire SG13 7NU
Tel: 01992 463353
Head: S A Westley MA
Type: Boys Boarding & Day B11-18 G16-18
No of Pupils: B298 VIth283 FB420
Fees: FB £13,338-£13,338 DAY £6405-£9672

Hitchin

THE PRINCESS HELENA COLLEGE
Preston, Hitchin, Hertfordshire SG4 7RT
Tel: 01462 432100
Head: J Jarvis OBE, BA, MSc, FIPD, FIMgt, FRGS
Type: Girls Boarding & Day G11-18
No of Pupils: G100 VIth40
Fees: FB £9990 DAY £6960

Kings Langley

RUDOLF STEINER SCHOOL
Langley Hill, Kings Langley, Hertfordshire WD4 9HG
Tel: 01923 262505
Type: Co-educational Day B3-19 G3-19
Fees: DAY £2145-£3450

Letchworth

ST CHRISTOPHER SCHOOL
Barrington Road, Letchworth, Hertfordshire SG6 3JZ
Tel: 01462 679301
Head: Colin Reid MA
Type: Co-educational Day & Boarding B2-18 G2-18
No of Pupils: B310 G206 VIth95
Fees: FB £9171-£11,454
DAY £1620-£6489

ST FRANCIS' COLLEGE
The Broadway, Letchworth, Hertfordshire SG6 3PJ
Tel: 01462 670511
Head: Miss M Hegarty BA, HDipEd, DHS
Type: Girls Day & Boarding B3-7 G3-18
No of Pupils: B13 G282 VIth52 FB60
Fees: FB £8325-£10,410 WB £6825-£10,200
DAY £2685-£5355

Rickmansworth

THE RICKMANSWORTH MASONIC SCHOOL
Rickmansworth Park, Rickmansworth, Hertfordshire WD3 4HF
Tel: 01923 773168
Head: Mrs I M Andrews MA(Oxon)
Type: Girls Day & Boarding G4-18
No of Pupils: G680
Fees: FB £5229-£8811 WB £5154-£8736
DAY £2760-£5361

St Albans

ST ALBANS HIGH SCHOOL FOR GIRLS
Townsend Avenue, St Albans, Hertfordshire AL1 3SJ
Tel: 01727 853800
Head: Mrs C Y Daly BSc
Type: Girls Day G7-18
No of Pupils: G720
Fees: DAY £4170-£5040

ST ALBANS SCHOOL
Abbey Gateway, St Albans, Hertfordshire AL3 4HB
Tel: 01727 855521
Head: Mr A R Grant MA(Cantab)
Type: Boys Day B11-18 G16-18
No of Pupils: B430 VIth220
Fees: DAY £5865

ST COLUMBA'S COLLEGE
King Harry Lane, St Albans, Hertfordshire AL3 4AW
Tel: 01727 855185
Head: J Stuart MA(Oxon)
Type: Boys Day B11-18
No of Pupils: B500
Fees: DAY £4140

Tring

THE ARTS EDUCATIONAL SCHOOL
Tring Park, Tring, Hertfordshire HP23 5LX
Tel: 01442 824255
Head: Mrs J D Billing GGSM(London), CertEd, FRSA
Type: Co-educational Boarding & Day B8-18 G8-18
No of Pupils: FB160
Fees: FB £8673-£11,340 DAY £5003-£7005

Ware

★ **ST EDMUND'S COLLEGE**
Old Hall Green, Ware, Hertfordshire SG11 1DS
Tel: 01920 821504
Head: D J J McEwen MA(Oxon), FRSA
Type: Co-educational Day & Boarding B3-18 G3-18
No of Pupils: B235 G140 VIth140 FB106 WB12
Fees: FB £10,320

Watford

NORTHFIELD SCHOOL
Church Road, Watford, Hertfordshire WD1 3QB
Tel: 01923 229758
Head: Mrs P Hargreaves BSc, MEd
Type: Girls Day B2-7 G2-18
No of Pupils: B20 G100
Fees: DAY £3180-£4023

ST MARGARET'S SCHOOL
Merryhill Road, Watford, Hertfordshire WD2 1DT
Tel: 0181 950 1548
Head: Miss M de Villiers BA
Type: Girls Boarding & Day G4-18
No of Pupils: G438 VIth66
Fees: FB £7935-£9210 DAY £3240-£5625

STANBOROUGH SCHOOL
Stanborough Park, Watford, Hertfordshire WD2 6JT
Tel: 01923 673268
Head: Dr A Luxton PhD
Type: Co-educational Day & Boarding B3-18 G3-18
Fees: FB £5890-£6690 DAY £2790

Welwyn

SHERRARDSWOOD SCHOOL
Lockleys, Welwyn, Hertfordshire AL6 0BJ
Tel: 01438 714282
Head: Martin Lloyd MA
Type: Co-educational Day & Boarding B4-18 G4-18
No of Pupils: B159 G138 VIth20
Fees: FB £6804-£8385
DAY £2706-£4437

Isle of Man

Castletown

KING WILLIAM'S COLLEGE
Castletown, Isle of Man IM9 1TP
Tel: 01624 822551
Head: K Fulton-Peebles MA
Type: Co-educational Day & Boarding B10-19 G10-19
No of Pupils: B163 G108 VIth45 FB95
Fees: FB £9330-£11,100
DAY £8250-£11,580

Lincolnshire

Grimsby

ST JAMES' SCHOOL
22 Bargate, Grimsby, Lincolnshire DN34 4SY
Tel: 01472 362093/4
Head: D J Berisford BA, CertEd
Type: Co-educational Boarding & Day B4-18 G4-18
No of Pupils: B134 G89 VIth23
Fees: FB £6273-£8163 WB £5874-£7764
DAY £2325-£4890

Isle of Wight

Bembridge

BEMBRIDGE SCHOOL
Hillway, Bembridge, Isle of Wight PO35 5PH
Tel: 01983 872101
Head: A R Doe BSc
Type: Co-educational Boarding & Day B9-16 G9-16
No of Pupils: B75 G45
Fees: FB £9640 WB £9640
DAY £4805

Ryde

RYDE SCHOOL
9 Vernon Square, Ryde, Isle of Wight PO33 2JG
Tel: 01983 611756
Principal: M D Featherstone
Type: Co-educational Day B2-18 G2-18
No of Pupils: B390 G293
Fees: FB £5451-£9231 DAY £1866-£4524

RYDE SCHOOL WITH UPPER CHINE
Queens Road, Ryde, Isle of Wight PO33 3BE
Tel: 01983 562229
Head: M D Featherstone MA
Type: Co-educational Day & Boarding B3-18 G3-18
No of Pupils: B305 G235 VIth135
Fees: FB £7374-£8877 WB £7374-£8877
DAY £1794-£4358

Kent

Ashford

ASHFORD SCHOOL
East Hill, Ashford, Kent TN24 8PB
Tel: 01233 625171/2
Head: Mrs P Metham BA(Hons) Bristol
Type: Girls Day & Boarding G11-18
No of Pupils: G366 VIth111
Fees: FB £9747-£11,319
DAY £626-£6513

Bromley

BASTON SCHOOL
Baston Road, Bromley, Kent BR2 7AB
Tel: 0181 462 1010
Head: Mr C R C Wimble MA(Cantab), PGTC
Type: Girls Day & Boarding G2-18
No of Pupils: G193 VIth28 FB24 WB3
Fees: FB £9222-£9222 WB £9072-£9072
DAY £1005-£4722

BISHOP CHALLONER SCHOOL
Bromley Road, Bromley, Kent BR2 0BS
Tel: 0181 460 3546
Head: T Robinson BSc
Type: Co-educational Day B3-18 G3-18
Fees: DAY £2250-£3585

BROMLEY HIGH SCHOOL GPDST
Blackbrook Lane, Bromley, Kent BR1 2TW
Tel: 0181 468 7981
Head: Mrs E J Hancock BA
Type: Girls Day G4-18
No of Pupils: G662 VIth129
Fees: DAY £3864-£4920

HOLY TRINITY COLLEGE
81 Plaistow Lane, Bromley, Kent BR1 3LL
Tel: 0181 313 0399
Heads: Mrs Doreen Bradshaw BA, MA, PGCE
& Miss Anne Murphy CertEd
Type: Girls Day B3-4 G3-18
No of Pupils: B30 G546 VIth72
Fees: DAY £1395-£4347

Canterbury

KENT COLLEGE
Whitstable Road, Canterbury, Kent CT2 9DT
Tel: 01227 763231
Head: E B Halse BSc (Wales)
Type: Co-educational Day & Boarding B3-18 G3-18
No of Pupils: B307 G218 VIth160
Fees: FB £8481-£10,770 DAY £6048

THE KING'S SCHOOL, CANTERBURY
Canterbury, Kent CT1 2ES
Tel: 01227 595501
Head: Rev Keith Wilkinson BA, MA, FRSA
Type: Co-educational Boarding & Day B13-18 G13-18
No of Pupils: B438 G302
Fees: FB £13,440 DAY £9285

ST EDMUND'S SCHOOL
Canterbury, Kent CT2 8HU
Tel: 01227 454575
Head: A N Ridley MA(Oxon)
Type: Co-educational Day & Boarding B3-18 G3-18
No of Pupils: B320 G170 VIth120
Fees: FB £12,030 DAY £3090-£8310

Chislehurst

★ **FARRINGTONS & STRATFORD HOUSE**
Perry Street, Chislehurst, Kent BR7 6LR
Tel: 0181 467 0256
Head: Mrs B J Stock BA(Hons)
Type: Girls Day & Boarding G11-18
No of Pupils: G280 VIth85
Fees: FB £10,278 DAY £5205

Cranbrook

★ **BEDGEBURY SCHOOL**
Bedgebury Park, Cranbrook, Kent TN17 2SH
Tel: 01580 211221/211954
Head: Mrs L J Griffin BA, BPhil
Type: Girls Boarding & Day B3-7 G3-19
No of Pupils: B13 G257 VIth97
Fees: FB £7425-£11,301 DAY £1641-£6996

BENENDEN SCHOOL
Cranbrook, Kent TN17 4AA
Tel: 01580 240592
Head: Mrs G duCharme MA
Type: Girls Boarding G11-18
No of Pupils: G440 VIth140
Fees: FB £13,260

BETHANY SCHOOL
Cranbrook, Kent TN17 1LB
Tel: 01580 211273
Head: W M Harvey MA(Oxon) DipEd
Type: Co-educational Boarding & Day B11-18 G11-18
No of Pupils: B245 G50 VIth84
Fees: FB £9819-£10,353 WB £9819-£10,353
DAY £6282-£6813

★ **CRANBROOK SCHOOL**
Waterloo Road, Cranbrook, Kent TN17 3JD
Tel: 01580 712163
Head: Mr P A Close MA, FRSA
Type: Co-educational Day & Boarding B13-18 G13-18
No of pupils: B155 G116
Fees: FB £5100

Dover

DOVER COLLEGE
Effingham Crescent, Dover, Kent CT17 9RH
Tel: 01304 205969
Head: M P G Wright BA, JP
Type: Co-educational Boarding & Day B11-18 G11-18
No of Pupils: B130 G120 VIth100
Fees: FB £6900-£11,820 WB £9450-£11,820
DAY £3900-£6450

DUKE OF YORK'S ROYAL MILITARY SCHOOL
Dover, Kent CT15 5EQ
Tel: 01304 245024
Head: Col G H Wilson BA, DipEd, MEd, FRSA
Type: Co-educational Boarding B11-18 G11-18
No of Pupils: VIth120
Fees: FB £795-£795

Gravesend

COBHAM HALL SCHOOL
Gravesend, Kent DA12 3BL
Tel: 01474 823371/824319
Head: Mrs R McCarthy BA
Type: Girls Boarding & Day G11-18
No of Pupils: G200 VIth70 FB160 WB10
Fees: FB £12,855 DAY £6600-£8250

Maidstone

SUTTON VALENCE SCHOOL WITH UNDERHILL
Maidstone, Kent ME17 3HN
Tel: 01622 842281
Head: N A Sampson MA
Type: Co-educational Day & Boarding B3-19 G3-19
No of Pupils: B373 G277 VIth125 FB115 WB4
Fees: FB £8850-£11,700 DAY £3150-£7485

Ramsgate

ST LAWRENCE COLLEGE IN THANET
Ramsgate, Kent CT11 7AE
Tel: 01843 587666
Head: Mark Slater, MA
Type: Co-educational Boarding & Day B4-18 G4-18
No of Pupils: B321 G204 VIth132 FB230
Fees: FB £8880-£11,835
DAY £5820-£7905

Rochester

GAD'S HILL SCHOOL
Rochester, Kent ME3 7PA
Tel: 01474 822366
Head: Mrs A Everitt BA(Hons), AKC, PGCE
Type: Co-educational Day B3-11 G3-18
No of Pupils: B40 G110 VIth1
Fees: DAY £1338-£2925

KING'S SCHOOL, ROCHESTER
Satis House, Rochester, Kent ME1 1TE
Tel: 01634 843913
Head: Dr I R Walker BA, PhD, LTh, ABIA, FCollP, FRSA
Type: Co-educational Day & Boarding B4-18 G4-18
No of Pupils: B435 G106 VIth127
Fees: FB £9735-£12,375 WB £9735-£12,375
DAY £3510-£7110

Sevenoaks

COMBE BANK SCHOOL
Sevenoaks, Kent TN14 6AE
Tel: 01959 562918
Heads: Miss N Spurr BSc(Senior), FRSA
& Mrs E Marsden BA
Type: Girls Day B3-5 G3-18
No of Pupils: B17 G389 VIth47
Fees: DAY £1950-£6030

SEVENOAKS SCHOOL
Sevenoaks, Kent TN13 1HU
Tel: 01732 455133
Head: R P Barker MA
Type: Co-educational Day & Boarding B11-18 G11-18
No of Pupils: B525 G415 FB331
Fees: FB £11,178-£11,961
DAY £6804-£7587

WALTHAMSTOW HALL
Sevenoaks, Kent TN13 3UL
Tel: 01732 451334
Head: Mrs J S Lang MA(Oxford)
Type: Girls Day & Boarding G3-18
No of Pupils: G370 VIth110
Fees: FB £10,035-£12,360 WB £10,035-£12,360
DAY £285-£6660

WEST HEATH SCHOOL
Sevenoaks, Kent TN13 1SR
Tel: 01732 452541
Head: Mrs A Williamson BSc, FRSA
Type: Girls Boarding & Day G11-18
No of Pupils: G75 VIth30
Fees: FB £11,040 DAY £7755

Tonbridge

SACKVILLE SCHOOL
Tonbridge Rd, Tonbridge, Kent TN11 9HN
Tel: 01732 838888
Head: Mrs M Sinclair MA
Type: Co-educational Day B11-18 G11-18
No of Pupils: B100 G16 VIth3
Fees: DAY £4806-£6024

TONBRIDGE SCHOOL
Tonbridge, Kent TN9 1JP
Tel: 01732 365555
Head: J M Hammond MA
Type: Boys Boarding & Day B13-18
No of Pupils: B680 FB430
Fees: FB £12,969 DAY £9153

Tunbridge

BEECHWOOD SACRED HEART
12 Pembury Road, Tunbridge Wells, Kent TN2 3QD
Tel: 01892 532747
Head: T S Hodkinson
Type: Girls Day & Boarding B2-11 G2-18
No of Pupils: B8 G151 VIth54
Fees: FB £8280-£11,211
DAY £2535-£6675

KENT COLLEGE, PEMBURY
Tunbridge Wells, Kent TN2 4AX
Tel: 01892 822006
Head: Miss B J Crompton BSc, CPhys, MInstP
Type: Girls Boarding & Day G3-18
No of Pupils: G327 VIth63 FB68 WB32
Fees: FB £8760-£11,700 WB £7710-£10,905
DAY £3345-£6960

Westgate-on-Sea

URSULINE COLLEGE
225 Canterbury Road, Westgate-on-Sea, Kent CT8 8LX
Tel: 01843 834431
Head: Sr Alice Montgomery OSU, MEd
Type: Co-educational Boarding & Day B5-18 G5-18
No of Pupils: B130 G190 VIth120
Fees: FB £9969-£11,124
DAY £3750-£5640

Lancashire

Blackburn

QUEEN ELIZABETH'S GRAMMAR SCHOOL
West Park Road, Blackburn, Lancashire BB2 6DF
Tel: 01254 59911
Head: Dr D S Hempsall MA, PhD, FRSA
Type: Boys Day B7-19 G16-18
No of Pupils: B1123 G66
Fees: DAY £2944-£3720

TAUHEEDUL ISLAM GIRLS HIGH SCHOOL
31 Bicknell Street, Blackburn, Lancashire BB1 7EY
Tel: 01254 54021
Head: I M Patel BA, BEd
Type: Girls Day G11-16
No of Pupils: G134
Fees: DAY £400

WESTHOLME SCHOOL
Wilmar Lodge, Blackburn, Lancashire BB2 6QU
Tel: 01254 53447
Head: Mrs L Croston BSc(Hons), PGCE(Cantab), ALCM
Type: Girls Day B3-7 G3-18
No of Pupils: G749 VIth120
Fees: DAY £2625-£3690

Blackpool

★ **ARNOLD SCHOOL**
Lytham Road, Blackpool, Lancashire FY4 1JG
Tel: 01253 346391
Head: W T Gillen MA
Type: Co-educational Day B3-18 G3-18
No of Pupils: B411 G402 VIth223
Fees: DAY £3900

ELMSLIE GIRLS' SCHOOL
194 Whitegate Drive, Blackpool, Lancashire FY3 9HL
Tel: 01253 763775
Head: Miss E M Smithies MA(Oxon)
Type: Girls Day B2-7 G2-18
No of Pupils: B16 G230 VIth40
Fees: DAY £2985-£4140

Bury

BURY GRAMMAR SCHOOL
Tenterden Street, Bury, Lancashire BL9 0HN
Tel: 0161 797 2700
Head: K Richards MA
Type: Boys Day B7-18
No of Pupils: B700 VIth165
Fees: DAY £2763-£3876

BURY GRAMMAR SCHOOL (GIRLS)
Bridge Road, Bury, Lancashire BL9 0HH
Tel: 0161 797 2808
Head: Miss J M Lawley BA
Type: Girls Day B4-7 G4-18
No of Pupils: B72 G697 VIth210
Fees: DAY £3876

Clitheroe

STONYHURST COLLEGE
Clitheroe, Lancashire BB7 9PZ
Tel: 01254 826345
Head: A J F Aylward MA(Oxon), PGCE
Type: Co-educational Boarding & Day B13-18 G16-18
No of Pupils: B383 G9 VIth165 FB331
Fees: FB £11,472 DAY £7125

Fleetwood

ROSSALL SCHOOL
Fleetwood, Lancashire FY7 8JW
Tel: 01253 774247/774201
Head: R D W Rhodes JP, BA
Type: Co-educational Boarding & Day B11-18 G11-18
No of Pupils: B165 G96 VIth135 FB297
Fees: FB £7710-£11,400 WB £7710-£11,400 DAY £4200

Lancaster

BENTHAM GRAMMAR SCHOOL
Lancaster, Lancashire LA2 7DB
Tel: 01524 261275
Head: T Halliwell BSc, MA
Type: Co-educational Boarding & Day B3-18 G3-18
No of Pupils: B113 G96 VIth50 FB127
Fees: FB £7950-£9450 WB £7950-£9450 DAY £2850-£4710

Lytham-St-Annes

KING EDWARD VII SCHOOL
Clifton Drive, Lytham-St-Annes, Lancashire FY8 1DT
Tel: 01253 736459
Head: P J Wilde MA(Oxon)
Type: Boys Day B3-18 G3-11
No of Pupils: B450 G70 VIth115
Fees: DAY £3870

QUEEN MARY SCHOOL
Lytham-St-Annes, Lancashire FY8 1DS
Tel: 01253 723246
Head: Miss M C Ritchie JP, BSc
Type: Co-educational Day B3-10 G3-18
No of Pupils: B105 G605 VIth100
Fees: DAY £3870

ST ANNE'S COLLEGE GRAMMAR SCHOOL
293 Clifton Drive South, Lytham-St-Annes, Lancashire FY8 1HN
Tel: 01253 725815
Heads: Mr & Mrs S Welsby
Type: Co-educational Day B2-18 G2-18
No of Pupils: B106 G106
Fees: DAY £1950-£2475

Oldham

HULME GRAMMAR SCHOOL FOR GIRLS
Chamber Road, Oldham, Lancashire OL8 4BX
Tel: 0161 624 2523
Head: Miss M S Smolenski BSc
Type: Girls Day G7-18
No of Pupils: G635 VIth130
Fees: DAY £2535-£3549

THE HULME GRAMMAR SCHOOL
Chamber Road, Oldham, Lancashire OL8 4BX
Tel: 0161 624 4497
Head: T J Turvey BSc, DipEd, CBiol, FIBiol, FLS
Type: Boys Day B7-18
No of Pupils: B632 VIth165
Fees: DAY £3501

Ormskirk

SCARISBRICK HALL SCHOOL
Ormskirk, Lancashire L40 9RQ
Tel: 01704 880200
Head: D M Raynor BA, DipEd
Type: Co-educational Day B3-18 G3-18
No of Pupils: B280 G250
Fees: DAY £1869-£2817

Preston

KIRKHAM GRAMMAR SCHOOL
Ribby Road, Preston, Lancashire PR4 2BH
Tel: 01772 671079
Head: B Stacey MA, DipEd(Oxon), FRSA
Type: Co-educational Day & Boarding B4-18 G4-18
No of Pupils: B446 G385
Fees: FB £6651 DAY £2775-£3675

Southport

KINGSWOOD SCHOOLS
26 Westcliffe Rd, Southport, Lancashire PR8 2BU
Tel: 01704 563211
Head: E J Borowski BSc, GRIC, CertEd
Type: Co-educational Day B1-18 G1-18
No of Pupils: B177 G233
Fees: DAY £1030-£2880

Leicestershire

Leicester

DARUL ULOOM LEICESTER
119 Loughborough Road, Leicester LE4 5LN
Tel: 0116 2668922/2611278
Head: Molana (Islamic Doctor)
Type: Boys Boarding

★ **LEICESTER GRAMMAR SCHOOL**
8 Peacock Lane, Leicester LE1 5PX
Tel: 0116 291 0500
Head: J B Sugden MA(Cantab), MPhil, FRSA
Type: Co-educational Day B10-18 G10-18
No of Pupils: B325 G287 VIth150
Fees: DAY £4320

LEICESTER HIGH SCHOOL FOR GIRLS
454 London Road, Leicester LE2 2PP
Tel: 0116 2705338
Head: Mrs P A Watson BSc
Type: Girls Day G3-18
No of Pupils: G420 VIth50
Fees: DAY £2850-£4500

RATCLIFFE COLLEGE
Fosse Way, Leicester LE7 4SG
Tel: 01509 817000
Head: T A Kilbride BA
Type: Co-educational Boarding & Day B10-18 G10-18
No of Pupils: B264 G113 VIth115
Fees: FB £9459 WB £7521 DAY £5016-£6309

Loughborough

★ **LOUGHBOROUGH GRAMMAR SCHOOL**
6 Burton Walks, Loughborough, Leicestershire LE11 2DU
Tel: 01509 233233
Head: D N Ireland MA
Type: Boys Day & Boarding B10-18
No of Pupils: B940 VIth270
Fees: FB £8586 WB £7551 DAY £4662

LOUGHBOROUGH HIGH SCHOOL
Burton Walks, Loughborough, Leicestershire LE11 2DU
Tel: 01509 212348
Head: Miss J E L Harvatt BA
Type: Girls Day G11-18
No of Pupils: G386 VIth143
Fees: DAY £4194

OUR LADY'S CONVENT SCHOOL
Burton Street, Loughborough, Leicestershire LE11 2DT
Tel: 01509 263901
Head: Sr Shelagh Fynn
Type: Girls Day B3-5 G3-18
No of Pupils: B11 G565 VIth45
Fees: DAY £2160-£3660

Market Bosworth

DIXIE GRAMMAR SCHOOL
Station Road, Market Bosworth, Leicestershire CV13 0LE
Tel: 01455 292244
Head: R S Willmott MA
Type: Co-educational Day B0-18 G0-18
No of Pupils: B210 G185 VIth42
Fees: DAY £2820-£3750

Oakham

OAKHAM SCHOOL
Chapel Close, Oakham, Leicestershire LE15 6DT
Tel: 01572 722487
Head: Mr A R M Little MA
Type: Co-educational Boarding & Day B10-18 G10-18
No of Pupils: B514 G526
Fees: FB £11,760 DAY £6450-£6450

Rutland

UPPINGHAM SCHOOL
Rutland, Leicestershire LE15 9QE
Tel: 01572 822216
Head: Dr S C Winkley MA, DPhil
Type: Boys Boarding & Day B11-18 G16-18
No of Pupils: B613 VIth323
Fees: FB £12,750 DAY £5970-£7650

Lincolnshire

Lincoln

LINCOLN MINSTER SCHOOL
Upper Lindum Street, Lincoln LN2 5RW
Tel: 01522 543764
Head: Mrs M Bradley MEd
Type: Girls Day & Boarding G7-18
No of Pupils: G210
Fees: FB £6900-£7215
DAY £3435-£3885

Stamford

STAMFORD HIGH SCHOOL
St Martin's, Stamford, Lincolnshire PE9 2LJ
Tel: 01780 62330
Head: Miss G K Bland BA
Type: Girls Day & Boarding B4-8 G4-18
No of Pupils: B58 G1069 FB103 WB19
Fees: FB £7356-£8178 WB £7284-£8100
DAY £3273-£4089

STAMFORD SCHOOL
St Paul's Street, Stamford, Lincolnshire PE9 2BS
Tel: 01780 62171
Head: J Hale BSc(London)
Type: Boys Day & Boarding B8-18
No of Pupils: B900 FB205
Fees: FB £7752-£8616
DAY £3444-£4308

London

London

★ **ALLEYN'S SCHOOL**
Townley Road, London SE22 8SU
Tel: 0181 693 3422
Head: Dr C H R Niven MA, DipEd, Dr de l'Univ(Lille)
Type: Co-educational Day B5-18 G5-18
No of Pupils: B452 G472 VIth258
Fees: DAY £5895

ASHBOURNE MIDDLE SCHOOL
17 Old Court Place, London W8 4PL
Tel: 0171 376 0360/937 3858
Head: M J Hatchard-Kirby MSc, BApSc
Type: Co-educational Day B16-19 G16-19
Fees: DAY £8325-£10,500

★ **BLACKHEATH HIGH SCHOOL GPDST**
Vanbrugh Park, London SE3 7AG
Tel: 0181 853 2929
Head: Miss R K Musgrave MA(Oxon)
Type: Girls Day G4-18
No of Pupils: G616 VIth70
Fees: DAY £4920

★ **CHANNING SCHOOL**
Highgate, London N6 5HG
Tel: 0181 340 2328
Head: Mrs I R Raphael MA(Cantab)
Type: Girls Day G4-18
No of Pupils: G479 VIth35
Fees: DAY £5880

CHRIST'S COLLEGE
4 St Germans Place, London SE3 ONJ
Tel: 0181 858 0692
Head: R Bellerby MA, BSc, FInstM, FBIS, GradCertEd
Type: Co-educational Day & Boarding B4-19 G4-19
No of Pupils: B100 G28 VIth29
Fees: FB £7125-£8925 WB £6645-£8445
DAY £2685-£4485

CITY OF LONDON SCHOOL
Queen Victoria Street, London EC4V 3AL
Tel: 0171 489 0291
Head: R M Dancey MA
Type: Boys Day B10-18
No of Pupils: B616 VIth252
Fees: DAY £6120

★ **CITY OF LONDON SCHOOL FOR GIRLS**
Barbican, London EC2Y 8BB
Tel: 0171 628 0841
Head: Dr Y A Burne BA, PhD, FRSA
Type: Girls Day G7-18
No of Pupils: G497 VIth161
Fees: DAY £5427

COLFE'S SCHOOL
Horn Park Lane, London SE12 8AW
Tel: 0181 852 2283
Head: Dr D Richardson PhD, BA, FRSA
Type: Boys Day B3-18 G16-18
No of Pupils: B896 G39 VIth206
Fees: DAY £3465-£5370

★ **DULWICH COLLEGE**
London SE21 7LD
Tel: 0181 693 3601
Head: G G Able MA, MA
Type: Boys Day & Boarding B7-18
No of Pupils: B1380 VIth370
Fees: FB £12,636 WB £12,126
DAY £6318

EALING COLLEGE UPPER SCHOOL
83 The Avenue, London W13 8JS
Tel: 0181 997 4346
Head: Mr Barrington Webb MA
Type: Boys Day B11-18 G16-18
No of Pupils: B158 G5 VIth60
Fees: DAY £4080

ELTHAM COLLEGE
Grove Park Road, London SE9 4QF
Tel: 0181 857 1455
Head: D M Green MA, FRSA
Type: Boys Day & Boarding B7-18 G16-18
No of Pupils: B705 G50 VIth183 FB9
Fees: FB £11,481-£12,801
DAY £4410-£5724

EMANUEL SCHOOL
Battersea Rise, London SW11 1HS
Tel: 0181 870 4171
Head: T Jones-Parry MA
Type: Co-educational Day B10-18 G10-18
No of Pupils: B732 G19 VIth178
Fees: DAY £4650-£4950

FOREST BOYS SCHOOL
College Place, London E17 3PY
Head: A G Boggis MA(Oxon)
Type: Co-educational Boarding & Day B7-18 G7-18
No of Pupils: B807 FB23
Fees: FB £9087 DAY £5790

FOREST GIRLS SCHOOL
London E17 3PY
Tel: 0181 520 1744
Head: A G Boggis MA(Oxon)
Type: Girls Day G11-18
No of Pupils: G360
Fees: DAY £5790

★ **FRANCIS HOLLAND SCHOOL**
Clarence Gate, Ivor Place, London NW1 6XR
Tel: 0171 723 0176
Head: Mrs P H Parsonson MA(Oxon)
Type: Girls Day G11-18
No of Pupils: G380 VIth99
Fees: DAY £5295

★ **FRANCIS HOLLAND SCHOOL**
39 Graham Terrace, London SW1W 8JF
Tel: 0171 730 2971
Head: Mrs J A Anderson MA(Cantab), MA(London)
Type: Girls Day G4-18
No of Pupils: G365 VIth50
Fees: DAY £6330

★ **THE GODOLPHIN AND LATYMER SCHOOL**
Iffley Road, London W6 0PG
Tel: 0181 741 1936
Head: Miss M Rudland BSc
Type: Girls Day G11-18
No of Pupils: G700 VIth191
Fees: DAY £5625

HELLENIC COLLEGE OF LONDON
67 Pont Street, London SW1X 0BD
Tel: 0171 581 5044
Head: J Wardrobe MA
Type: Co-educational Day B2-18 G2-18
No of Pupils: B108 G100
Fees: DAY £3885-£5070

HIGHGATE SCHOOL
Highgate, London N6 4AY
Tel: 0181 340 1524
Head: R P Kennedy MA
Type: Boys Day B13-18
No of Pupils: B412 VIth204
Fees: DAY £7515

INTERNATIONAL COMMUNITY SCHOOL
4 York Terrace East, London NW1 4PT
Tel: 0171 935 1206
Head: P Hurd
Type: Co-educational Day B3-18 G3-18
Fees: DAY £5100-£6750

INTERNATIONAL SCHOOL OF LONDON
139 Gunnersbury Avenue, London W3 8LG
Tel: 0181 992 5823
Head: Richard Hermon MA
Type: Co-educational Day B4-18 G4-18
No of Pupils: B108 G81 VIth27
Fees: DAY £5550-£8760

Directory - Independent Schools with Sixth Form entry

★ **JAMES ALLEN'S GIRLS' SCHOOL**
East Dulwich Grove, London SE22 8TE
Tel: 0181 693 1181
Head: Mrs M Gibbs BA, MLitt
Type: Girls Day G11-18
No of Pupils: G543 VIth207
Fees: DAY £6150

KING ALFRED SCHOOL
North End Road, London NW11 7HY
Tel: 0181 457 5200
Head: F P Moran MA(Cantab), PGCE
Type: Co-educational Day B4-18 G4-18
No of Pupils: B213 G235 VIth39
Fees: DAY £3975-£6702

KING FAHAD ACADEMY
Bromyard Avenue, London W3 7HD
Tel: 0181 743 0131
Head: Dr Ibtissam Al-Bassam
Type: Co-educational Day B3-18 G3-18
No of Pupils: B520 G570
Fees: DAY £1672-£2272

KING'S COLLEGE SCHOOL
Southside, London SW19 4TT
Tel: 0181 255 5352
Head: A C V Evans
Type: Boys Day B13-18
No of Pupils: B720
Fees: DAY £6840

★ **LATYMER UPPER SCHOOL**
King Street, London W6 9LR
Tel: 0181 741 1851
Head: C Diggory BSc, CMath, FIMA, FRSA
Type: Boys Day B7-18 G16-18
No of Pupils: B940 G35 VIth280
Fees: DAY £6180

LUBAVITCH HOUSE GRAMMAR SCHOOL
107-115 Stamford Hill, London N16 5RP
Tel: 0181 800 0022
Head: Rabbi T M Hertz
Type: Co-educational Day B2-18 G2-16
No of Pupils: B350 G150

★ **LYCÉE FRANCAIS CHARLES DE GAULLE**
35 Cromwell Road, London SW7 2DG
Tel: 0171 584 6322
Proviseur: Dr H L Brusa BA, MA, PhD(La Sorbonne)
Type: Co-educational Day B4-19 G4-19
No of Pupils: B1400 G1500 VIth355
Fees: DAY £3354

MENORAH GRAMMAR SCHOOL
Beverley Gardens, London NW11 9DG
Tel: 0181 458 8354
Head: Rabbi A M Goldblatt MA(Oxon)
Type: Boys Day B11-18
No of Pupils: B115 VIth10
Fees: DAY £3870

★ **MILL HILL SCHOOL**
The Ridgeway, Mill Hill Village, London NW7 1QS
Tel: 0181 959 1176
Head: William R Winfield MA
Type: Boys Boarding & Day B4-18 G4-18
Fees: FB £12,045 DAY £7815

MORE HOUSE SCHOOL
22-24 Pont Street, London SW1X 0AA
Tel: 0171 235 2855
Head: Miss M Connell MA(Oxon)
Type: Girls Day G11-18
No of Pupils: G230 VIth36
Fees: DAY £5940

★ **THE MOUNT SCHOOL**
Milespit Hill, London NW7 2RX
Tel: 0181 959 3403
Head: Mrs M Pond BSc(Lond), MIBiol
Type: Girls Day G5-18
No of Pupils: G335 VIth50
Fees: DAY £3195-£3750

NOTTING HILL & EALING HIGH SCHOOL
2 Cleveland Road, London W13 8AX
Tel: 0181 997 5744
Head: Mrs S Whitfield MA(Cantab)
Type: Girls Day G5-18
No of Pupils: G832 VIth140
Fees: DAY £3864-£4920

PORTLAND PLACE SCHOOL
56-58 Portland Place, London W1N 3DG
Tel: 0171 307 8700
Head: R Walker BSc, CChem, MRSC
Type: Co-educational Day B11-18 G11-18
No of Pupils: B85 G35
Fees: DAY £5835-£6435

PUTNEY HIGH SCHOOL
35 Putney Hill, London SW15 6BH
Tel: 0181 788 4886
Head: Mrs E Merchant BSc
Type: Girls Day G4-18
No of Pupils: G831 VIth138
Fees: DAY £3864-£4920

★ **QUEEN'S COLLEGE**
43-49 Harley Street, London W1N 2BT
Tel: 0171 636 2446
Head: The Hon Lady Goodhart MA(Oxon)
Type: Girls Day G11-18
No of Pupils: G386 VIth101
Fees: DAY £6105

QUEEN'S GATE SCHOOL
133 Queen's Gate, London SW7 5LE
Tel: 0171 589 3587
Head: Mrs A M Holyoak CertEd
Type: Girls Day G4-18
No of Pupils: G310 VIth46
Fees: DAY £3480-£5400

THE ROYAL BALLET SCHOOL
155 Talgarth Road, London W14 9DE
Tel: 0181 748 6335
Head: J Mitchell
Type: Co-educational Boarding & Day B11-18 G11-18
No of Pupils: B70 G181 FB128
Fees: FB £16,323 DAY £9459

THE ROYAL SCHOOL, HAMPSTEAD
65 Rosslyn Hill, London NW3 5UD
Tel: 0171 794 7707
Head: Mrs C A Sibson BA(Oxon)
Type: Girls Day & Boarding G4-18
No of Pupils: G180
Fees: FB £7500-£9300 WB £5760-£7500
DAY £3450-£4050

SCHILLER INTERNATIONAL UNIVERSITY
Royal Waterloo House, London SE1 8TX
Tel: 0171 928 1372
Head: Dr Richard Taylor PhD
Type: Co-educational Day

SOUTH HAMPSTEAD HIGH SCHOOL GPDST
3 Maresfield Gardens, London NW3 5SS
Tel: 0171 435 2899
Head: Mrs J G Scott BSc
Type: Girls Day G4-18
No of Pupils: G912 VIth155
Fees: DAY £4044-£4920

SOUTHBANK INTERNATIONAL SCHOOL
36-38 Kensington Park Road, London W11 3BU
Tel: 0171 229 8230
Head: M E Toubkin BA
Type: Co-educational Day B5-18 G5-18
Fees: DAY £7290-£8910

ST AUGUSTINE'S PRIORY
Hillcrest Road, London W5 2JL
Tel: 0181 997 2022
Head: Mrs F J Gumley-Mason MA(Cantab)
Type: Girls Day G4-19
No of Pupils: G365 VIth40
Fees: DAY £2505-£3795

ST BENEDICT'S SCHOOL
54 Eaton Rise, London W5 2ES
Tel: 0181 862 2010
Head: Dr A J Dachs MA, PhD(Cantab), FRSA
Type: Boys Day B11-18 G16-18
No of Pupils: B407 VIth186
Fees: DAY £5220

★ **ST DUNSTAN'S COLLEGE**
Stanstead Road, Catford, London SE6 4TY
Tel: 0181 690 1274
Head: J D Moore MA
Type: Co-educational Day B4-18 G4-18
No of Pupils: B155 G26
Fees: DAY £5370

★ **ST JAMES INDEPENDENT SCHOOL FOR GIRLS**
19 Pembridge Villas, London W11 3EP
Tel: 0171 229 2253
Principal: Mrs Laura Hyde CertEd
Type: Girls Day G16-18
No of pupils: 28-30
Fees: DAY £4995

★ **ST JAMES INDEPENDENT SCHOOL FOR BOYS**
Pope's Villa, Cross Deep, Twickenham, Middlesex TW1 4QG
Tel: 0181 892 2002
Principal: Nicholas Debenham MA(Cantab)
Type: Boys Day B16-18
No of pupils: B30-40
Fees: DAY £4995

ST PAUL'S GIRLS' SCHOOL
Brook Green, London W6 7BS
Tel: 0171 603 2288
Head: Miss J Gough MA
Type: Girls Day G11-18
No of Pupils: G410 VIth200
Fees: DAY £6627

ST PAUL'S SCHOOL
Lonsdale Road, London SW13 9JT
Tel: 0181 748 9162
Head: R S Baldock MA(Cantab)
Type: Boys Day & Boarding B13-18
No of Pupils: B467 VIth318 WB100
Fees: FB £12,765 WB £12,765
DAY £8490

STREATHAM HILL & CLAPHAM HIGH SCHOOL
42 Abbotswood Road, London SW16 1AW
Tel: 0181 677 8400
Head: Miss G M Ellis BSc(Hons)(Glasgow)
Type: Girls Day G4-18
No of Pupils: G581 VIth95
Fees: DAY £3864-£4920

SYDENHAM HIGH SCHOOL GPDST
19 Westwood Hill, London SE26 6BL
Tel: 0181 778 8737
Head: Mrs G Baker BSc, FZS
Type: Girls Day G4-18
No of Pupils: G470 VIth110
Fees: DAY £3864-£4920

UNIVERSITY COLLEGE SCHOOL
Frognal, London NW3 6XH
Tel: 0171 435 2215
Head: K J Durham BA
Type: Boys Day B11-18
No of Pupils: B500 VIth200
Fees: DAY £6735-£7200

Directory - Independent Schools with Sixth Form entry

★ **VIRGO FIDELIS CONVENT**
Central Hill, Upper Norwood, London SE19 1RS
Tel: 0181 670 6917
Head: Sr Madeleine BA, DipEd
Type: Girls Day G11-18
No of Pupils: G150
Fees: DAY £4275

WESTMINSTER SCHOOL
17 Dean's Yard, London SW1P 3PB
Tel: 0171 963 1003
Head: D M Summerscale MA
Type: Boys Boarding & Day B13-18 G16-18
No of Pupils: B320 VIth361 FB185
Fees: FB £13,530 WB £13,530
DAY £9300-£10,125

WIMBLEDON HIGH SCHOOL
Mansel Road, London SW19 4AB
Tel: 0181 946 1756
Head: Dr J L Clough BA(London), PhD(Hull)
Type: Girls Day G4-18
No of Pupils: G718 VIth143
Fees: DAY £3855-£4920

★ **WOODSIDE PARK SCHOOL**
Friern Barnet Road, London N11 3DR
Tel: 0181 368 3777
Head: R F Metters BEd
Type: Co-educational Day B11-18 G11-18
No of Pupils: B374 G136
Fees: DAY £6000-£9000

Greater Manchester

Bolton

BOLTON SCHOOL (BOYS' DIVISION)
Chorley New Road, Bolton,
Greater Manchester BL1 4PA
Tel: 01204 840201
Head: A W Wright BSc
Type: Boys Day B8-18
No of Pupils: B800 VIth225
Fees: DAY £3333-£4626

BOLTON SCHOOL (GIRLS' DIVISION)
Chorley New Road, Bolton,
Greater Manchester BL1 4PB
Tel: 01204 840201
Head: Miss E J Panton MA(Oxon), FRSA
Type: Girls Day B4-8 G4-18
No of Pupils: B100 G832 VIth222
Fees: DAY £3333-£4626

Manchester

BRIDGEWATER SCHOOL
Drywood Hall, Worsley Road, Manchester M28 2WQ
Tel: 0161 794 1463
Head: Mrs Nairn
Type: Co-educational Day B3-18 G3-18
No of Pupils: B245 G235 VIth50
Fees: DAY £2000-£3995

CHETHAM'S SCHOOL OF MUSIC
Long Millgate, Manchester M3 1SB
Tel: 0161 834 9644
Head: Rev P F Hullah BD, AKC, FRSA
Type: Co-educational Boarding & Day B8-18 G8-18
No of Pupils: B127 G157
Fees: FB £15,600 DAY £12,075

JEWISH HIGH SCHOOL FOR GIRLS
10 Radford Street, Manchester M7 4NT
Tel: 0161 792 2118
Head: Rabbi C Goldblatt
Type: Girls Day G11-18
No of Pupils: G160
Fees: DAY £3300

MANCHESTER GRAMMAR SCHOOL
Old Hall Lane, Manchester M13 0XT
Tel: 0161 224 7201
Head: Dr G M Stephen
Type: Boys Day B11-18
No of Pupils: B1004 VIth400
Fees: DAY £4140

MANCHESTER HIGH SCHOOL FOR GIRLS
Grangethorpe Road, Manchester M14 6HS
Tel: 0161 224 0447
Head: Miss E M Diggory BA, FRSA
Type: Girls Day G4-18
No of Pupils: G790 VIth165
Fees: DAY £2805-£4185

MANCHESTER JEWISH GRAMMAR SCHOOL
Charlton Avenue, Manchester M25 0PH
Tel: 0161 773 1789
Head: Mr Pink BSc(Econ), DipEd
Type: Boys Day B11-18
No of Pupils: B170
Fees: DAY £3900

ST BEDE'S COLLEGE
Alexandra Park, Manchester M16 8HX
Tel: 0161 226 3323
Head: J Byrne BA, MEd
Type: Co-educational Day B11-19 G11-19
No of Pupils: B570 G330
Fees: DAY £3720

WILLIAM HULME'S GRAMMAR SCHOOL
Spring Bridge Road, Manchester M16 8PR
Tel: 0161 226 2054
Head: P D Briggs MA
Type: Co-educational Day B11-18 G11-18
No of Pupils: B386 G183 VIth192
Fees: DAY £4215

WITHINGTON GIRLS' SCHOOL
Wellington Road, Manchester M14 6BL
Tel: 0161 224 1077
Head: Mrs M Kenyon MA
Type: Girls Day G7-18
No of Pupils: G484 VIth136
Fees: DAY £2730-£3930

Merseyside

Birkenhead

BIRKENHEAD HIGH SCHOOL GPDST
86 Devonshire Place, Birkenhead,
Merseyside L43 1TY
Tel: 0151 652 5777
Head: Mrs K R Irving BSc
Type: Girls Day G3-18
No of Pupils: G972
Fees: DAY £2928-£3984

BIRKENHEAD SCHOOL
The Lodge, Birkenhead, Merseyside L43 2JD
Tel: 0151 652 4014
Head: S J Haggett MA
Type: Boys Day B3-18
No of Pupils: B875 VIth189
Fees: DAY £2982-£3897

Liverpool

THE BELVEDERE SCHOOL GPDST
17 Belvedere Road, Liverpool, Merseyside L8 3TF
Tel: 0151 727 1284
Head: Mrs C H Evans BA
Type: Girls Day G3-18
No of Pupils: G535 VIth113
Fees: DAY £2832-£4140

LIVERPOOL COLLEGE
North Mossley Hill Road, Liverpool,
Merseyside L18 8BE
Tel: 0151 724 4000
Head: B R Martin MA, MBA, MIMgt, FRSA
Type: Co-educational Day B3-18 G3-18
No of Pupils: B534 G274 VIth146
Fees: DAY £2685-£4290

MERCHANT TAYLORS' SCHOOL
Crosby, Liverpool, Merseyside L23 0QP
Tel: 0151 928 3308
Head: S J R Dawkins MA
Type: Boys Day B7-18
No of Pupils: B651 VIth197
Fees: DAY £2529-£3744

MERCHANT TAYLORS' SCHOOL FOR GIRLS
Liverpool Road, Liverpool, Merseyside L23 5SP
Tel: 0151 924 3140
Head: Mrs J I Mills BA
Type: Girls Day B4-11 G4-18
No of Pupils: B66 G865 VIth160
Fees: DAY £2421-£3744

ST EDWARD'S COLLEGE
Sandfield Park, Liverpool, Merseyside L12 1LF
Tel: 0151 228 3376
Head: J E Waszek BSc, MA, FRSA, FIMgt
Type: Co-educational Day B3-18 G3-18
No of Pupils: B537 G430 VIth189
Fees: DAY £2550-£3798

ST MARY'S COLLEGE
Crosby, Liverpool, Merseyside L23 3AB
Tel: 0151 924 3926
Head: W Hammond MA
Type: Co-educational Day B3-18 G3-18
No of Pupils: B407 G346 VIth156
Fees: DAY £2022-£3894

South Wirral

MOSTYN HOUSE SCHOOL
Parkgate, South Wirral, Cheshire L64 6SG
Tel: 0151 336 1010
Head: A D J Grenfell MA(Oxon)
Type: Co-educational Day B4-18 G4-18
No of Pupils: B212 G135 VIth36
Fees: DAY £1320-£4485

Middlesex

Ashford

★ **ST DAVID'S SCHOOL**
Church Road, Ashford, Middlesex TW15 3DZ
Tel: 01784 252494
Head: Mrs J G Osborne BA(Hons), DipEd
Type: Girls Day & Boarding G3-18
No of Pupils: G360 VIth100 FB25 WB20
Fees: FB £8985 WB £8460 DAY £4950

Edgware

NORTH LONDON COLLEGIATE SCHOOL
Canons Drive, Edgware, Middlesex HA8 7RJ
Tel: 0181 952 0912
Head: Mrs J L Clanchy MA
Type: Girls Day G4-18
No of Pupils: G1019 VIth227
Fees: DAY £4137-£5124

Enfield

ST JOHN'S SENIOR SCHOOL
North Lodge, Enfield, Middlesex EN2 8BE
Tel: 0181 363 4439
Head: A Tardios LLB(Hons), BA(Hons), CertEd
Type: Co-educational Day B11-18 G11-18
No of Pupils: B51 G58
Fees: DAY £3600-£3900

Feltham

HOUNSLOW COLLEGE
The Old Rectory, Feltham, Middlesex TW13 6PN
Tel: 0181 751 1710
Head: R C Boyd BA, DipPhysEd
Type: Co-educational Day B10-18 G10-18
No of Pupils: B17 G18
Fees: DAY £2595

Hampton

HAMPTON SCHOOL
Hanworth Road, Hampton, Middlesex TW12 3HD
Tel: 0181 979 5526
Head: B R Martin MA(Cantab), MBA MIMgt
Type: Boys Day B11-18
No of Pupils: B930 VIth280
Fees: DAY £5280

THE LADY ELEANOR HOLLES SCHOOL
102 Hanworth Road, Hampton, Middlesex TW12 3HF
Tel: 0181 979 1601
Head: Miss E M Candy BSc, FRSA
Type: Girls Day G7-18
No of Pupils: G705 VIth171
Fees: DAY £4620-£5520

Harrow

BUCKINGHAM COLLEGE SENIOR SCHOOL
15 Hindes Road, Harrow, Middlesex HA1 1SH
Tel: 0181 427 1220
Head: D T F Bell MA, PGCE
Type: Boys Day B11-18 G16-18
Fees: DAY £3705-£4335

HARROW SCHOOL
1 High Street, Harrow, Middlesex HA1 3HW
Tel: 0181 869 1200
Head: N R Bomford MA, FRSA
Type: Boys Boarding B13-18
No of Pupils: B780 VIth320
Fees: FB £13,830

THE JOHN LYON SCHOOL
Middle Road, Harrow, Middlesex HA2 0HN
Tel: 0181 422 2046
Head: Revd T J Wright BD, AKC
Type: Boys Day B11-18
No of Pupils: B525 VIth136
Fees: DAY £5790

Harrow on the Hill

THE PURCELL SCHOOL, LONDON
Mount Park Road, Harrow on the Hill, Middlesex HA1 3JS
Tel: 0181 422 1284
Head: K J Bain MA, FRSA
Type: Co-educational Day & Boarding B8-18 G8-18
No of Pupils: B34 G56 VIth59
Fees: FB £12,699-£14,400 DAY £6969-£8514

Northwood

MERCHANT TAYLORS' SCHOOL
Sandy Lodge, Northwood, Middlesex HA6 2HT
Tel: 01923 820644
Head: J R Gabitass MA(Oxon)
Type: Boys Day & Boarding B11-18
No of Pupils: B492 VIth254
Fees: FB £11,520 DAY £6920

NORTHWOOD COLLEGE
Maxwell Road, Northwood, Middlesex HA6 2YE
Tel: 01923 825446
Head: Mrs A Mayou MA
Type: Girls Day G3-18
No of Pupils: G714 VIth106
Fees: DAY £3420-£5172

ST HELEN'S SCHOOL FOR GIRLS
Eastbury Road, Northwood, Middlesex HA6 3AS
Tel: 01923 828511
Head: Mrs D M Jefkins MA(Cantab), CPhys
Type: Girls Day & Boarding G4-18
No of Pupils: G965 VIth168 FB40 WB12
Fees: FB £8103-£9576 DAY £3294-£5082

Pinner

HEATHFIELD SCHOOL GPDST
Beaulieu Drive, Pinner, Middlesex HA5 1NB
Tel: 0181 868 2346
Head: Miss C M Juett BSc
Type: Girls Day G3-18
No of Pupils: G486 VIth68
Fees: DAY £3444-£4920

Shepperton

★ **HALLIFORD SCHOOL**
Russell Road, Shepperton, Middlesex TW17 9HX
Tel: 01932 223593
Head: J R Crook CertEd(Lond), BA(Wales)
Type: Boys Day B11-19 G16-19
No of Pupils: B284 VIth53
Fees: DAY £2580-£4680

Uxbridge

AMERICAN COMMUNITY SCHOOL
Hillingdon Court, Uxbridge, Middlesex UB10 0BE
Tel: 01895 259771
Head: Paul Berg
Type: Co-educational Day B4-18 G4-18
No of Pupils: B290 G288

Norfolk

Holt

GRESHAM'S SCHOOL
Holt, Norfolk NR25 6EA
Tel: 01263 713271
Head: J H Arkell MA
Type: Co-educational Boarding & Day B13-19 G13-19
No of Pupils: B183 G128 VIth209 FB327 WB7
Fees: FB £12,435 WB £11,190
DAY £8700

Norwich

CAWSTON COLLEGE
Cawston, Norwich, Norfolk NR10 4JD
Tel: 01603 871204
Head: B Harrison BA(Hons), PGCE
Type: Co-educational Boarding & Day B5-17 G5-17
No of Pupils: B93 G30 FB70 WB70
Fees: FB £6534-£8205 WB £6381-£8049
DAY £2226-£4497

HETHERSETT OLD HALL SCHOOL
Hethersett, Norwich, Norfolk NR9 3DW
Tel: 01603 810390
Head: Mrs V M Redington MA, DipEd(Oxon)
Type: Girls Boarding & Day G7-18
No of Pupils: G199 VIth44
Fees: FB £2475-£3075 WB £2475-£3075
DAY £1175-£1550

LANGLEY SCHOOL
Langley Park, Norwich, Norfolk NR14 6BJ
Tel: 01508 520210
Head: S J W McArthur BSc, BA, CertEd, FCoIP
Type: Co-educational Boarding & Day B10-18 G10-18
No of Pupils: B147 G47 VIth51
Fees: FB £8655-£10,500 WB £7410-£8520
DAY £4455-£5460

NORWICH HIGH SCHOOL FOR GIRLS GPDST
95 Newmarket Road, Norwich, Norfolk NR2 2HU
Tel: 01603 453265
Head: Mrs V C Bidwell BA, PGCE, FRSA
Type: Girls Day G4-18
No of Pupils: G850 VIth160
Fees: DAY £3036-£4140

NORWICH SCHOOL
71A The Close, Norwich, Norfolk NR1 4DQ
Tel: 01603 623194
Head: C D Brown MA
Type: Boys Day B8-18 G16-18
No of Pupils: B731 G46
Fees: DAY £4353-£4530

Thetford

THETFORD GRAMMAR SCHOOL
Bridge Street, Thetford, Norfolk IP24 3AF
Tel: 01842 752840
Head: J R Weeks MA, MLitt
Type: Co-educational Day B7-18 G7-18
No of Pupils: B186 G145 VIth59
Fees: DAY £4029-£4377

Northamptonshire

Blackthorn

ST PETER'S INDEPENDENT SCHOOL
Lingswood Park, Blackthorn, Northamptonshire NN3 4TA
Tel: 01604 411745
Head: G J Smith BA, CertEd
Type: Co-educational Day B4-18 G4-18
Fees: DAY £2040

Northampton

NORTHAMPTON HIGH SCHOOL
Newport Pagnell Road, Northampton NN4 6UU
Tel: 01604 765765
Head: Mrs L A Mayne BSc
Type: Girls Day G3-18
No of Pupils: G718 VIth130
Fees: DAY £2535-£4275

NORTHAMPTONSHIRE GRAMMAR SCHOOL
Pitsford Hall, Northampton NN6 9AX
Tel: 01604 880306
Head: Dr M D W Tozer
Type: Boys Day B8-18
No of Pupils: B227
Fees: DAY £4455

★ **QUINTON HOUSE**
Upton Hall, Upton, Northampton NN5 4UX
Tel: 01604 752050
Head: G H Griffiths BA, DASE, FRGS
Type: Co-educational Day B3-18 G3-18
No of Pupils: B165 G160 VIth27
Fees: DAY £3861

Towcester

FALCON MANOR SCHOOL
Greens Norton, Towcester, Northamptonshire NN12 8BN
Tel: 01327 350544
Head: G D Priest
Type: Co-educational Boarding & Day B8-19 G8-19
No of Pupils: B75 G29 VIth16 FB120
Fees: FB £7350-£8700
DAY £3000-£4800

Wellingborough

WELLINGBOROUGH SCHOOL
Wellingborough, Northamptonshire NN8 2BX
Tel: 01933 222427
Head: F R Ullmann MA, ACP, FCollP
Type: Co-educational Day & Boarding B13-18 G13-18
No of Pupils: B246 G134 VIth 136
Fees: FB £9300 WB £8370
DAY £2490-£5175

Northumberland

Alnwick

ST OSWALDS
Spring Gardens, Alnwick, Northumberland NE66 2NU
Tel: 01665 602739
Head: Dr A J Rodd BSc, PhD, PGCE, CChem, MRSC
Type: Co-educational Day B4-13 G4-18
No of Pupils: B40 G76
Fees: DAY £1980-£2970

Berwick-upon-Tweed

LONGRIDGE TOWERS SCHOOL
Longridge Towers, Berwick-upon-Tweed,
Northumberland TD15 2XH
Tel: 01289 307584
Head: Dr M J Barron BSc, PhD
Type: Co-educational Day & Boarding B4-18 G4-18
No of Pupils: B120 G125 VIth45 FB76 WB8
Fees: FB £7245-£8340 WB £7245-£8340
DAY £2475-£4170

Nottingham

Newark

RODNEY SCHOOL
Newark, Nottingham NG22 8NB
Tel: 01636 813281
Head: Miss G R T Howe BEd(Hons)
Type: Co-educational Boarding & Day B7-18 G7-18
No of Pupils: B46 G42 VIth9
Fees: FB £5850 WB £5850
DAY £2910-£3450

Nottingham

NOTTINGHAM HIGH SCHOOL
Waverley Mount, Nottingham NG7 4ED
Tel: 0115 9786056
Head: C S Parker BA, FRSA
Type: Boys Day B11-18
No of Pupils: B782 VIth242
Fees: DAY £4644-£4950

NOTTINGHAM HIGH SCHOOL FOR GIRLS GPDST
9 Arboretum Street, Nottingham NG1 4JB
Tel: 0115 9417663
Head: Mrs A Rees MA(Oxon)
Type: Girls Day G4-18
No of Pupils: G1100 VIth260
Fees: DAY £3036-£4140

TRENT COLLEGE
Derby Road, Nottingham NG10 4AD
Tel: 0115 9732737
Head: J S Lee MA(Oxon)
Type: Co-educational Boarding & Day B11-18 G11-18
No of Pupils: B313 G151 VIth240 FB260
Fees: FB £9198-£10,899
DAY £6198-£6690

Worksop

WORKSOP COLLEGE
Worksop, Nottingham S80 3AP
Tel: 01909 537100
Head: R A Collard MA
Type: Co-educational Boarding & Day B13-18 G13-18
No of Pupils: B150 G60 VIth120 FB130 WB60
Fees: FB £11,325 WB £11,325
DAY £7800

Oxfordshire

Abingdon

ABINGDON SCHOOL
Park Road, Abingdon, Oxfordshire OX14 1DE
Tel: 01235 521563
Head: M St John Parker MA
Type: Boys Boarding & Day B11-18
No of Pupils: B770 VIth270
Fees: FB £9849 WB £9849
DAY £5262

THE EUROPEAN SCHOOL
Culham, Abingdon, Oxfordshire OX14 3DZ
Tel: 01235 522621
Head: Mrs Barco
Type: Co-educational Day B4-18 G4-18

OUR LADY'S CONVENT SENIOR SCHOOL
Radley Road, Abingdon, Oxfordshire OX14 3PS
Tel: 01235 524658
Head: Mrs G Butt MA(Oxon)
Type: Girls Day G11-18
No of Pupils: G225 VIth77
Fees: DAY £3750

RADLEY COLLEGE
Radley, Abingdon, Oxfordshire OX14 2HR
Tel: 01235 543000
Head: R M Morgan MA
Type: Boys Boarding B13-18
No of Pupils: B370 VIth240 FB600
Fees: FB £12,300

THE SCHOOL OF ST HELEN & ST KATHARINE
Faringdon Road, Abingdon, Oxfordshire OX14 1BE
Tel: 01235 520173
Head: Mrs C Hall MA(Oxon)
Type: Girls Day G10-18
No of Pupils: G552 VIth126
Fees: DAY £4500

Banbury

BLOXHAM SCHOOL
Banbury, Oxfordshire OX15 4PE
Tel: 01295 720206
Head: D K Exham MA
Type: Boys Boarding & Day B11-18 G16-18
No of Pupils: B187 VIth173
Fees: FB £12,735 DAY £6660-£9990

SIBFORD SCHOOL
Sibford Ferris, Banbury, Oxfordshire OX15 5QL
Tel: 01295 780441
Head: Susan Freestone MA, BEd
Type: Co-educational Boarding & Day B5-18 G5-18
No of Pupils: B147 G86 VIth140
Fees: FB £7230-£10,035 DAY £3225-£5310

TUDOR HALL SCHOOL
Wykham Park, Banbury, Oxfordshire OX16 9UR
Tel: 01295 263434
Head: Miss N Godfrey BA
Type: Girls Boarding & Day G11-18
No of Pupils: G185 VIth78
Fees: FB £10,545 DAY £6570

Henley-on-Thames

SHIPLAKE COLLEGE
Henley-on-Thames, Oxfordshire RG9 4BS
Tel: 01734 402455
Head: N V Bevan MA(Oxon)
Type: Boys Boarding & Day B13-18
No of Pupils: B280 VIth90 FB230
Fees: FB £11,175 DAY £7530

Oxford

★ **D'OVERBROECK'S**
1 Park Town, Oxford OX2 6SN
Tel: 01865 310000
Heads: Mr S N Cohen BSc & Dr R M Knowles MA, DPhil
Type: Co-educational Day & Boarding B14-19 G14-19
No of Pupils: B130 G120 FB134
Fees: FB £10,800 DAY £7200

HEADINGTON SCHOOL
Oxford OX3 7TD
Tel: 01865 741968
Head: Mrs H A Fender BA(Exeter)
Type: Girls Day & Boarding B4-7 G4-18
No of Pupils: B15 G600 VIth154 FB137 WB60
Fees: FB £8070-£9600 WB £7974-£9504
DAY £2550-£4830

KINGHAM HILL SCHOOL
Kingham, Oxford OX7 6TH
Tel: 01608 658999
Head: M H Payne BSc, PGCE
Type: Co-educational Boarding & Day B11-18 G11-18
No of Pupils: B112 G38 VIth70 FB190
Fees: FB £9435-£9945
DAY £5655-£5970

MAGDALEN COLLEGE SCHOOL
Cowley Place, Oxford OX4 1DZ
Tel: 01865 242191
Head: P M Tinniswood MA, MBA
Type: Boys Day B9-18
No of Pupils: B382 VIth136 FB20
Fees: DAY £5094

OXFORD HIGH SCHOOL GPDST
Belbroughton Road, Oxford OX2 6XA
Tel: 01865 559888
Head: Mrs J Townsend MA, MSc
Type: Girls Day G9-18
No of Pupils: G500 VIth150
Fees: DAY £3036-£4140

RYE ST ANTONY SCHOOL
Pullens Lane, Oxford OX3 0BY
Tel: 01865 62802
Head: Miss A M Jones BA, PGCE
Type: Girls Boarding & Day G8-18
No of Pupils: G400 FB120 WB30
Fees: FB £7185-£7950 WB £6885-£7575 DAY £2775-£4875

ST CLARE'S, OXFORD
139 Banbury Road, Oxford OX2 7AL
Tel: 01865 552031
Head: Mrs M Skarland BA, PGCE(Manchester)
Type: Co-educational Boarding & Day B16-20 G16-20
No of Pupils: B72 G107
Fees: FB £12,820 DAY £8020

ST EDWARD'S SCHOOL
Woodstock Road, Oxford OX2 7NN
Tel: 01865 319200
Head: D Christie BA, BSc(Econ)
Type: Boys Boarding & Day B13-18 G16-18
No of Pupils: B302 VIth271
Fees: FB £12,270 DAY £9210

★ **WYCHWOOD SCHOOL**
74 Banbury Road, Oxford OX2 6JR
Tel: 01865 557976
Head: Mrs M L Duffill CertEd(Oxon)
Type: Girls Boarding & Day G11-18
No of Pupils: G192 VIth33
Fees: FB £7185 WB £6930 DAY £4530

Wallingford

CARMEL COLLEGE
Mongewell Park, Wallingford, Oxfordshire OX10 8BT
Tel: 01491 837505
Head: P D Skelker MA, FRSA
Type: Co-educational Boarding & Day B11-18 G11-18
No of Pupils: B132 G68 FB204
Fees: FB £9300-£13,500 WB £9300-£13,500 DAY £7500

Wantage

★ **ST MARY'S SCHOOL, WANTAGE**
Wantage, Oxfordshire OX12 8BZ
Tel: 01235 763571
Head: Mrs S Bodinham BSc, AKC, AdvDipEd
Type: Girls Boarding G11-18
No of Pupils: G225
Fees: FB £11,550

Witney

COKETHORPE SCHOOL
Cokethorpe, Witney, Oxfordshire OX8 7PU
Tel: 01993 703921
Head: P J S Cantwell BA
Type: Co-educational Boarding & Day B9-18 G9-18
No of Pupils: B184 G42 VIth27 FB48 WB22
Fees: FB £9885-£12,420 DAY £4350-£8010

Shropshire

Bucknell

BEDSTONE COLLEGE
Bucknell, Shropshire SY7 0BG
Tel: 01547 530303
Head: M S Symonds BSc, PGCE
Type: Co-educational Boarding & Day B7-18 G7-18
No of Pupils: B75 G75 VIth50
Fees: FB £6519-£9639 DAY £4335-£6000

Ellesmere

ELLESMERE COLLEGE
Ellesmere, Shropshire SY12 9AB
Tel: 01691 622321
Head: B J Wignall MA, MIMgt
Type: Co-educational Boarding & Day B9-18 G9-18
No of Pupils: B270 G90 VIth127 FB222
Fees: FB £11,100 DAY £4800-£7350

Oswestry

★ **MORETON HALL**
Weston Rhyn, Oswestry, Shropshire SY11 3EW
Tel: 01691 773671
Head: J Forster BA, FRSA
Type: Girls Boarding & Day G10-18
No of Pupils: G280 VIth90
Fees: FB £11,700 DAY £8100

★ **OSWESTRY SCHOOL**
Upper Brook Street, Oswestry, Shropshire SY11 2TL
Tel: 01691 655711
Head: P K Smith MA(Cantab), MEd, FRGS
Type: Co-educational Boarding & Day B9-18 G9-18
No of Pupils: B179 G103 FB107
Fees: DAY £5550

Shrewsbury

ADCOTE SCHOOL FOR GIRLS
Little Ness, Shrewsbury, Shropshire SY4 2JY
Tel: 01939 260202
Head: Mrs S B Cecchet BSc, PGCE
Type: Girls Boarding & Day G5-18
No of Pupils: G106 VIth14 FB38 WB12
Fees: FB £8655-£9540 WB £6645-£9540
DAY £2955-£5295

CONCORD COLLEGE
Acton Burnell Hall, Shrewsbury, Shropshire SY5 7PF
Tel: 01694 731631
Head: A L Morris BA, DipEd
Type: Co-educational Day & Boarding B12-18 G12-18
No of Pupils: B20 G20 VIth230
Fees: FB £11,850 DAY £4230

SHREWSBURY HIGH SCHOOL GPDST
32 Town Walls, Shrewsbury, Shropshire SY1 1TN
Tel: 01743 362872
Head: Miss S Gardner MA
Type: Girls Day G4-18
No of Pupils: G490 VIth88
Fees: DAY £3036-£4140

SHREWSBURY SCHOOL
The Schools, Shrewsbury, Shropshire SY3 7BA
Tel: 01743 344537
Head: F E Maidment MA
Type: Boys Boarding & Day B13-18
No of Pupils: B418 VIth274
Fees: FB £12,375 DAY £8700

Telford

WREKIN COLLEGE
Telford, Shropshire TF1 3BG
Tel: 01952 240131
Head: P M Johnson MA
Type: Co-educational Boarding & Day B11-18 G11-18
No of Pupils: B165 G105
Fees: FB £3540-£3970 DAY £1850-£2180

Somerset

Bath

BATH HIGH SCHOOL GPDST
Hope House, Bath, Somerset BA1 5ES
Tel: 01225 422931
Head: Miss M A Winfield BA
Type: Girls Day G4-18
No of Pupils: G670
Fees: DAY £2928-£3984

DOWNSIDE SCHOOL
Bath, Somerset BA3 4RJ
Tel: 01761 232206
Head: Dom Antony Sutch MA
Type: Boys Boarding & Day B10-19
No of Pupils: B350 G2
Fees: FB £8928-£11,130
DAY £5340-£5940

KING EDWARD'S SCHOOL BATH
North Road, Bath, Somerset BA2 6HU
Tel: 01225 464313
Head: P J Winter MA(Oxon)
Type: Co-educational Day B7-18 G7-18
No of Pupils: B780 G50
Fees: DAY £3411-£4548

KINGSWOOD SCHOOL
Bath, Somerset BA1 5RG
Tel: 01225 734200
Head: G M Best MA
Type: Co-educational Boarding & Day B11-18 G11-18
No of Pupils: B184 G136 VIth133
Fees: FB £9321-£11,829 WB £9321-£11,829
DAY £5757-£7350

MONKTON COMBE SCHOOL
Bath, Somerset BA2 7HG
Tel: 01225 721102
Head: M J Cuthbertson MA
Type: Co-educational Boarding & Day B3-18 G3-18
No of Pupils: B510 G247 VIth142 FB123
Fees: FB £8685-£12,195
DAY £3360-£8400

PRIOR PARK COLLEGE
Bath, Somerset BA2 5AH
Tel: 01225 835353
Head: R G G Mercer MA, DPhil
Type: Co-educational Boarding & Day B11-18 G11-18
No of Pupils: B291 G224 VIth139
Fees: FB £10,758 WB £10,758
DAY £5697-£5949

THE ROYAL SCHOOL, BATH
Bath, Somerset BA1 5SZ
Tel: 01225 313877
Head: Mrs Christine Edmundson
Type: Girls Boarding & Day B3-7 G3-18
No of Pupils: B12 G289 VIth80
Fees: FB £9261-£11,001 DAY £2781-£5886

Bruton

★ **BRUTON SCHOOL FOR GIRLS**
Sunny Hill, Bruton, Somerset BA10 0NT
Tel: 01749 812277
Head: Mrs J M Wade BSc(Hons), MSc(York)
Type: Girls Boarding & Day G8-18
No of Pupils: G540 VIth94
Fees: FB £7761 DAY £4011

KING'S SCHOOL
Bruton, Somerset BA10 0ED
Tel: 01749 813326
Head: R I Smyth MA
Type: Co-educational Boarding & Day B13-18 G13-18
No of Pupils: B227 VIth108 FB231
Fees: FB £11,055 DAY £8055

Street

MILLFIELD
Street, Somerset BA16 0YD
Tel: 01458 442291
Head: C S Martin MA
Type: Co-educational Boarding & Day B13-19 G13-19
No of Pupils: B722 G498 VIth539
Fees: FB £13,785 DAY £8820

Taunton

KING'S COLLEGE
Taunton, Somerset TA1 3DX
Tel: 01823 334222
Head: R S Funnell MA(Cantab)
Type: Co-educational Boarding & Day B13-18 G13-18
No of Pupils: B307 G139
Fees: FB £11,490 DAY £7560

QUEEN'S COLLEGE
Trull Road, Taunton, Somerset TA1 4QS
Tel: 01823 272559
Head: Christopher T Bradnock MA(Cantab)
Type: Co-educational Boarding & Day B2-18 G2-18
No of Pupils: B257 G221 VIth147 FB170
Fees: FB £4320-£9270 DAY £2790-£6075

TAUNTON SCHOOL
Taunton, Somerset TA2 6AD
Tel: 01823 349223
Head: B B Sutton MA
Type: Co-educational Boarding & Day B3-18 G3-18
No of Pupils: B501 G421 VIth196 FB269
Fees: FB £4395-£11,355 DAY £1350-£7260

Wellington

WELLINGTON SCHOOL
South Street, Wellington, Somerset TA21 8NT
Tel: 01823 668800
Head: A J Rogers MA
Type: Co-educational Boarding & Day B10-18 G10-18
No of Pupils: B316 G261 VIth198
Fees: FB £8394 DAY £4596

Wells

WELLS CATHEDRAL SCHOOL
Wells, Somerset BA5 2ST
Tel: 01749 672117
Head: J S Baxter BA(Dunelm), DipEd(Oxon), MBIM, FRSA
Type: Co-educational Boarding & Day B3-18 G3-18
No of Pupils: VIth181 FB272
Fees: FB £9651 DAY £5667

Yeovil

CHILTON CANTELO SCHOOL
Chilton Cantelo, Yeovil, Somerset BA22 8BG
Tel: 01935 850555
Head: D S von Zeffman LLB Barrister
Type: Co-educational Boarding & Day B8-18 G8-18
No of Pupils: B66 G55 VIth2 FB80
Fees: FB £6555-£8760 WB £6555-£8760
DAY £3315-£5010

Winscombe

★ **SIDCOT SCHOOL**
Winscombe, Somerset BS25 1PD
Tel: 01934 843102
Head: Dr C Greenfield MA, MEd, EdD
Type: Co-educational Boarding & Day B9-18 G9-18
No of Pupils: B221 G193 VIth125 FB170 WB10
Fees: FB £9930 DAY £5925

Staffordshire

Brewood

ST DOMINIC'S SCHOOL
32 Bargate Street, Brewood, Staffordshire ST19 9BA
Tel: 01902 850248
Head: Mrs K S Butwilowska JP, BA, MEd
Type: Girls Day B2-7 G2-18
No of Pupils: B6 G431 VIth38
Fees: DAY £2460-£3825

Cannock

CHASE ACADEMY
Lyncroft House, Cannock, Staffordshire WS11 3UR
Tel: 01543 502388
Head: R Edgar BSc, CPhys, MInstP
Type: Co-educational Day & Boarding B3-18 G3-18
No of Pupils: B70 G70 VIth30
Fees: FB £5502-£8820 WB £5502-£8820
DAY £2586-£4005

Newcastle-under-Lyme

NEWCASTLE-UNDER-LYME SCHOOL
Mount Pleasant, Newcastle-under-Lyme,
Staffordshire ST5 1DB
Tel: 01782 633604
Head: Dr R M Reynolds BSc
Type: Co-educational Day B8-18 G8-18
No of Pupils: B557 G563 VIth302
Fees: DAY £3303-£3785

Lichfield

ABBOTS BROMLEY
School of S Mary & S Anne, Nr Lichfield,
Staffordshire WS15 3BW
Tel: 01283 840232
Head: A J Grigg BA, MPhil
Type: Girls Boarding & Day G5-18
No of Pupils: G291
Fees: FB £9495-£11,205
DAY £2625-£7485

Stafford

STAFFORD GRAMMAR SCHOOL
Burton Manor, Stafford ST18 9AT
Tel: 01785 249752
Head: M S James MA(Oxon), MSc
Type: Co-educational Day B11-18 G11-18
No of Pupils: B153 G130
Fees: DAY £3945

Stoke-on-Trent

ST JOSEPH'S COLLEGE
Trent Vale, Stoke-on-Trent, Staffordshire ST4 5NT
Tel: 01782 848008
Head: J E Stoer
Type: Co-educational Day B4-18 G4-18
No of Pupils: B353 G117
Fees: DAY £1893-£3168

Stone

ST DOMINIC'S PRIORY SCHOOL
21 Station Road, Stone, Staffordshire ST15 8EN
Tel: 01785 814181/814411
Head: Mrs J W Hildreth BA, MEd
Type: Girls Day B3-8 G3-18
No of Pupils: B22 G279 VIth45
Fees: DAY £2070-£3294

Uttoxeter

ABBOTSHOLME SCHOOL
Rocester, Uttoxeter, Staffordshire ST14 5BS
Tel: 01889 590217
Head: D J Farrant MA, DipEd, FRSA
Type: Co-educational Boarding & Day B11-18 G11-18
No of Pupils: B108 G70 VIth65
Fees: FB £11,850 WB £11,850
DAY £7920

DENSTONE COLLEGE
Uttoxeter, Staffordshire ST14 5HN
Tel: 01889 590484
Head: Mr David Derbyshire
Type: Co-educational Boarding & Day B11-18 G11-18
No of Pupils: B205 G92 VIth88
Fees: FB £11,328 DAY £5580-£8082

Suffolk

Bawdsey

ALEXANDERS INTERNATIONAL SCHOOL
Bawdsey College, Bawdsey, Suffolk IP12 3AZ
Tel: 01394 411633
Head: Niels Toettcher
Type: Co-educational Boarding B11-18 G11-18
No of Pupils: B60 G40
Fees: FB £9000

Bury St Edmunds

CULFORD SCHOOL
Bury St Edmunds, Suffolk IP28 6TX
Tel: 01284 728615
Head: J S Richardson MA(Cantab)
Type: Co-educational Boarding & Day B2-18 G2-18
No of Pupils: B367 G259 VIth140 FB200 WB25
Fees: FB £7656-£10,920 WB £7656-£10,920
DAY £5460-£7107

Ipswich

IPSWICH HIGH SCHOOL GPDST
Ipswich, Suffolk IP9 1AZ
Tel: 01473 780201
Head: Miss V C MacCuish BA
Type: Girls Day G3-18
No of Pupils: G705 VIth90
Fees: DAY £3036-£4140

IPSWICH SCHOOL
Henley Road, Ipswich, Suffolk IP1 3SG
Tel: 01473 255313
Head: Ian Galbraith MA
Type: Boys Day & Boarding B11-18 G16-18
No of Pupils: B394 VIth201 FB18 WB7
Fees: FB £7905-£9111 WB £7767-£8853
DAY £4887-£5331

ROYAL HOSPITAL SCHOOL
Holbrook, Ipswich, Suffolk IP9 2RX
Tel: 01473 326200
Head: N K D Ward BSc
Type: Co-educational Boarding B11-18 G11-18
No of Pupils: B300 G200 VIth160 FB650
Fees: FB £7875 DAY £4275

ST JOSEPH'S COLLEGE WITH THE SCHOOL OF JESUS & MARY
Ipswich, Suffolk IP2 9DR
Tel: 01473 690281
Head: John Regan BA, MEd
Type: Co-educational Boarding & Day B3-18 G3-18
No of Pupils: B570 G180 VIth146 FB45 WB5
Fees: FB £8772 WB £8397 DAY £5022

Southwold

ST FELIX SCHOOL
Southwold, Suffolk IP18 6SD
Tel: 01502 722175
Head: Mrs S R Campion MA(Cantab)
Type: Girls Boarding & Day G11-18
No of Pupils: G206 VIth57 FB192
Fees: FB £10,305 DAY £6705

Stowmarket

FINBOROUGH SCHOOL
Great Finborough, Stowmarket, Suffolk IP14 3EF
Tel: 01449 674479
Head: J Sinclair BSc(Econ), FCA
Type: Co-educational Boarding & Day B2-18 G2-18
No of Pupils: B75 G65 VIth25 FB230
Fees: FB £4500-£8310 WB £4500-£8310
DAY £1800-£3900

Woodbridge

FRAMLINGHAM COLLEGE
Woodbridge, Suffolk IP13 9EY
Tel: 01728 723789
Head: Mrs G M Randall BA
Type: Co-educational Boarding & Day B13-18 G13-18
No of Pupils: B281 G176 VIth190
Fees: FB £9687 DAY £6216

WOODBRIDGE SCHOOL
Woodbridge, Suffolk IP12 4JH
Tel: 01394 385547
Head: S H Cole MA, CPhys, MInstP
Type: Co-educational Day & Boarding B4-18 G4-18
No of Pupils: B301 G295 VIth159
Fees: FB £8796 WB £8796
DAY £2718-£5352

Surrey

Ashtead

CITY OF LONDON FREEMEN'S SCHOOL
Ashtead Park, Ashtead, Surrey KT21 1ET
Tel: 01372 277933
Head: D C Haywood MA
Type: Co-educational Day & Boarding B7-18 G7-18
No of Pupils: B295 G326 VIth120 FB26 WB21
Fees: FB £8286-£9888 WB £7893-£9585 DAY £4689-£6291

PARSONS MEAD SCHOOL
Ottways Lane, Ashtead, Surrey KT21 2PE
Tel: 01372 276401
Head: Miss E B Plant BA(Hons), PGCE
Type: Girls Day & Boarding G3-18
No of Pupils: G355 VIth40 WB12
Fees: WB £7940 DAY £3090-£5280

Banstead

GREENACRE SCHOOL
Sutton Lane, Banstead, Surrey SM7 3RA
Tel: 01737 352114
Head: Mrs P M Wood BA
Type: Girls Day G3-18
No of Pupils: G351 VIth46
Fees: DAY £1350-£5250

Camberley

ELMHURST BALLET SCHOOL
Heathcote Road, Camberley, Surrey GU15 2EV
Tel: 01276 65301
Head: John McNamara BA, MPhil
Type: Co-educational Boarding & Day B9-19 G9-19
No of Pupils: B15 G134 VIth72 FB193
Fees: FB £9570 DAY £7020

Caterham

★ **CATERHAM SCHOOL**
Harestone Valley Road, Caterham, Surrey CR3 6YA
Tel: 01883 343028
Head: R A E Davey MA(Dublin)
Type: Co-educational Day & Boarding B3-18 G3-18
No of Pupils: B500 G200 VIth210
Fees: FB £11,130-£11,730 DAY £6090

Chertsey

SIR WILLIAM PERKINS'S SCHOOL
Guildford Road, Chertsey, Surrey KT16 9BN
Tel: 01932 562161
Head: Miss S A Ross BSc
Type: Girls Day G11-18
No of Pupils: G460 VIth130
Fees: DAY £4170

Cobham

AMERICAN COMMUNITY SCHOOLS
Heywood, Cobham, Surrey KT11 1BL
Tel: 01932 867251
Head: T Lehman
Type: Co-educational Boarding & Day B3-18 G3-18
No of Pupils: B666 G584

NOTRE DAME SENIOR SCHOOL
Burwood House, Cobham, Surrey KT11 1HA
Tel: 01932 863560
Head: Sr Faith Ede MA
Type: Girls Day G11-18
No of Pupils: G300 VIth57
Fees: DAY £4500-£4734

REED'S SCHOOL
Sandy Lane, Cobham, Surrey KT11 2ES
Tel: 01932 863076
Head: D E Prince MA(Cantab)
Type: Boys Boarding & Day B11-18 G16-18
No of Pupils: B340 VIth75
Fees: FB £8277-£9894
DAY £6207-£7479

YEHUDI MENUHIN SCHOOL
Stoke Road, Cobham, Surrey KT11 3QQ
Tel: 01932 864739
Head: N Chisholm MA
Type: Co-educational Boarding B8-18 G8-18
No of Pupils: B20 G30 VIth15 FB57
Fees: FB £20,205

Cranleigh

CRANLEIGH SCHOOL
Horseshoe Lane, Cranleigh, Surrey GU6 8QQ
Tel: 01483 273666
Head: G de W Waller MA, MSc, FRSA
Type: Boys Boarding & Day B13-18 G16-18
No of Pupils: B591 G71 VIth247
Fees: FB £12,990
DAY £9615

Croydon

OLD PALACE SCHOOL
Old Palace Road, Croydon, Surrey CR0 1AX
Tel: 0181 688 2027
Head: Miss K L Hilton BA, PGCE
Type: Girls Day G4-18
No of Pupils: G820
Fees: DAY £2925-£3978

ROYAL RUSSELL SCHOOL
Coombe Lane, Croydon, Surrey CR9 5BX
Tel: 0181 657 4433
Head: Dr J R Jennings BSc, PhD
Type: Co-educational Boarding & Day B3-18 G3-18
No of Pupils: B380 G200 VIth120 FB100 WB50
Fees: FB £10,530 WB £10,530 DAY £1305-£5550

TRINITY SCHOOL
Shirley Park, Croydon, Surrey CR9 7AT
Tel: 0181 656 9541
Head: B J Lenon MA
Type: Boys Day B10-18
No of Pupils: B675 VIth215
Fees: DAY £5622

Dorking

BOX HILL SCHOOL
Dorking, Surrey RH5 6EA
Tel: 01372 373382
Head: Dr R A S Atwood BA, PhD
Type: Co-educational Boarding & Day B11-18 G11-18
No of Pupils: B176 G93 FB140 WB23
Fees: FB £10,530 WB £10,080
DAY £5100-£6300

ST TERESA'S SCHOOL
Effingham Hill, Dorking, Surrey RH5 6ST
Tel: 01372 452037
Head: L Allan BA, MEd
Type: Girls Boarding & Day G3-18
No of Pupils: G580
Fees: FB £8250-£9330 DAY £2250-£4590

Egham

TASIS ENGLAND AMERICAN SCHOOL
Coldharbour Lane, Egham, Surrey TW20 8TE
Tel: 01932 565252
Head: L D Rigg BA, MA, EdM
Type: Co-educational Boarding & Day B4-18 G4-18
No of Pupils: B324 G309
Fees: FB £11,850-£12,160 DAY £6730-£7685

Epsom

EPSOM COLLEGE
Epsom, Surrey KT17 4JQ
Tel: 01372 723621
Head: A H Beadles MA
Type: Co-educational Boarding & Day B13-18 G13-18
No of Pupils: B335 VIth316
Fees: FB £11,595 WB £11,436 DAY £8616

EWELL CASTLE SCHOOL
Church Street, Epsom, Surrey KT17 2AW
Tel: 0181 393 1413
Head: R A Fewtrell MA, JP
Type: Co-educational Day B3-18 G3-11
No of Pupils: B350 G20 VIth60
Fees: DAY £2352-£4425

STUDY ASSOCIATES INTERNATIONAL
Gold Peak House, Epsom, Surrey KT18 7EH
Tel: 01372 275005
Head: Mrs B A Legge
Type: Co-educational Day

Esher

CLAREMONT FAN COURT SCHOOL
Claremont Drive, Esher, Surrey KT10 9LY
Tel: 01372 467841
Head: Mrs P B Farrar TCert
Type: Co-educational Day & Boarding B3-18 G3-18
No of Pupils: B285 G297 VIth63
Fees: FB £9090-£9435 DAY £3495-£5970

Farnham

FRENSHAM HEIGHTS SCHOOL
Farnham, Surrey GU10 4EA
Tel: 01252 792134
Head: P de Voil MA, FRSA
Type: Co-educational Boarding & Day B3-18 G3-18
No of Pupils: B123 G130 VIth86
Fees: FB £11,985 DAY £7770

Godalming

CHARTERHOUSE
Godalming, Surrey GU7 2DX
Tel: 01483 291601
Head: Rev John Witheridge MA
Type: Boys Boarding & Day B13-18 G16-18
No of Pupils: B627 G78 FB679
Fees: FB £13,341 DAY £11,022

★ **KING EDWARD'S SCHOOL WITLEY**
Petworth Road, Godalming, Surrey GU8 5SG
Tel: 01428 682572
Head: R J Fox MA, CMath, FIMA
Type: Co-educational Boarding & Day B11-18 G11-18
No of Pupils: B159 G153 VIth146
Fees: FB £9450

★ **PRIOR'S FIELD SCHOOL**
Priorsfield Road, Godalming, Surrey GU7 2RH
Tel: 01483 810551
Head: Mrs J M McCallum BA(Hons)
Type: Girls Boarding & Day G11-18
No of Pupils: G230 VIth40
Fees: FB £10,287 DAY £6867

Guildford

GUILDFORD HIGH SCHOOL
London Road, Guildford, Surrey GU1 1SJ
Tel: 01483 561440
Head: Mrs S H Singer BA
Type: Girls Day G4-18
No of Pupils: G679 VIth132
Fees: DAY £3024-£5100

ROYAL GRAMMAR SCHOOL
High Street, Guildford, Surrey GU1 3BB
Tel: 01483 502424
Head: T M S Young MA
Type: Boys Day B11-18
No of Pupils: B600 VIth250
Fees: DAY £5715-£5985

★ **ST CATHERINE'S SCHOOL**
Bramley, Guildford, Surrey GU5 0DF
Tel: 01483 893363
Head: Mrs C M Oulton MA(Oxon)
Type: Girls Day & Boarding G4-18
No of Pupils: G664 VIth103
Fees: FB £10,350 DAY £6300

TORMEAD SCHOOL
27 Cranley Road, Guildford, Surrey GU1 2JD
Tel: 01483 575101
Head: Mrs H E M Alleyne
Type: Girls Day G5-18
No of Pupils: G615
Fees: DAY £2625-£4860

Haslemere

★ **THE ROYAL SCHOOL**
Farnham Lane, Haslemere, Surrey GU27 1HQ
Tel: 01428 605805
Head: C Brooks BA(Hons), AdDipEd, CertEd, FRGS, FRMetS
Type: Girls Day & Boarding G4-18
No of Pupils: G395 VIth65 FB100 WB63
Fees: FB £9507 DAY £6057

WISPERS SCHOOL
High Lane, Haslemere, Surrey GU27 1AD
Tel: 01428 643646
Head: L H Beltran BA(Hons), PGCE
Type: Girls Boarding & Day G11-18
No of Pupils: G120
Fees: FB £9135 DAY £5880

Kingston upon Thames

KINGSTON GRAMMAR SCHOOL
70 London Road, Kingston upon Thames, Surrey KT2 6PY
Tel: 0181 546 5875
Head: C D Baxter MA(Oxon), FRSA
Type: Co-educational Day B10-19 G10-19
No of Pupils: B310 G152 VIth138
Fees: DAY £5560-£5830

MARYMOUNT INTERNATIONAL SCHOOL
George Road, Kingston upon Thames, Surrey KT2 7PE
Tel: 0181 949 0571
Head: Sr Rosaleen Sheridan RSHM, MSc
Type: Girls Day & Boarding G11-18
No of Pupils: G222 VIth45 FB105 WB9
Fees: FB £13,100-£14,000 WB £12,900-£13,800
DAY £7200-£8100

SURBITON HIGH SCHOOL
Surbiton Crescent, Kingston upon Thames, Surrey KT1 2JT
Tel: 0181 546 5245
Head: Miss M G Perry BSc, MEd
Type: Girls Day B4-11 G4-18
No of Pupils: B116 G795
Fees: DAY £2901-£4875

Leatherhead

ST JOHN'S SCHOOL
Epsom Road, Leatherhead, Surrey KT22 8SP
Tel: 01372 372021
Head: C H Tongue MA
Type: Boys Boarding & Day B13-18 G16-18
No of Pupils: B350 G50 VIth186 FB25 WB100
Fees: FB £10,500 WB £10,500 DAY £7200

Lingfield

NOTRE DAME SCHOOL
Lingfield, Surrey RH7 6PH
Tel: 01342 833176
Head: Mrs N E Shepley BA
Type: Co-educational Day B2-18 G2-18
Fees: DAY £2190-£4440

Purley

COMMONWEAL LODGE SCHOOL
Woodcote Lane, Purley, Surrey CR8 3HB
Tel: 0181 660 3179
Head: Mrs S C Law BEd, MA, LRAM, FRSA
Type: Girls Day G3-18
No of Pupils: G160 VIth12
Fees: DAY £1515-£4725

OAKWOOD
Godstone Road, Purley, Surrey CR8 2AN
Tel: 0181 668 8080
Head: Mrs P M Shanks
Type: Co-educational Day

Reigate

DUNOTTAR SCHOOL
High Trees Road, Reigate, Surrey RH2 7EL
Tel: 01737 761945
Head: Miss M Skinner JP, BSc(Hons)
Type: Girls Day G4-18
No of Pupils: G413 VIth63
Fees: DAY £2970-£4875

REIGATE GRAMMAR SCHOOL
Reigate Road, Reigate, Surrey RH2 0QS
Tel: 01737 222231
Head: P V Dixon MA
Type: Co-educational Day B10-18 G10-18
No of Pupils: B488 G98 VIth219
Fees: DAY £5160

South Croydon

CROHAM HURST SCHOOL
79 Croham Road, South Croydon, Surrey CR2 7YN
Tel: 0181 680 3064
Head: Miss S C Budgen BA
Type: Girls Day G3-18
No of Pupils: G558 VIth63
Fees: DAY £2370-£4890

CROYDON HIGH SCHOOL GPDST
Old Farleigh Road, South Croydon, Surrey CR2 8YB
Tel: 0181 651 5020
Head: Mrs P E Davies BSc, MEd
Type: Girls Day G4-18
No of Pupils: G819 VIth189
Fees: DAY £3036-£4140

WHITGIFT SCHOOL
Haling Park, South Croydon, Surrey CR2 6YT
Tel: 0181 688 9222
Head: Dr C A Barnett MA, Phil
Type: Boys Day B10-18
No of Pupils: B1100
Fees: DAY £5826

Sutton

SUTTON HIGH SCHOOL (GPDST)
55 Cheam Road, Sutton, Surrey SM1 2AX
Tel: 0181 642 0594
Head: Mrs Anne Coutts BSc, MEd
Type: Girls Day G4-18
No of Pupils: G636 VIth140
Fees: DAY £3864-£4920

Weybridge

ST GEORGE'S COLLEGE
Weybridge Road, Weybridge, Surrey KT15 2QS
Tel: 01932 854811
Head: Joseph A Peake MA(Oxon), PGCE
Type: Boys Day B11-18 G16-18
No of Pupils: B350 VIth190
Fees: DAY £5985-£6795

ST MAUR'S SCHOOL
Thames Street, Weybridge, Surrey KT13 8NL
Tel: 01932 851411
Head: Mrs M E Dodds BA(Hons), MA
Type: Girls Day G2-18
No of Pupils: G509 VIth50
Fees: DAY £1395-£4725

Woldingham

WOLDINGHAM SCHOOL
Marden Park, Woldingham, Surrey CR3 7YA
Tel: 01883 349431
Head: Dr P Dineen BA, PhD
Type: Girls Boarding & Day G11-18
No of Pupils: G410 VIth140
Fees: FB £12,009 DAY £7281

East Sussex

Battle

BATTLE ABBEY SCHOOL
Battle, East Sussex TN33 0AD
Tel: 01424 772385
Head: D J A Teall BSc(Newcastle)
Type: Co-educational Day & Boarding B2-18 G2-18
No of Pupils: B95 G95 VIth20 FB60 WB12
Fees: FB £7590-£9465
DAY £3225-£5865

WILTON HOUSE SCHOOL
Catsfield Place, Battle, East Sussex TN33 9BS
Tel: 01424 830234
Head: J Shrine MA
Type: Co-educational Boarding & Day B13-18 G13-18
Fees: FB £6327-£7950
DAY £2880-£4638

Brighton

BRIGHTON & HOVE HIGH SCHOOL
Montpellier Road, Brighton, East Sussex BN1 3AT
Tel: 01273 734112
Head: Miss R A Woodbridge MA
Type: Girls Day G4-18
No of Pupils: G641 VIth102
Fees: DAY £3036-£4140

BRIGHTON COLLEGE
Eastern Road, Brighton, East Sussex BN2 2AL
Tel: 01273 704202
Head: J D Leach MA
Type: Co-educational Day & Boarding B13-18 G13-18
No of Pupils: B334 G141
Fees: FB £12,450 WB £11,130
DAY £8190

ROEDEAN SCHOOL
Brighton, East Sussex BN2 5RQ
Tel: 01273 603181
Head: Mrs A R Longley MA
Type: Girls Boarding & Day G10-18
No of Pupils: G450
Fees: FB £13,635 DAY £7740

ST MARY'S HALL
Eastern Road, Brighton, East Sussex BN2 5JF
Tel: 01273 606061
Head: Mrs P J James BA
Type: Girls Day & Boarding B3-8 G3-18
No of Pupils: B5 G352 VIth51
Fees: FB £9315 WB £6975-£8940
DAY £1230-£6180

Eastbourne

EASTBOURNE COLLEGE
Old Wish Road, Eastbourne, East Sussex BN21 4JX
Tel: 01323 452300
Head: C M P Bush MA
Type: Co-educational Boarding & Day B13-18 G13-18
No of Pupils: B224 G38 VIth234
Fees: FB £12,084 DAY £8936

MOIRA HOUSE SCHOOL
Upper Carlisle Road, Eastbourne, East Sussex BN20 7TD
Tel: 01323 644144
Head: A R Underwood BA(Hons), MA
Type: Girls Boarding & Day G11-18
No of Pupils: G230 VIth70 FB130
Fees: FB £11,340 WB £10,320
DAY £3810-£7320

Forest Row

GREENFIELDS SCHOOL EDUCATIONAL TRUST LTD
Priory Road, Forest Row, East Sussex RH18 5JD
Tel: 01342 822845
Head: Mr A M McQuade MA(Oxon)
Type: Co-educational Day & Boarding B3-18 G3-18
No of Pupils: B88 G77
Fees: FB £8979-£9801 WB £8979-£9801
DAY £969-£5247

MICHAEL HALL SCHOOL
Kidbrooke Park, Forest Row, East Sussex RH18 5JB
Tel: 01342 822275
Head: E Van-Manen
Type: Co-educational Day & Boarding B3-18 G3-18
No of Pupils: B232 G264 VIth55
Fees: FB £6075-£8100
DAY £2310-£3750

Hailsham

ST BEDE'S SCHOOL
Upper Dicker, Hailsham, East Sussex BN27 3QH
Tel: 01323 843252
Head: R A Perrin MA
Type: Co-educational Boarding & Day B12-18 G12-18
No of Pupils: B295 G155 VIth180
Fees: FB £11,925 DAY £7200

Lewes

THE OLD GRAMMAR SCHOOL
High Street, Lewes, East Sussex BN7 1XS
Tel: 01273 472634
Head: Dr A N L Hodd MA(Cantab), PhD
Type: Co-educational Day B4-18 G4-18
No of Pupils: B222 G101 VIth65
Fees: DAY £2460-£4527

Mayfield

ST LEONARDS-MAYFIELD SCHOOL
The Old Palace, Mayfield, East Sussex TN20 6PH
Tel: 01435 873055
Head: Sr J Sinclair BSc, PGCE
Type: Girls Boarding & Day G11-18
No of Pupils: G525
Fees: FB £9735 DAY £6490

Seaford

NEWLANDS SCHOOL
Eastbourne Road, Seaford, East Sussex BN25 4NP
Tel: 01323 892334
Head: B F Underwood MA, DipEd(Oxon)
Type: Co-educational Boarding & Day B2-18 G2-18
No of Pupils: B424 G228 VIth70
Fees: FB £8430-£9300
DAY £4380-£5895

Wadhurst

BELLERBYS COLLEGE MAYFIELD AND WADHURST
(Central Admissions), Wadhurst, East Sussex TN5 6JA
Tel: 01892 782000
Heads: Jorg Muller MA & Eric Reynolds BA(Hons), PGCE
Type: Co-educational Boarding & Day B11-18 G11-18
No of Pupils: B133 G184 VIth71
Fees: FB £4200 DAY £1000-£2140

West Sussex

Arundel

SLINDON COLLEGE
Slindon House, Arundel, West Sussex BN18 0RH
Tel: 01243 814320
Head: P D Morris BEd, MA(Oxon)
Type: Boys Boarding & Day B11-18
No of Pupils: B70 VIth15
Fees: FB £9495 DAY £5985

Burgess Hill

BURGESS HILL SCHOOL FOR GIRLS (SNR)
Keymer Road, Burgess Hill, West Sussex RH15 0EG
Tel: 01444 241050
Head: Mrs R F Lewis BSc
Type: Girls Day & Boarding G11-18
No of Pupils: G280 VIth60 FB56
Fees: FB £9675 DAY £2664-£5730

Chichester

LAVANT HOUSE ROSEMEAD
Chichester, West Sussex PO18 9AB
Tel: 01243 527211
Head: Mrs S E Watkins BA
Type: Girls Day & Boarding B3-8 G3-18
No of Pupils: B5 G146 FB30
Fees: FB £8325-£10,425 WB £8325-£10,425
DAY £1425-£5850

Crawley

WORTH SCHOOL
Crawley, West Sussex RH10 4SD
Tel: 01342 710200
Head: Rev P C Jamison MA(Oxon)
Type: Boys Boarding & Day B10-18
No of Pupils: B256 VIth129
Fees: FB £8490-£11,952
DAY £5892-£8109

Hassocks

HURSTPIERPOINT COLLEGE
Hassocks, West Sussex BN6 9JS
Tel: 01273 833636
Head: S D A Meek MA
Type: Co-educational Boarding & Day B6-18 G6-18
No of Pupils: B415 G86 VIth161
Fees: FB £8025-£11,940
DAY £5955-£9330

Haywards Heath

ARDINGLY COLLEGE
Haywards Heath, West Sussex RH17 6SQ
Tel: 01444 892577/892429
Head: J W Flecker MA
Type: Co-educational Boarding & Day B13-18 G13-18
No of Pupils: B256 G191 FB292
Fees: FB £11,085 DAY £8805

Horsham

CHRIST'S HOSPITAL
Horsham, West Sussex RH13 7LS
Tel: 01403 252547/211293
Head: Peter C D Southern MA, PhD
Type: Co-educational Boarding B11-18 G11-18
No of Pupils: B351 G237 VIth244 FB804
Fees: FB £11,124

★ FARLINGTON SCHOOL
Strood Park, Horsham, West Sussex RH12 3PN
Tel: 01403 254967
Head: Mrs P M Mawer BA
Type: Girls Day & Boarding G4-18
No of Pupils: G350 VIth50
Fees: FB £6435-£9870
DAY £2655-£6090

Lancing

LANCING COLLEGE
Lancing, West Sussex BN15 0RW
Tel: 01273 452213
Head: C J Saunders MA
Type: Boys Boarding & Day B13-18 G16-18
No of Pupils: B450 G70
Fees: FB £12,030 DAY £9045

Petworth

SEAFORD COLLEGE
Lavington Park, Petworth, West Sussex GU28 0NB
Head: R C Hannaford BSc, MIBiol, CertEd
Type: Boys Boarding B11-18 G16-18
No of Pupils: B324
Fees: FB £7935-£9255
DAY £4950-£5550

Worthing

OUR LADY OF SION SCHOOL
Gratwicke Road, Worthing, West Sussex BN11 4BL
Tel: 01903 204063
Head: B Sexton MA, BEd
Type: Co-educational Day B2-18 G2-18
No of Pupils: B216 G262
Fees: DAY £2985-£4455

Tyne & Wear

Newcastle upon Tyne

CENTRAL NEWCASTLE HIGH SCHOOL
Eskdale Terrace, Newcastle upon Tyne,
Tyne & Wear NE2 4DS
Tel: 0191 281 1768
Head: Mrs A M Chapman BA
Type: Girls Day G4-18
No of Pupils: G711 VIth205
Fees: DAY £3036-£4140

DAME ALLAN'S BOYS' SCHOOL
Fowberry Crescent, Newcastle upon Tyne,
Tyne & Wear NE4 9YJ
Tel: 0191 275 0608
Head: Mr D W Welsh
Type: Boys Day B8-18 G16-18
Fees: DAY £2679-£3432

DAME ALLAN'S GIRLS' SCHOOL
Fowberry Crescent, Newcastle upon Tyne,
Tyne & Wear NE4 9YJ
Tel: 0191 275 0708
Head: Mr D W Welsh
Type: Girls Day B16-18 G8-18
Fees: DAY £2679-£3432

EASTCLIFFE GRAMMAR SCHOOL
The Grove, Newcastle upon Tyne,
Tyne & Wear NE3 1NE
Tel: 0191 285 4873
Head: G D Pearson BA, DipEd, FRSA
Type: Co-educational Day B3-18 G3-18
No of Pupils: B142 G60 VIth28
Fees: DAY £2580-£4260

LA SAGESSE HIGH SCHOOL
Newcastle upon Tyne, Tyne & Wear NE2 3RJ
Tel: 0191 281 3474
Head: Miss Linda Clark BEd(Hons), MA
Type: Girls Day G3-18
No of Pupils: G540
Fees: DAY £2250-£3915

ROYAL GRAMMAR SCHOOL
Eskdale Terrace, Newcastle upon Tyne,
Tyne & Wear NE2 4DX
Tel: 0191 281 5711
Head: J F X Miller MA
Type: Boys Day B8-18
No of Pupils: B795 VIth280
Fees: DAY £3195-£3885

THE NEWCASTLE UPON TYNE CHURCH HIGH SCHOOL
Tankerville Terrace, Newcastle upon Tyne,
Tyne & Wear NE2 3BA
Tel: 0191 281 4306
Head: Mrs L G Smith BA, FRSA, FIMgt
Type: Girls Day G3-18
No of Pupils: G572 VIth86
Fees: DAY £2781-£3960

WESTFIELD SCHOOL
Oakfield Road, Newcastle upon Tyne, Tyne & Wear NE3 4HS
Tel: 0191 285 1948
Head: Mrs M Farndale BA(Hons)(Lon), PGCE(Oxon), FRSA
Type: Girls Day G3-18
No of Pupils: G315 VIth50
Fees: DAY £1398-£4140

North Shields

THE KING'S SCHOOL (HMC)
Huntington Place, North Shields, Tyne & Wear NE30 4RF
Tel: 0191 258 5995
Head: Dr D Younger MSc, PhD, DipEd
Type: Co-educational Day B4-18 G4-18
No of Pupils: B583 G158 VIth177
Fees: DAY £2580-£3720

Sunderland

SUNDERLAND HIGH SCHOOL
Mowbray Road, Sunderland, Tyne & Wear SR2 8HY
Tel: 0191 567 4984
Head: Miss C M Rendle-Short MEd, BMus, AAco
Type: Co-educational Day B3-18 G3-18
No of Pupils: B240 G278 VIth35
Fees: DAY £2850-£4065

Warwickshire

Atherstone

TWYCROSS HOUSE SCHOOL
Atherstone, Warwickshire CV9 3PL
Tel: 01827 880651
Head: R V Kirkpatrick MEd
Type: Co-educational Day B8-18 G8-18
No of Pupils: B127 G123 VIth40
Fees: DAY £1300-£3330

Kenilworth

ST JOSEPH'S SCHOOL
Kenilworth, Warwickshire CV8 2FT
Tel: 01926 855348
Head: Mrs L P A Cox BSc
Type: Girls Day B4-7 G4-18
No of Pupils: B10 G244
Fees: DAY £2820-£3450

Leamington Spa

THE KINGSLEY SCHOOL
Beauchamp Avenue, Leamington Spa, Warwickshire CV32 5RD
Tel: 01926 425127
Head: Mrs M A Webster BA, MEd, FRSA
Type: Girls Day B2-7 G2-18
No of Pupils: B6 G473 VIth105
Fees: DAY £3015-£4485

Rugby

PRINCETHORPE COLLEGE
Leamington Road, Rugby, Warwickshire CV23 9PX
Tel: 01926 632147
Head: Rev Alan Whelan BA
Type: Boys Day & Boarding B11-18 G16-18
No of Pupils: B399 G8
Fees: FB £6912-£7659 DAY £3570-£3570

RUGBY SCHOOL
Rugby, Warwickshire CV22 5EH
Tel: 01788 543465
Head: M B Mavor
Type: Co-educational Boarding & day B13-18 G13-18
No of Pupils: B508 G171 FB539
Fees: FB £12,270 DAY £4380-£9195

Warwick

THE KING'S HIGH SCHOOL FOR GIRLS
Smith Street, Warwick, Warwickshire CV34 4HJ
Tel: 01926 494485
Head: Mrs J M Anderson BA, DipEd
Type: Girls Day G10-18
No of Pupils: G437 VIth134
Fees: DAY £4095

WARWICK SCHOOL
Myton Road, Warwick, Warwickshire CV34 6PP
Tel: 01926 492484
Head: Dr P J Cheshire BSc, PhD
Type: Boys Day & Boarding B7-18
No of Pupils: B1006 VIth240 FB30 WB28
Fees: FB £9300-£9840 WB £8640-£9180
DAY £4050-£4590

Wiltshire

Calne

ST MARY'S SCHOOL
Calne, Wiltshire SN11 0DF
Tel: 01249 815899
Head: Mrs C J Shaw BA(London)
Type: Girls Boarding & Day G11-18
No of Pupils: G376 VIth80
Fees: FB £4040 DAY £2390

Devizes

DAUNTSEY'S SCHOOL
High Street, Devizes, Wiltshire SN10 4HE
Tel: 01380 818441
Head: C Evans MA
Type: Co-educational Day & Boarding B11-18 G11-18
No of Pupils: B239 G195 VIth187
Fees: FB £10,542 DAY £6492

Marlborough

MARLBOROUGH COLLEGE
Marlborough, Wiltshire SN8 1PA
Tel: 01672 892200
Head: E J H Gould MA
Type: Co-educational Boarding & Day B13-18 G13-18
No of Pupils: B280 G120 VIth369
Fees: FB £12,750 DAY £8985

Marshfield

★ **THE INTERNATIONAL SCHOOL OF CHOUEIFAT**
Ashwicke Hall, Marshfield, Wiltshire SN14 8AG
Tel: 01225 891841
Director: Salah Ayche BSc, MSc
Type: Co-educational Boarding B9-18 G9-18
No of Pupils: B100 G20
Fees: FB £9300-£9900

Melksham

STONAR SCHOOL
Cottles Park, Melksham, Wiltshire SN12 8NT
Tel: 01225 702309
Head: Mrs S Hopkinson BA(Oxon)
Type: Girls Boarding & Day G4-18
No of Pupils: G376 VIth104
Fees: FB £8742-£9546
DAY £2340-£5289

Salisbury

LA RETRAITE SCHOOL
& The Swan School at La Retraite, Salisbury, Wiltshire SP1 3BQ
Tel: 01722 333094
Head: Mrs R Simmons BSc
Type: Girls Day B2-11 G2-18
No of Pupils: B120 G185
Fees: DAY £2550-£4575

THE GODOLPHIN SCHOOL
Milford Hill, Salisbury, Wiltshire SP1 2RA
Tel: 01722 333059
Head: Mrs H A Fender BA(Hons)
Type: Girls Boarding & Day G7-18
No of Pupils: G346 VIth102
Fees: FB £10,779 DAY £5199-£6456

Warminster

WARMINSTER SCHOOL
Church Street, Warminster, Wiltshire BA12 8PJ
Tel: 01985 213038
Head: M J Pipes BA
Type: Co-educational Day & Boarding B3-18 G3-18
No of Pupils: B271 G172 VIth75
Fees: FB £8460-£9270 WB £8460-£9270
DAY £1650-£5370

West Midlands

Birmingham

AL-FURQAN SCHOOL
Stanfield House, Birmingham, West Midlands B11 2JR
Tel: 0121 764 5373
Head: Mrs Zahida P Hussain BSc, PGCE, MEd
Type: Co-educational Day B4-18 G4-18
No of Pupils: B63 G213
Fees: DAY £1050

EDGBASTON CHURCH OF ENGLAND COLLEGE
31 Calthorpe Road, Birmingham, West Midlands B15 1RX
Tel: 0121 454 1392
Head: Mrs A Varley-Tipton MA, FRSA
Type: Girls Day G2-18
No of Pupils: G235 VIth35
Fees: DAY £2580-£4185

EDGBASTON HIGH SCHOOL FOR GIRLS
Westbourne Road, Birmingham, West Midlands B15 3TS
Tel: 0121 454 5831
Head: Mrs S J Horsman MA
Type: Girls Day G2-18
No of Pupils: G826 VIth124
Fees: DAY £1680-£4215

HIGHCLARE SCHOOL
10 Sutton Road, Birmingham, West Midlands B23 6QL
Tel: 0121 373 7400
Head: Mrs C A Hanson BSc(Hons)
Type: Girls Day B16-18 G1-18
No of Pupils: B40 G357 VIth31
Fees: DAY £2265-£4380

HOLY CHILD SCHOOL
39 Sir Harry's Road, Birmingham, West Midlands B15 2UR
Tel: 0121 440 4103
Head: Mrs J M C Hill BA
Type: Girls Day B2-11 G2-18
No of Pupils: B39 G227 VIth28
Fees: DAY £2475-£4625

KING EDWARD VI HIGH SCHOOL FOR GIRLS
Edgbaston Park Road, Birmingham, West Midlands B15 2UB
Tel: 0121 472 1834
Head: S H Evans BA, MA
Type: Girls Day G11-18
No of Pupils: G387 VIth163
Fees: DAY £4500

KING EDWARD'S SCHOOL
Edgbaston Park Road, Birmingham, West Midlands B15 2UA
Tel: 0121 472 1672
Head: H R Wright MA
Type: Boys Day B11-18
No of Pupils: B625 VIth250
Fees: DAY £4725

Coventry

BABLAKE SCHOOL
Coundon Road, Coventry, West Midlands CV1 4AU
Tel: 01203 228388/251374
Head: Dr S Nuttall FRSA
Type: Co-educational Day B11-18 G11-18
No of Pupils: B328 G319 VIth217
Fees: DAY £2775-£3825

KING HENRY VIII SCHOOL
Warwick Road, Coventry, West Midlands CV3 6AQ
Tel: 01203 673442
Head: T J Vardon MA, FRSA, ARCM
Type: Co-educational Day B7-18 G7-18
No of Pupils: B533 G485 VIth220
Fees: DAY £2940-£3975

Solihull

SAINT MARTIN'S SCHOOL
Brueton Avenue, Solihull, West Midlands B91 3EN
Tel: 0121 705 1265
Head: Mrs S J Williams MA, DipEd, FRSA
Type: Girls Day G2-18
No of Pupils: G444 VIth38
Fees: DAY £1440-£4419

SOLIHULL SCHOOL
Warwick Road, Solihull, West Midlands B91 3DJ
Tel: 0121 705 0958
Head: P S J Derham MA
Type: Boys Day B7-18 G16-18
No of Pupils: B707 VIth265
Fees: DAY £2976-£4284

Wolverhampton

TETTENHALL COLLEGE
Wood Road, Wolverhampton, West Midlands WV6 8QX
Tel: 01902 751119
Head: Dr P C Bodkin BSc, PhD
Type: Co-educational Day & Boarding B7-18 G7-18
No of Pupils: B185 G91 VIth65
Fees: FB £7509-£9147 WB £6090-£7611
DAY £4512-£5640

THE ROYAL WOLVERHAMPTON SCHOOL
Penn Road, Wolverhampton, West Midlands WV3 0EG
Tel: 01902 341230
Head: Mrs B A Evans BSc, HNC Mech.Eng
Type: Co-educational Day & Boarding B2-18 G2-18
No of Pupils: B332 G217 VIth80
Fees: FB £8610-£10,545 DAY £2580-£5385

WOLVERHAMPTON GRAMMAR SCHOOL
Compton Road, Wolverhampton, West Midlands WV3 9RB
Tel: 01902 21326
Head: Mr Bernard Trafford MA, MEd, FRSA
Type: Co-educational Day B11-18 G11-18
No of Pupils: B477 G140 VIth246
Fees: DAY £5100

North Yorkshire

Great Ayton

AYTON SCHOOL
High Green, Great Ayton, North Yorkshire TS9 6BN
Tel: 01642 722141
Head: Mrs Alice Meager BA(Hons), MA
Type: Co-educational Day & Boarding B4-18 G4-18
No of Pupils: B112 G98 VIth9 FB40
Fees: FB £9495 WB £8355 DAY £2445-£4500

Harrogate

ASHVILLE COLLEGE
Green Lane, Harrogate, North Yorkshire HG2 9JP
Tel: 01423 566358
Head: M H Crosby MA(Cantab)
Type: Co-educational Day & Boarding B4-18 G4-18
No of Pupils: B458 G312 VIth60 FB135 WB37
Fees: FB £7974-£8754 DAY £2400-£4680

HARROGATE LADIES' COLLEGE
Clarence Drive, Harrogate, North Yorkshire HG1 2QG
Tel: 01423 504543
Head: Dr Margaret J Hustler BSc, PhD
Type: Girls Boarding & Day G10-18
No of Pupils: G235 VIth85
Fees: FB £9225-£9495 DAY £6144-£6324

Scarborough

SCARBOROUGH COLLEGE
Filey Road, Scarborough, North Yorkshire YO11 3BA
Tel: 01723 360620
Head: T L Kirkup MA, ARCM
Type: Co-educational Day & Boarding B11-18 G11-18
No of Pupils: B153 G125 VIth82
Fees: FB £9843 DAY £5337

Selby

READ SCHOOL
Drax, Selby, North Yorkshire YO8 8NL
Tel: 01757 618248
Head: A J Saddler MA(Cantab)
Type: Co-educational Day & Boarding B5-18 G5-18
No of Pupils: B138 G45 VIth20
Fees: FB £6345-£7455 DAY £2595-£3615

Settle

GIGGLESWICK SCHOOL
Giggleswick, Settle, North Yorkshire BD24 0DE
Tel: 01729 823545
Head: A P Millard BSc(Econ), FRSA
Type: Co-educational Boarding & Day B7-18 G7-18
No of Pupils: B210 G122 VIth116
Fees: FB £8451-£11,100 DAY £5643-£7362

Whitby

FYLING HALL SCHOOL
Robin Hood's Bay, Whitby, North Yorkshire YO22 4QD
Tel: 01947 880261/353
Head: Michael Bayes BA, MA
Type: Co-educational Boarding & Day B3-18 G3-18
No of Pupils: B84 G75 VIth20 FB153
Fees: FB £5655-£6615
DAY £2445-£2725

★ ST HILDA'S SCHOOL
Sneaton Castle, Whitby, North Yorkshire YO21 3QN
Tel: 01947 600051
Head: Mrs M E Blain BEd, MA
Type: Co-educational Boarding & Day B2-18 G2-18
No of Pupils: B78 G146
Fees: FB £7425-£8850
DAY £2820-£4800

Yarm

YARM SCHOOL
The Friarage, Yarm, North Yorkshire TS15 9EJ
Tel: 01642 786023
Head: R N Tate MA, BSc
Type: Boys Day B4-18 G16-18
No of Pupils: B740 G36 VIth176
Fees: DAY £2469-£5136

York

AMPLEFORTH COLLEGE
York, North Yorkshire YO6 4ER
Tel: 01439 766000
Head: Rev G F L Chamberlain OSB, MA
Type: Boys Boarding & Day B13-18
No of Pupils: B300 VIth240 FB531
Fees: FB £12,015 DAY £6195

BOOTHAM SCHOOL
York, North Yorkshire YO3 7BU
Tel: 01904 623636
Head: I M Small BA, FRSA
Type: Co-educational Boarding & Day B11-18 G11-18
No of Pupils: B154 G76 VIth106 FB91
Fees: FB £10,161 WB £10,161
DAY £6594

★ POCKLINGTON SCHOOL
West Green, York, North Yorkshire YO4 2NJ
Tel: 01759 303125
Head: J N D Gray BA
Type: Co-educational Day & Boarding B7-18 G7-18
No of Pupils: B460 G301 VIth194 FB143
Fees: FB £8904 DAY £5109

QUEEN ETHELBURGA'S COLLEGE
Thorpe Underwood Hall, York, North Yorkshire YO5 9SZ
Tel: 01423 331480
Head: Mrs G L Richardson BA(Hons)
Type: Girls Boarding & Day G2-18
No of Pupils: B25 G270
Fees: FB £6525-£9585
DAY £1425-£6075

QUEEN MARGARET'S SCHOOL
Escrick Park, York, North Yorkshire YO4 6EU
Tel: 01904 728261
Head: Dr G A H Chapman MA(Oxon), DLitt et Phil(SA), FRSA
Type: Girls Boarding & Day G11-18
No of Pupils: G265 VIth100
Fees: FB £10,218 DAY £6474

ST PETER'S SCHOOL
Clifton, York, North Yorkshire YO3 6AB
Tel: 01904 623213
Head: A F Trotman MA
Type: Co-educational Day & Boarding B13-18 G13-18
No of Pupils: B239 G142 VIth97
Fees: FB £10419-£10698
DAY £6066-£6369

THE MOUNT SCHOOL, YORK
Dalton Terrace, York, North Yorkshire YO2 4DD
Tel: 01904 667500
Head: Miss B J Windle MA(Cantab)
Type: Girls Boarding & Day G11-18
No of Pupils: G200 VIth140 FB120
Fees: FB £10,170 DAY £2925-£6165

East Riding of Yorkshire

Hull

HULL HIGH SCHOOL FOR GIRLS
Tranby Croft, Hull, East Riding of Yorkshire HU10 7EH
Tel: 01482 657016
Head: Mrs M A Benson BA
Type: Girls Day B3-8 G3-18
No of Pupils: B65 G258 VIth37
Fees: DAY £2640-£4125

HYMERS COLLEGE
Hymers Avenue, Hull, East Riding of Yorkshire HU3 1LW
Tel: 01482 343555
Head: J C Morris MA
Type: Co-educational Day B8-18 G8-18
No of Pupils: B430 G308 VIth210
Fees: DAY £3285-£3735

Kingston-upon-Hull

HULL GRAMMAR SCHOOL
Cottingham Road, Kingston-upon-Hull,
East Riding of Yorkshire HU5 2DL
Tel: 01482 440144
Head: R Haworth MA(Cantab)
Type: Co-educational Day B2-18 G2-18
No of Pupils: B235 G139 VIth58
Fees: DAY £2085-£4050

South Yorkshire

Sheffield

BIRKDALE SCHOOL
Oakholme Road, Sheffield, South Yorkshire S10 3DH
Tel: 0114 2668408
Head: Rev M D A Hepworth MA
Type: Boys Day B4-18 G16-18
No of Pupils: B645 VIth131
Fees: DAY £3243-£4599

★ **SHEFFIELD HIGH SCHOOL GPDST**
10 Rutland Park, Sheffield, South Yorkshire S10 2PE
Tel: 0114 2660324
Head: Mrs M A Houston BA, PGCE
Type: Girls Day G4-18
No of Pupils: G563 VIth117
Fees: DAY £4140

West Yorkshire

Apperley Bridge

WOODHOUSE GROVE SCHOOL
Apperley Bridge, West Yorkshire BD10 0NR
Tel: 0113 250 2477
Head: D C Humphries BA
Type: Co-educational Day & Boarding B3-18 G3-18
No of Pupils: B505 G294
Fees: FB £8100-£9450
DAY £3150-£5565

Batley

BATLEY GRAMMAR SCHOOL
Carlinghow Hill, BATLEY, West Yorkshire WF17 0AD
Tel: 01924 474980
Head: W M Duggan MA
Type: Boys Day B11-18 G16-18
No of Pupils: B370 G28 VIth162
Fees: DAY £3882

Bradford

BRADFORD GIRLS' GRAMMAR SCHOOL
Squire Lane, Bradford, West Yorkshire BD9 6RB
Tel: 01274 545395
Head: Mrs L J Warrington MEd
Type: Girls Day B3-8 G3-18
No of Pupils: G681 VIth193
Fees: DAY £2520-£4200

BRADFORD GRAMMAR SCHOOL
Keighley Road, Bradford, West Yorkshire BD9 4JP
Tel: 01274 545461
Head: D A G Smith JP, MA
Type: Boys Day B8-18 G16-18
No of Pupils: B983 G0 VIth293
Fees: DAY £3492-£4428

FEVERSHAM COLLEGE
Feversham Street, Bradford, West Yorkshire BD3 9QL
Tel: 01274 743428
Head: Mrs R Shasquat
Type: Girls Day G13-18
No of Pupils: G180 VIth40
Fees: DAY £2100-£2100

Halifax

HIPPERHOLME GRAMMAR SCHOOL
Bramley Lane, Halifax, West Yorkshire HX3 8JE
Tel: 01422 202256
Head: C C Robinson MA
Type: Co-educational Day B11-18 G11-18
No of Pupils: B135 G135 VIth55
Fees: DAY £3750-£3975

RISHWORTH SCHOOL
Rishworth, Halifax, West Yorkshire HX6 4QA
Tel: 01422 822217
Head: M J Elford BSc
Type: Co-educational Day & Boarding B3-18 G3-18
No of Pupils: B304 G256 VIth92 FB100
Fees: FB £8298-£9660 DAY £2490-£4995

Leeds

FULNECK SCHOOL
Fulneck, Leeds, West Yorkshire LS28 8DS
Tel: 0113 2570235
Head: Mrs H S Gordon BA(Hons), PGCE
Type: Co-educational Day & Boarding B3-18 G3-18
No of Pupils: B218 G216 VIth72 FB37 WB9
Fees: FB £6780-£9075 WB £7140-£8085
DAY £3015-£4845

GATEWAYS SCHOOL
Harewood, Leeds, West Yorkshire LS17 9LE
Tel: 0113 2886345
Head: Mrs J E Stephen BSc
Type: Girls Day G3-18
No of Pupils: G320 VIth45
Fees: DAY £2760-£3750

LEEDS GIRLS' HIGH SCHOOL
Headingley Lane, Leeds, West Yorkshire LS6 1BN
Tel: 0113 2744000
Head: Miss P A Randall BA, MA(Ed)
Type: Girls Day B3-8 G3-19
No of Pupils: B20 G960
Fees: DAY £2094-£4092

LEEDS GRAMMAR SCHOOL
Alwoodley Gates, Leeds, West Yorkshire LS17 8GS
Tel: 0113 236 1552
Head: B W Collins MSc, MEd
Type: Boys Day B4-18
No of Pupils: B1200 VIth200
Fees: DAY £2997-£5316

Pontefract

ACKWORTH SCHOOL
Barnsley Road, Pontefract, West Yorkshire WF7 7LT
Tel: 01977 611401
Head: Martin Dickinson MA(Cantab)
Type: Co-educational Day & Boarding B7-18 G7-18
No of Pupils: B202 G213
Fees: FB £9705 DAY £5529

Wakefield

QUEEN ELIZABETH GRAMMAR SCHOOL
154 Northgate, Wakefield, West Yorkshire WF1 3QY
Tel: 01924 373943
Head: Robert Mardling
Type: Boys Day B7-18
No of Pupils: B790 VIth210
Fees: DAY £4122

SILCOATES SCHOOL
Wrenthorpe, Wakefield, West Yorkshire WF2 0PD
Tel: 01924 291614
Head: P Spillane BA
Type: Co-educational Day B7-18 G7-18
No of Pupils: B346 G168 VIth84
Fees: DAY £3216-£5394

WAKEFIELD GIRLS' HIGH SCHOOL
Wentworth Street, Wakefield, West Yorkshire WF1 2QS
Tel: 01924 372490
Heads: Mrs P A Langham BA, MEd &
Mrs D Robinson BSc(Durham)
Type: Girls Day B4-7 G4-18
No of Pupils: B43 G1004
Fees: DAY £3084-£4368

Ireland

County Antrim

Belfast

BELFAST ROYAL ACADEMY
7 Cliftonville Road, Belfast, County Antrim BT14 6JL
Tel: 01232 740423
Head: W M Sillery MA
Type: Co-educational Day B11-18 G11-18
No of Pupils: B489 G521 VIth359
Fees: DAY £65

CAMPBELL COLLEGE
Belfast, County Antrim BT4 2ND
Tel: 01232 763076
Head: Dr R J I Pollock BSc, MEd, PhD
Type: Boys Day & Boarding B11-18
No of Pupils: B700 VIth190 FB25 WB43
Fees: FB £5293 WB £5293 DAY £860-£993

HUNTERHOUSE COLLEGE
Finaghy, Belfast BT10 0LE
Tel: 01232 612293
Head: Miss D E M Hunter BA, DipEd
Type: Girls Day & Boarding G5-18
No of Pupils: G544 VIth143 FB30 WB50
Fees: FB £2895 WB £2895

LAGAN COLLEGE
63 Church Road, Belfast, County Antrim BT
Tel: 01232 401810
Head: Dr B H Lambkin
Type: Co-educational Day

METHODIST COLLEGE
1 Malone Road, Belfast, County Antrim BT9 6BY
Tel: 01232 669558
Head: T W Mulryne MA
Type: Co-educational Day & Boarding B4-19 G4-19
No of Pupils: B723 G577 VIth553 FB192
Fees: FB £3320-£5892 DAY £80-£230

ROYAL BELFAST ACADEMICAL INSTITUTION
College Square East, Belfast, County Antrim BT1 6DL
Tel: 01232 240461
Head: R M Ridley MA
Type: Boys Day B4-18
No of Pupils: B1005 VIth270
Fees: DAY £425-£1400

ST MARY'S CHRISTIAN BROTHERS GRAMMAR SCHOOL
Glen Road, Belfast, County Antrim BT11 8NR
Tel: 01232 615321
Head: Rev Br D Gleeson
Type: Boys Day B12-18
No of Pupils: B112

VICTORIA COLLEGE BELFAST
Cranmore Park, Belfast, County Antrim BT9 6JA
Tel: 01232 661506
Head: Mrs M Andrews BSc, PGDICE
Type: Girls Day & Boarding G3-18
No of Pupils: G860 VIth199 FB40
Fees: FB £3795-£5190 WB £3795-£5190 DAY £225-£1395

Lisburn

★ **FRIENDS' SCHOOL LISBURN**
6 Magheralave Road, Lisburn, County Antrim BT28 3BH
Tel: 01846 662156
Head: J T Green MA
Type: Co-educational Day & Boarding B5-18 G5-18
No of Pupils: B457 G488 VIth232 FB19 WB31
Fees: FB £5935 WB £5805 DAY £2607

County Armagh

Armagh

THE ROYAL SCHOOL
College Hill, Armagh, County Armagh BT61 9DH
Tel: 01861 522807
Head: T Duncan MA, BSc, DASE
Type: Co-educational Boarding & Day B11-18 G11-18
No of Pupils: B257 G289 VIth141
Fees: FB £2080-£3465 WB £2080-£3465 DAY £105

County Down

Bangor

BANGOR GRAMMAR SCHOOL
13 College Avenue, Bangor, County Down BT20 5HJ
Tel: 01247 473734
Head: T W Patton MA
Type: Boys Day B11-18
No of Pupils: B696 VIth223
Fees: DAY £160-£1200

County Fermanagh

Enniskille

PORTORA ROYAL SCHOOL
Enniskillen, County Fermanagh BT74 7HA
Tel: 01365 322658
Head: R L Bennett MA, DipEd
Type: Boys Day B11-18
No of Pupils: B360 VIth100

County Londonderry

Coleraine

COLERAINE ACADEMICAL INSTITUTION
Castlerock Road, Coleraine, County Londonderry BT51 3LA
Tel: 01265 44331
Head: R S Forsythe BSc, DASE
Type: Boys Day & Boarding B11-18
No of Pupils: B650 VIth198 FB50 WB50
Fees: FB £3360-£360

County Tyrone

Dungannon

ROYAL SCHOOL DUNGANNON
Northland Row, Dungannon, County Tyrone BT71 6AP
Tel: 01868 722710
Head: P D Hewitt MA, DipEd, FRSA, FInstMgt
Type: Co-educational Day & Boarding B4-19 G4-19
No of Pupils: B344 G360 VIth173 FB12 WB8
Fees: FB £6324 DAY £2940

Scotland

Aberdeenshire

Aberdeen

ALBYN SCHOOL FOR GIRLS
17-23 Queens Road, Aberdeen AB15 4PB
Tel: 01224 322408
Head: Miss N H Smith BSc, DipEd
Type: Girls Day B2-5 G2-18
No of Pupils: B28 G391 VIth32
Fees: DAY £1210-£3925

INTERNATIONAL SCHOOL OF ABERDEEN
'Fairgirth', 296 North Deeside Rd, Aberdeen AB13 6AB
Tel: 01224 732267
Head: Dr Robert Morrisson
Type: Co-educational Day B4-18 G4-18
Fees: DAY £8000

ROBERT GORDONS COLLEGE
Schoolhill, Aberdeen AB10 1FE
Tel: 01224 646346
Head: Brian R W Lockhart MA, DipEd
Type: Co-educational Day B5-18 G5-18
No of Pupils: B809 G414 VIth123
Fees: DAY £2550-£4185

ST MARGARET'S SCHOOL FOR GIRLS
17 Albyn Place, Aberdeen, Aberdeen AB10 1RU
Tel: 01224 584466
Head: Miss Lorna M Ogilvie BSc, MSc, FRMetS
Type: Girls Day G3-18
No of Pupils: G410 VIth65
Fees: DAY £732-£3924

Argyll & Bute

Helensburgh

LOMOND SCHOOL
10 Stafford Street, Helensburgh, Argyll & Bute G84 9JX
Tel: 01436 672476
Head: A D MacDonald MA(Hons)(Cantab), DipEd
Type: Co-educational Day & Boarding B3-18 G3-18
No of Pupils: B218 G221 VIth85 FB70 WB1
Fees: FB £9685-£10,305
DAY £1350-£4770

South Ayrshire

Ayr

WELLINGTON SCHOOL
Carleton Turrets, Ayr, South Ayrshire KA7 2XH
Tel: 01292 269321/2
Head: Mrs D A Gardner
Type: Girls Day G3-18
No of Pupils: G400
Fees: DAY £4470

Clackmannanshire

Dollar

DOLLAR ACADEMY
Dollar, Clackmannanshire FK14 7DU
Tel: 01259 742511
Head: J S Robertson MA
Type: Co-educational Day & Boarding B5-18 G5-18
No of Pupils: B452 G418 VIth246 FB115 WB27
Fees: FB £8181-£9195 WB £8181-£9195
DAY £3135-£4149

Dumbarton & Clydebank

Dumbarton

KEIL SCHOOL
Helenslee Road, Dumbarton, Dumbarton & Clydebank G82 4AL
Tel: 01389 763855
Head: J Cummings BA, MA
Type: Co-educational Boarding & Day B10-18 G10-18
No of Pupils: B144 G76 FB125
Fees: FB £9192-£9354
DAY £4494-£5241

Dumfries & Galloway

Thornhill

CADEMUIR INTERNATIONAL SCHOOL
Crawfordton House, Thornhill, Dumfries & Galloway DG3 4HG
Tel: 01848 200212
Head: Robert Mulvey DIL
Type: Co-educational Boarding & Day B3-19 G3-19
No of Pupils: B50 G20 VIth16
Fees: FB £10,500 WB £9450
DAY £1800-£5700

Dundee City

Dundee

THE HIGH SCHOOL OF DUNDEE
P O Box 16, Dundee DD1 9BP
Tel: 01382 202921
Head: R Nimmo OBE, MA, MEd, FIMgt, FRSA
Type: Co-educational Day B5-18 G5-18
No of Pupils: B450 G450 VIth240
Fees: DAY £2928-£4170

City of Edinburgh

Edinburgh

DANIEL STEWART'S & MELVILLE COLLEGE
Queensferry Road, Edinburgh EH4 3EZ
Tel: 0131 332 7925
Head: P F J Tobin MA, FRSA
Type: Boys Day & Boarding B12-18
No of Pupils: B790 FB50
Fees: FB £8640 DAY £4320

THE EDINBURGH ACADEMY
42 Henderson Row, Edinburgh EH3 5BL
Tel: 0131 556 4603
Head: J V Light MA
Type: Boys Day & Boarding B11-18 G16-18
No of Pupils: B484 VIth224
Fees: FB £9687-£11,265 DAY £2574-£5283

FETTES COLLEGE
Carrington Road, Edinburgh EH4 1QX
Tel: 0131 332 2281
Head: M T Thyne MA
Type: Co-educational Boarding & Day B10-18 G10-18
No of Pupils: B278 G216 VIth164
Fees: FB £8775-£12,810
DAY £5505-£8655

GEORGE HERIOT'S SCHOOL
Lauriston Place, Edinburgh EH3 9EQ
Tel: 0131 229 7263
Head: K P Pearson
Type: Co-educational Day B3-18 G3-18
No of Pupils: B930 G707
Fees: DAY £700-£3936

GEORGE WATSON'S COLLEGE
Colinton Road, Edinburgh EH10 5EG
Tel: 0131 447 7931
Head: F E Gerstenberg MA(Cantab), FRSA, FIMgt
Type: Co-educational Day & Boarding B3-18 G3-18
No of Pupils: B1217 G982 FB46
Fees: FB £8646 DAY £969-£4299

THE MARY ERSKINE SCHOOL
Ravelston, Edinburgh EH4 3NT
Tel: 0131 337 2391
Head: P F J Tobin MA, FRSA
Type: Girls Day & Boarding G12-18
No of Pupils: G665 VIth197 FB30
Fees: FB £8280 DAY £4140

MERCHISTON CASTLE SCHOOL
294 Colinton Road, Edinburgh EH13 0PU
Tel: 0131 441 1567
Head: D M Spawforth MA
Type: Boys Boarding & Day B10-18
No of Pupils: B262 VIth130
Fees: FB £8310-£11,505 DAY £5310-£7440

RUDOLF STEINER SCHOOL OF EDINBURGH
60 Spylaw Road, Edinburgh EH10 5BR
Tel: 0131 337 3410
Head: Chairman of The College of Teachers
Type: Co-educational Day B4-18 G4-18
No of Pupils: B132 G148 VIth15
Fees: DAY £1290-£3702

ST DENIS AND CRANLEY SCHOOL
Ettrick Road, Edinburgh EH10 5BJ
Tel: 0131 229 1500
Head: Mrs S M Duncanson MA
Type: Girls Day & Boarding B3-9 G3-18
No of Pupils: B3 G140 VIth25
Fees: FB £9975 DAY £5085

ST GEORGE'S SCHOOL FOR GIRLS
Garscube Terrace, Edinburgh EH12 6BG
Tel: 0131 332 4575
Head: Dr J McClure MA, DPhil(Oxon)
Type: Girls Day & Boarding G3-18
No of Pupils: G884
Fees: FB £7044-£8247
DAY £2292-£4272

ST MARGARET'S
East Suffolk Road, Edinburgh EH16 5PJ
Tel: 0131 668 1986
Head: Miss A C Mitchell MA
Type: Girls Day & Boarding B3-8 G3-18
No of Pupils: B10 G610 VIth52 FB50 WB15
Fees: FB £6660-£8685
DAY £2445-£4305

ST MARY'S MUSIC SCHOOL
Coates Hall, 25 Grosvenor Crescent, Edinburgh EH12 5EL
Tel: 0131 538 7766
Head: Mrs J Jennifer Rimer BMus(Hons), LRAM, DipEd
Type: Co-educational Day & Boarding B8-19 G8-19
No of Pupils: B26 G15 VIth12
Fees: FB £17,596-£19,061
DAY £12,421-£13,886

ST SERF'S SCHOOL
5 Wester Coates Gardens, Edinburgh EH12 5LT
Tel: 0131 337 1015
Head: Mrs K D Hume BSc
Type: Co-educational Day B5-18 G5-18
No of Pupils: B91 G91 VIth21
Fees: DAY £1580-£2060

Fife

St Andrews

ST LEONARDS SCHOOL
St Andrews, Fife KY16 9QU
Tel: 01334 472126
Head: Mrs M C James BA(Hons) York St Anne's College Oxford
Type: Girls Boarding & Day G7-18
No of Pupils: G325 VIth99
Fees: FB £9369-£12,366
DAY £3465-£6540

City of Glasgow

Glasgow

BELMONT HOUSE
Sandringham Avenue, Glasgow G77 5DU
Tel: 0141 639 2922
Head: J Mercer
Type: Boys Day B3-18
No of Pupils: B347 VIth19
Fees: DAY £2795-£3810

CRAIGHOLME SCHOOL
72 St Andrews Drive, Glasgow G41 4HS
Tel: 0141 427 0375
Head: Mrs G Burt
Type: Girls Day B3-8 G3-18
Fees: DAY £1200-£3795

FERNHILL SCHOOL
Fernbrae Avenue, Glasgow G73 4SG
Tel: 0141 634 2674
Head: Mrs L M McLay MA
Type: Girls Day B4-11 G4-18
No of Pupils: B52 G270 VIth14
Fees: DAY £2850-£3060

THE GLASGOW ACADEMY
Colebrooke Street, Glasgow G12 8HE
Tel: 0141 334 8558
Head: Rector D Comins MA
Type: Co-educational Day B4-18 G4-18
No of Pupils: B643 G348 VIth195
Fees: DAY £2865-£4485

THE HIGH SCHOOL OF GLASGOW
637 Crow Road, Glasgow G13 1PL
Tel: 0141 954 9628
Head: R G Easton OBE, MA, DipEd
Type: Co-educational Day B3-18 G3-18
No of Pupils: B402 G414 VIth170
Fees: DAY £1494-£4266

HUTCHESONS' GRAMMAR SCHOOL
21 Beaton Road, Glasgow G41 4NW
Tel: 0141 423 2933
Head: D R Ward MA
Type: Co-educational Day B4-18 G4-18
No of Pupils: B784 G714 VIth366
Fees: DAY £3114-£3654

THE KELVINSIDE ACADEMY
33 Kirklee Road, Glasgow G12 0SW
Tel: 0141 357 3376
Head: J H Duff MA
Type: Boys Day B2-18
No of Pupils: B425 G10 VIth125
Fees: DAY £1440-£4728

LAUREL PARK SCHOOL
4 Lilybank Terrace, Glasgow G12 8RX
Tel: 0141 339 9127
Head: Mrs E Surber MA, PGCE
Type: Girls Day B3-5 G3-18
No of Pupils: B10 G432 VIth118
Fees: DAY £2583-£3969

ST ALOYSIUS COLLEGE
45 Hill Street, Glasgow G3 6RJ
Tel: 0141 332 3190
Head: Rev Adrian Porter SJ
Type: Co-educational Day B3-18 G3-18
No of Pupils: B701 G488 VIth99
Fees: DAY £2850-£3160

South Lanarkshire

Hamilton

HAMILTON COLLEGE
Bothwell Road, Hamilton, South Lanarkshire ML3 0AY
Tel: 01698 282700
Head: Mr A J Leach BD, FRSA
Type: Co-educational Day B4-18 G4-18
No of Pupils: B403 G343
Fees: DAY £2250-£3030

East Lothian

Musselburgh

LORETTO SCHOOL
Musselburgh, East Lothian EH21 7RE
Tel: 0131 665 2567
Head: Keith J Budge MA
Type: Co-educational Boarding & Day B13-18 G13-18
No of Pupils: B250 G58 VIth146
Fees: FB £11,610 DAY £7740

Moray

Elgin

GORDONSTOUN
Elgin, Moray IV30 2RF
Tel: 01343 830445
Head: M C S-R Pyper BA
Type: Co-educational Boarding & Day B13-18 G13-18
No of Pupils: B258 G162 VIth180
Fees: FB £12,480 DAY £8055

Perthshire & Kinross

Crieff

MORRISON'S ACADEMY
Crieff, Perthshire & Kinross PH7 3AN
Tel: 01764 653885
Head: G H Edwards MA(Oxon)
Type: Co-educational Day & Boarding B5-18 G5-18
Fees: FB £9996-£11,121
DAY £2550-£3828

Dunkeld

THE NEW SCHOOL
Butterstone, Dunkeld, Perthshire & Kinross PH8 0HJ
Tel: 01350 724216
Head: Dr William Marshall BSc, PhD
Type: Co-educational Boarding B12-18 G12-18
No of Pupils: B19 G21
Fees: WB £11,100 DAY £8400

Perth

GLENALMOND COLLEGE, PERTH
Perth, Perthshire & Kinross PH1 3RY
Tel: 01738 880442
Head: I G Templeton MA, BA
Type: Co-educational Boarding & Day B12-18 G12-18
No of Pupils: B140 G40 VIth140
Fees: FB £9000-£12,000 DAY £6000-£8000

★ **KILGRASTON SCHOOL**
(A Scared Heart School), Perthshire PH2 9BQ
Tel: 01738 812257
Head: Mrs Juliet L Austin BA(Hons)
Type: Girls Boarding & Day B5-8 G5-18
No of Pupils: B3 G250 VIth55
Fees: FB £10,335 DAY £5955

STRATHALLAN SCHOOL
Perth, Perthshire & Kinross PH2 9EG
Tel: 01738 812546
Head: A W McPhail MA(Oxon)
Type: Co-educational Boarding & Day B10-18 G10-18
No of Pupils: B438 G228 VIth183 FB465
Fees: FB £9120-£11,775 DAY £6651-£8211

Pitlochry

RANNOCH SCHOOL
Pitlochry, Perthshire & Kinross PH17 2QQ
Tel: 01882 632332
Head: M Barratt MA
Type: Co-educational Boarding & Day B10-18 G10-18
No of Pupils: B180 G55 VIth80 FB235
Fees: FB £8964-£10,764 DAY £5655

Stirlingshire

Dunblane

QUEEN VICTORIA SCHOOL
Dunblane, Stirlingshire FK15 0JY
Tel: 01786 822288
Head: B Raine BA(Hons), PGCE
Type: Co-educational Boarding B11-18 G11-18
No of Pupils: B195 G40 VIth25

Stirling

BEACONHURST SCHOOL
52 Kenilworth Road, Stirling, Stirlingshire FK9 4RR
Tel: 01786 832146
Head: D R Clegg BMus, ARCO
Type: Co-educational Day B3-18 G3-18
No of Pupils: B124 G136
Fees: DAY £350-£1415

Wales

Aberconwy & Colwyn

Colwyn Bay

RYDAL PENHROS SENIOR SCHOOL CO-ED DIVISION
Pwllycrochan Avenue, Colwyn Bay,
Aberconwy & Colwyn LL29 7BT
Tel: 01492 530155
Head: N W Thorne BEd, MSc
Type: Co-educational Boarding & Day B11-18 G11-18
No of Pupils: B170 G90 VIth120 FB170
Fees: FB £8877-£10,383
DAY £6486-£7515

RYDAL PENHROS SENIOR SCHOOL GIRLS' DIVISION
Llannerch Road East, Colwyn Bay,
Aberconwy & Colwyn LL28 4DA
Tel: 01492 530333
Head: C M J Allen MA, MSc
Type: Girls Boarding & Day G11-18
No of Pupils: G164 VIth52 FB118
Fees: FB £8595-£9720 WB £8595-£9720
DAY £6225-£6660

Bridgend

Porthcawl

ST CLARE'S CONVENT
Arosfa, Porthcawl, Bridgend CF36 5NR
Tel: 01656 782509
Head: Miss A Jarrett
Type: Co-educational Day B3-18 G3-18
No of Pupils: B138 G218 VIth30
Fees: DAY £1830-£3795

Cardiff

HOWELL'S SCHOOL, LLANDAFF GPDST
Cardiff Road, Cardiff CF5 2YD
Tel: 01222 562019
Head: Mrs C J Fitz BSc
Type: Girls Day G3-18
No of Pupils: G564 VIth152
Fees: DAY £3036-£4140

KINGS MONKTON SCHOOL
The Parade, Cardiff CF2 3UA
Tel: 01222 483130
Head: R Griffin BA, BEd, MSc
Type: Co-educational Day B3-18 G3-18
No of Pupils: B221 G114 VIth29
Fees: DAY £2385-£3465

KINGS MONKTON SCHOOL
Clive Road, Cardiff CF2 1AR
Tel: 01222 482854
Head: R N Griffin BA, BEd(Hons), MSc
Type: Co-educational Day B2-18 G2-18
No of Pupils: B58 G26
Fees: DAY £2385-£2862

NEW COLLEGE AND SCHOOL
Bute Terrace, Cardiff CF1 2TE
Tel: 01222 463355
Head: W Hoole BSc(Hons), CChem, PhC, MPS
Type: Co-educational Day B3-18 G3-18
No of Pupils: B101 G60 VIth170
Fees: DAY £7725-£10,365

Carmarthenshire

Llandovery

LLANDOVERY COLLEGE
Llandovery, Carmarthenshire SA20 0EE
Tel: 01550 720315
Head: Dr C E Evans CChem, MRSC
Type: Co-educational Boarding & Day B11-18 G11-18
No of Pupils: B167 G73
Fees: FB £8460-£9987
DAY £5796-£6516

Llanelli

ST MICHAEL'S SCHOOL
Llanelli, Carmarthenshire SA14 9TU
Tel: 01554 820325
Head: D T Sheehan BSc(Hons), PGCE
Type: Co-educational Day B4-18 G4-18
No of Pupils: B160 G115 VIth38
Fees: DAY £2115-£3585

Denbighshire

Denbigh

HOWELL'S SCHOOL
Denbigh, Denbighshire LL16 3EN
Tel: 01745 813631
Head: Mrs Mary Steel BA
Type: Girls Boarding & Day G2-18
No of Pupils: G248 VIth64
Fees: FB £5685-£10,485
DAY £2820-£6840

ST BRIGIDS SCHOOL
Plas yn Green, Denbigh, Denbighshire LL16 4BH
Tel: 01745 815228
Head: Sr E Kelly CSB
Type: Girls Day & Boarding B3-11 G3-18
No of Pupils: FB33 WB44
Fees: FB £5610-£6555 WB £4890-£5700
DAY £1950-£3600

Ruthin

RUTHIN SCHOOL
Ruthin, Denbighshire LL15 1EE
Tel: 01824 702543
Head: J S Rowlands BSc
Type: Co-educational Day & Boarding B3-18 G3-18
No of Pupils: B140 G58 VIth42 FB63 WB27
Fees: FB £7005-£10,350 WB £7005-£8505
DAY £2250-£6510

Gwynedd

Bangor

ST GERARD'S SCHOOL
Ffriddoedd Road, Bangor, Gwynedd LL57 2EL
Tel: 01248 351656
Head: Miss Anne Parkinson BA(Hons)
Type: Co-educational Day B3-18 G3-18
No of Pupils: B132 G193 VIth27
Fees: DAY £2670

Llandudno

ST DAVID'S COLLEGE
Gloddaeth Hall, Llandudno, Gwynedd LL30 1RD
Tel: 01492 875974
Head: W Seymour MA
Type: Boys Boarding & Day B11-18
No of Pupils: B230 VIth60
Fees: FB £9978 DAY £6489

Monmouthshire

Monmouth

HABERDASHERS' MONMOUTH SCHOOL FOR GIRLS
Hereford Road, Monmouth NP5 3XT
Tel: 01600 714214
Head: Mrs D L Newman BA, PGCE
Type: Girls Day & Boarding G7-18
No of Pupils: G481 VIth167 FB65 WB66
Fees: FB £7272-£8346
DAY £3501-£4575

MONMOUTH SCHOOL
Monmouth NP5 3XP
Tel: 01600 713143
Head: Timothy H P Haynes BA
Type: Boys Day & Boarding B11-18
No of Pupils: B558 VIth166
Fees: FB £3175-£8175
DAY £4908-£4908

Newport

Newport

ROUGEMONT SCHOOL
Llantarnam Hall, Newport NP9 6QB
Tel: 01633 855560
Head: I Brown
Type: Co-educational Day B3-18 G3-18
No of Pupils: B220 G215 VIth60
Fees: DAY £2646-£4599

Powys

Brecon

CHRIST COLLEGE
Brecon, Powys LD3 8AG
Tel: 01874 623359
Head: S W Hockey MA(Cantab)
Type: Boys Boarding & Day B11-18 G16-18
Fees: FB £8913 DAY £6804

ST DAVID'S SCHOOL
Glamorgan Street, Brecon, Powys LD3 7DN
Tel: 01874 622806
Head: Mrs J A Jones MA, CPhys, MInstP
Type: Co-educational Day & Boarding B0-18 G0-18
No of Pupils: B31 G90 VIth8 WB10
Fees: WB £5250-£6300
DAY £1605-£3810

Swansea

Swansea

FFYNONE HOUSE SCHOOL
36 St James's Crescent, Swansea SA1 6DR
Tel: 01792 464967
Head: John Rhys Thomas BSc, DipEd, FRSA
Type: Co-educational Day B8-18 G11-18
No of Pupils: B130 G80 VIth40
Fees: DAY £2760-£3984

Vale of Glamorgan

Barry

ATLANTIC COLLEGE
St Donat's Castle, Barry, Vale of Glamorgan CF6 9WF
Tel: 01446 792530
Head: C Jenkins
Type: Co-educational Day

Channel Islands

Guernsey

ELIZABETH COLLEGE
Guernsey, Channel Islands GY1 2PY
Tel: 01481 726544
Head: J H F Doulton MA, FRSA
Type: Boys Day & Boarding B4-18 G16-18
No of Pupils: B526 VIth150
Fees: FB £6660 DAY £2610

THE LADIES' COLLEGE
Les Gravees, Guernsey, Channel Islands GY1 1RW
Tel: 01481 721602
Head: Miss M E Macdonald MA, DipEd
Type: Girls Day B3-4 G3-18
No of Pupils: B27 G440 VIth90
Fees: DAY £2250-£2370

Jersey

BEAULIEU CONVENT SCHOOL
Wellington Road, Jersey, Channel Islands JE2 4RJ
Tel: 01534 31280
Head: Mrs R A Hill BSc(Hons)
Type: Girls Day G4-18
No of Pupils: G538 VIth70
Fees: DAY £1800

VICTORIA COLLEGE
Jersey, Channel Islands JE1 4HT
Tel: 01534 37591
Head: J Hydes MA, MEd
Type: Boys Day B11-18
No of Pupils: B464 VIth160
Fees: DAY £0-£1782

Display Listings of Schools and Colleges offering the International Baccalaureate

A full list of schools and colleges offering the International Baccalaureate appears on page 183.

Hereford & Worcester

Malvern College

Malvern,
Worcestershire WR14 3DF
Tel: 01684 892333 Fax: 01684 572398 E-mail: inquiry@malcol.worcs.sch.uk

Head: Hugh C.K. Carson, BA

Member of HMC

Courses offered: More than 20 A level courses, AS courses and the International Baccalaureate.

No of students: Male 428 (223 in Sixth Form) Female 181 (96 in Sixth Form)

Nature of tuition: Classes, small groups.

Average size of class or group: 10-12

Teacher/student ratio: 1: 9

Range of fees as at 1.1.97: Tuition: £3090 per term
Accommodation: £1160 per term

Arrangements for accommodation:
Fully residential on campus.

Fully co-educational from 3-18, day and boarding school. Beautiful rural setting close to M5 and 40 minutes from Birmingham Airport. New extensively equipped Technology Centre.

Malvern College, a registered charity, exists to provide a quality all round education for pupils aged 3 to 18.

London

Woodside Park School

*Friern Barnet Road,
London N11 3DR
Tel: 0181 368 3777*

Head: Mr Robin F. Metters
Member of IAPS, ECIS

Courses offered: Students prepare for the International Baccalaureate Diploma by studying six subjects which must include their native language, a foreign language, mathematics, a science and a social science. At least three, and not more than four of the six subjects are taken at the Higher level, the others at subsidiary level. In addition, students must write an Extended Essay on a topic of their choice; follow a course entitled Theory of Knowledge; and devote time to the Creativity, Action and Service (CAS) programme.

As an alternative to the full Diploma programme, students may enrol in individual IB courses for the purpose of acquiring IB certificates.

No of students: Male 374 Female 136
Age range: 3-18

Nature of tuition: Classes, small groups, one-to-one.
Range of fees as at 1.1.97:
Tuition: £6000 to £9000

Facilities

Students have their own common room and have immediate access to modern technology, including the Internet. A new multi-media centre is at their disposal. Through our video conferencing facility students can keep in contact with the IB students in our New York school.

Entry requirements and procedures

Students should have at least five or six GCSE passes at grades C or higher, with preferably high grades (B, A, A*) in the subjects they wish to study at Higher Level.

Applicants will be interviewed by the IB Coordinator and will be advised over the choice of subjects and levels. They will need to take an entrance examination in early February in each of the three subjects they propose to take at Higher level. Scholarships will be available for exceptionally able students.

Aims and objectives of the institution

The School aims to create a secure, well-ordered and happy environment at the core of which is the learning process.

Emphasis is placed on the successful development of the whole individual in all areas of achievement including creative, musical, sporting and practical activities. The importance of learning to work with other students as team members and, where appropriate, as leaders is also emphasised.

Students are given a thorough preparation for adult life and an active role in society, including the ability to learn independently and to adapt confidently to new situations.

The School aims to serve a cosmopolitan community and importance is attached to empathising with the cultures, religions and backgrounds of its students. The School is keen to foster and encourage good relations with the international community and its students.

Display Listings of Professional Schools and Colleges

Business and Secretarial

Cookery

Teacher Training (Nursery and Infant)

The Arts

Business and Secretarial

Lucie Clayton College

*4 Cornwall Gardens,
Kensington, London SW7 4AJ
Tel: 0171 581 0024*

Business and Secretarial Training

1, 2 and 3 Term Executive Courses in Computing, Word Processing, Shorthand and Touch Typing. Options in PR, Law and Finance.

Nursery Nursing

1 and 3 Term courses in Childcare and Education. Professional Qualifications gained.

Range of fees: £1000-£2100 per term

Accommodation in the college hostel is available.

The College has its own exclusive Placement Bureau for graduates from the above courses.

Cookery

Leith's School of Food and Wine

*21 St Alban's Grove,
London W8 5BP
Tel: 0171 229 0177*

Principal: Caroline Waldegrave
Vice Principals: Alison Cavaliero and C.J. Jackson
Recognised by IACP
Courses offered: Professional one year or two term Diploma course and single term certificates. Four day, one week or four week courses. Three day

Chalet Cooking. Evening classes, Saturday demonstrations.
No. of students enrolled as at 11.10.96: 96
Male: 15 Female: 81
Age range: 18+
Nature of tuition: Lectures and demonstrations.
Average size of class or group: 16

Teacher/student ratio: 2:16

Range of fees inclusive of VAT as at 1.1.97:
Tuition: Diploma £8700. Four week £1310, one week £385

Average amount required to cover educational 'extras' is £160 on a Diploma course.

Accommodation: list and advice available.

Details of individual courses: Diploma in Food and Wine; Beginners, Intermediate and Advanced Certificates in Food and Wine; 3 day Chalet Cook; Basic Certificate in Practical Cookery; four week Intensive courses, Beginner's or Advanced; evening classes in Practical Cookery, Beginner's or Advanced; evening classes in Wine Knowledge and Appreciation; Saturday morning demonstrations; evening course in starting a restaurant; Summer evening demonstrations. Specialist weeks.

Subject specialities and academic track record: European and ethnic cooking, wine appreciation, basic nutrition and food hygiene, costing and catering management. 95% pass rate.

Examinations offered including Boards: Leith's Diploma in Food and Wine; Leith's Certificate (Beginners, Intermediate or Advanced) in Food and Wine; Leith's Certificate in Practical Cookery; Leith's Certificate or Advanced Certificate in Wine.

Destination and career prospects for leavers: Cooking in directors' boardrooms, catering companies, restaurants, wine bars, food stylists, writing for magazines, as freelance cooks, as chalet girls and in shooting lodges.

Academic and student facilities available: large demonstration room. Three large, well-equipped modern practical kitchens. Generous-sized student common room. Access to well-stocked library, kitchen equipment and bookshop.

The School is situated between High Street Kensington and Gloucester Road in spacious specifically converted premises just 5 minutes walk from the underground.

Teacher Training (Nursery & Infant)

The Norland College

Denford Park,
Hungerford, Berkshire RG17 0PQ
Tel: 01488 682252 Fax: 01488 685212

Principal: Mrs Louise Davis
Date of appointment: 1980
School foundation: 1892
College Specialising in Training of Nursery Nurses

Courses offered: A two year course leading to the award of the Diploma in Nursery Nursing, the Norland Diploma and the National Vocational Qualification in Child Care and Education.

Religious affiliation: None
Age range of pupils: Aged 17 and over
No. of students enrolled as at 1.9.96: 100
Average size of class: 25
Teacher/Pupil ratio: 1:18

Range of fees per term as at 1.8.97:
Tuition with tax relief available is £2600 per term.
Maintenance £1450 per term.
Bursary schemes are available

The demand for Norland Nurses in employment is such that students who successfully complete the course can be confident of choice of employment.

Entry requirements and procedures: Minimum three GCSEs at Grade C or above.

The College is situated in parkland together with the Norland Nursery School, Day Care Units and the Norland Childrens' Hotel.

The Arts

Fine Arts College

*85 Belsize Park Gardens,
London NW3 4NJ
Tel: 0171 586 0312
Fax: 0171 483 0355*

Principals: Candida Cave, CFA(Oxon) and Nicholas Cochrane, CFA(Oxon)

Courses offered: Portfolio and Pre-Foundation Courses in Art and Design. One and two year A level courses in all Arts subjects. One year GCSE courses.

No of students: 100 Male: 40% Female: 60%

Age range: 15 - 20

Nature of tuition: lectures, class, small groups

Average size of class: 7

Range of fees per term as at 1.10.96:
£2995 for 3 A levels;
£1095 for 1 A level;
£2995 for Pre-Foundation art course;
£2995 for Portfolio Course;
£2995 for Full-time one year GCSE course;
£765 per subject

Students may also be required to pay up to £160 for educational extras (*eg* theatre visits)

Arrangements for accommodation: available with local hostels.

Fine Arts College is the only Independent Sixth Form College in London to specialise in the Arts, preparing students for Arts degree courses at University as well as Foundation courses at Art School.

Most students follow further education courses after studying at Fine Arts College, so it is normally a requirement that students have passed five GCSEs before beginning the A level courses. However, exceptions can be made if the student is prepared to take the necessary GCSEs while sitting A levels.

A level courses are available in most arts subjects: Art, History of Art, Art and Crafts (Printmaking and Sculpture), Photography, English, Theatre Studies, Media Studies, Classical Civilisation, Archaeology, Ancient History, History, Philosophy, Psychology, Religious Studies, French, Italian, German, Spanish, Latin, Business Studies, Maths.

We offer an intensive one-year GCSE programme which is Arts and Humanities based but includes both Mathematics and Biology. Students are able to complete the full course of up to eight subjects within one year, and are then more prepared for studying arts based A level subjects either at Fine Arts College or elsewhere. Although GCSE students are fully integrated into the rest of the College, attention is paid to the specific differences of the GCSE programme.

The three month Portfolio Course and one year Pre-Foundation Course are suitable for those who have already taken A levels and wish to apply for a degree course at a University or a Foundation Course at Art School.

The nature of the two courses is broad and provides a basic introduction to Fine and Applied Art subjects: drawing, painting, sculpture and printmaking. There is a high level of success with Art School entry.

Fine Arts College, above all, offers an excellent opportunity to study all aspects of the Arts in a stimulating and friendly atmosphere, where every attention is given to the individual needs of the student to fulfil his/her academic potential.

The Heatherley School of Fine Art

*Upcerne Road,
London SW10 0SH
Tel: 0171 351 4190 Fax: 0171 351 6945*

SW1

Principal: John Walton, RP, DFA(Lond)
Courses offered:
Full-time Diploma in Portraiture
26hrs - £5296 per year
Part-time Diploma in Portraiture
15hrs - £3530 per year
Foundation/Portfolio course
2 terms - £3084, 1 year - £4240
Continuing Studies
15hrs - £2312, 30 hrs - £4624
Day and evening courses
5hrs - £260, 2½hrs - £130
Open Studio
Ten 2½hr sessions (25hrs) - £108
(Fees are for academic year 97/98)
Age range: 17-80 years
Nature of tuition: Lectures, classes, small groups, one-to-one tutorials.
Average size of class or group: 12
Teacher/student ratio: 1: 12
Arrangements for accommodation:
Accommodation advice only.
School founded 1845. Charity founded 1970. Purpose built studios in Chelsea for drawing, painting, printmaking, sculpture and design.
The Thomas Heatherley Educational Trust Ltd is a registered charity which exists to provide education in the arts and administers to the Heatherley School of Fine Art.

FOUNDER, PRINCIPAL & ARTISTIC DIRECTOR: **SORREL CARSON**
PATRON: **JOAN LITTLEWOOD**

- **Three Year Course**
  Intensive Full Time Training for a career in Theatre, Film and Television
- **One year Post Graduate**
  Actor's Course
- **Stage Management Course**

ALRA offers first class standards of tuition in a caring atmosphere and is a leading innovator in training for Theatre, Television and Film.

Superb facilities include the Southside Theatre, two Studio Theatres, Dance Studios and Rehearsal Rooms in a Grade One listed building.

Television classes take place in our fully equipped TV Studio under the direction of experienced professionals.

ALRA graduates have worked at the RSC, RNT, Royal Court, in the West End and in Television and Film.

Scholarships are available.

The Three Year Course is Accredited by the National Council for Drama Training.

- **Associate Evening Classes:-**
  Acting for Television, TV Presentation
  Evenings - Weekends - Summer School

**ACADEMY OF LIVE AND RECORDED ARTS
ROYAL VICTORIA BUILDING,
TRINITY ROAD, LONDON SW18 3SX**
TELEPHONE: 0181 870 6475   FAX: 0181 875 0789

Directory of Professional Schools and Colleges

Agriculture and Horticulture

Business and Secretarial

Computer, Electronics, Specialist

Cookery and Home Economics

Hairdressing

Health and Beauty

Hotel Training

Teaching Training (Nursery and Infant)

Other Specialist

Agriculture & Horticulture

ROYAL AGRICULTURAL COLLEGE
Cirencester, Gloucestershire GL7 6JS
Tel: 01285 652531
Principal: Professor Arthur Jones

ROYAL BOTANIC GARDEN
Inverleith Road, Edinburgh EH3 5LR
Tel: 0131 552 7171
Principal: G Anderson DHE, CertEd

THE ROYAL HORTICULTURAL SOCIETY'S GARDEN
Wisley, Woking, Surrey GU23 6QB
Tel: 01483 224234
Principal: W J Simpson

SCHOOL OF HORTICULTURE
Royal Botanic Gardens, Richmond, Surrey TW9 3AB
Tel: 0181 332 5545
Principal: Ian Leese BSc, MHort(RHS), DipHort(Kew), CertEd, FIHort

SCOTTISH AGRICULTURAL COLLEGE
Auchincruie, Ayr, South Ayrshire KA6 5HU
Tel: 01292 520331

THREAVE SCHOOL OF HORTICULTURE
National Trust for Scotland, Castle Douglas,
Dumfries & Galloway DG7 1R
Tel: 01556 502575
Principal: Trevor Jones

Business & Secretarial

BASIL PATERSON COLLEGE - SECRETARIAL & BUSINESS
Dugdale-McAdam House, Edinburgh EH3 6QE
Tel: 0131 556 7698
Principal: R R Mackenzie

BECKENHAM SECRETARIAL COLLEGE
31 Beckenham Road, Beckenham, Kent BR3 4PR
Tel: 0181 650 3321
Principal: Mrs E Wakeling

**BILINGUAL SECRETARIAL COLLEGE OF
THE FRENCH INSTITUTE**
14 Cromwell Place, London SW7 2JR
Tel: 0171 589 6211
Principal: Michel Richard

BRIERLEY PRICE PRIOR LTD
BBP House, Aldine Place, London W12 8AA
Tel: 0181 740 2222

BROADWAY SECRETARIAL TRAINING CENTRE
30-31 The Broadway, London W3 2NP
Tel: 0181 840 2762
Principal: Ms J Mattson

BROOKSIDE SECRETARIAL COLLEGE
2 Brookside, Cambridge CB2 1JE
Tel: 01223 364639
Principal: Mrs C Tuson

BUSINESS & OFFICE TRAINING CENTRE
3 Winchester Place, Poole, Dorset BH15 1NX
Tel: 01202 684646/570341 H/O
Principal: Ms L Shawe

THE CAMBRIDGE BUSINESS COLLEGE
16 Brooklands Avenue, Cambridge CB2 2BB
Tel: 01223 63159
Principals: Matthew Cole & Ms Jo Wainwright

CAMBRIDGE SECRETARIAL COURSES
6 Salisbury Villas, Cambridge CB1 2JF
Tel: 01223 369701
Principal: Mrs Christine Hodgson

CAVENDISH COLLEGE
209-212 Tottenham Court Road, London W1P 9AF
Tel: 0171 580 6043
Principal: Dr J Sanders BSc, MBA, PhD

CITY BUSINESS COLLEGE
178 Goswell Road, London EC1V 7DT
Tel: 0171 251 6473
Principal: M Nowaz BA, MABE, AIFA, ACII

CITY COLLEGE OF HIGHER EDUCATION
67-88 Seven Sisters Road, London N7 6BU
Tel: 0171 263 5937
Principal: A Andrews MBIM, FFA, FCEA, MABE

COLLEGE OF CENTRAL LONDON
213-215 Tottenham Court Road, London W1 4US
Tel: 0171 636 2212
Principal: N Kailides

COLLINS SECRETARIAL TRAINING
Victoria House, Epsom, Surrey KT17 1HH
Tel: 01372 728823
Principal: Mrs. Brooks

CROWN SECRETARIAL COLLEGE
121-129 North Road, Westcliff-on-Sea, Essex SS0 7AH
Tel: 01702 340121
Principal: Ms T Corsiwi

DAMAR TRAINING COLLEGE
36-38 St Petersgate, Stockport, Cheshire SK1 1HD
Tel: 0161 480 8171
Principal: Mrs D P Stafford

EMILE WOOLF COLLEGE
457-463 Caledonian Road, London N7 9BA
Tel: 0171 700 6438

EVEREST SECRETARIAL TRAINING
195 Cheltenham Road, Bristol BS6 5QX
Tel: 0117 9246248
Principal: Ruth Sowby

FOULKS LYNCH
6 Avonmouth Street, London SE1 6NX
Tel: 0181 8319990
Principal: D Rosebery

GREENWICH COLLEGE
Meridian House, London SE10 8RT
Tel: 0181 853 4484
Principal: W G Hunt BEd, MA

GUILDFORD SECRETARIAL COLLEGE
19 Chapel Street, Guildford, Surrey GU1 3UL
Tel: 01483 564885
Principal: Mrs D E White

HARROW SECRETARIAL COLLEGE
72 Station Road, Harrow, Middlesex HA1 2SQ
Tel: 0181 427 2939
Principal: Mrs R Bluston

HOVE BUSINESS COLLEGE
1-2 Ventnor Villas, Hove, East Sussex BN3 3DD
Tel: 01273 731352/727102
Principal: Mrs P Humphrey

INSTITUT FRANCAIS
14 Cromwell Place, London SW7 2JR
Tel: 0171 581 2701 or 0171 58962
Principal: Mrs L Towers

JHP BUSINESS CENTRE
28A Dyer Street, Cirencester, Gloucestershire GL7 2PF
Tel: 01203 667891 (Head Office)
Principal: Mrs R J Nunn

JORDAN COMMERCIAL COLLEGE
62 Bickerstaffe Street, St Helens, Lancashire
Tel: 01744 24547
Principal: Mrs J Kelly

KENSINGTON COLLEGE OF BUSINESS
52a Walham Grove, London SW6 1QR
Tel: 0171 381 6360
Principal: I R Pirie BA

LANSDOWNE SECRETARIAL COLLEGE
7-9 Palace Gate, London W8 5LS
Tel: 0171 581 4866
Principal: P Templeton BSc(Econ)

LONDON ACADEMY OF ADMINISTRATION STUDIES
Maritime House, London SW4 OJP
Tel: 0171 627 1299
Principal: Mr Filani

LONDON CITY COLLEGE
Royal Waterloo House, London SE1 8TX
Tel: 0171 928 0029/0938/0901
Principal: N Kyritsis MA, DMS, MCIM

LONDON COLLEGE OF ENGLISH & ADVANCED STUDIES
178 Goswell Road, London EC1V 7DT
Tel: 0171 250 0610
Principal: M Nowaz BA, MABE, AIFA, ACII

LONDON EXECUTIVE COLLEGE
Bank Chambers, London SW17 7BA
Tel: 0181 682 1011
Principal: The Head

★ **LUCIE CLAYTON SECRETARIAL COLLEGE**
4 Cornwall Gardens, London SW7 4AJ
Tel: 0171 581 0024
Principal: Georgina Blake

LUTON OFFICE TRAINING COLLEGE
14-16 Chapel Street, Luton, Bedfordshire LU1 2SU
Tel: 01582 451613/451588
Principal: Mrs B Gotch

MLS COLLEGE
7/8 Verulam Place, Bournemouth, Dorset BH1 IDW
Tel: 01202 291556/299552
Principal: Mr B Henwood

NEWTON SECRETARIAL SCHOOL
12Q Chesterbank Business Park, Chester, Cheshire CH4 8SL
Tel: 01244 681814/537265
Principal: Mrs A A Williams FIPS, FBSC

NORTH OF ENGLAND COLLEGE
Cavendish House, Leeds, West Yorkshire LS1 6AG
Tel: 0113 2453073
Principal: Mrs A Salama

NORTHERN BUSINESS/COMMERCIAL SCHOOL
Conservancy Buildings, Kingston-upon-Hull,
East Riding of Yorkshire HU1
Tel: 01482 325562
Principal: Mrs M Foers

OFFICE SKILLS CENTRE UK LTD
Dragon Court, London WC2B 5LX
Tel: 0171 242 0566
Principal: Jamie Dickson

OXFORD & COUNTY BUSINESS COLLEGE
34 St Giles, Oxford OX1 3LH
Tel: 01865 310100
Principal: Joy Thompson BA(Hons), FIMgt

OXFORD COLLEGE FOR BUSINESS STUDIES
15 King Edward Street, Oxford OX1 4HT
Tel: 01865 200830
Principal: S Hunter MA

OXFORD SCHOOL OF LEARNING
1 Bradmore Road, Oxford OX2 6QN
Tel: 01865 512428 or 773391 even
Principal: C Sivewright

PAMELA NEAVE TRAINING CENTRE
18 St Augustines Parade, Bristol BS1 4UL
Tel: 0117 9211831
Principal: Mrs J Derrick-Smith

PITMAN CENTRAL COLLEGE
154 Southampton Row, London WC1B 5AX
Tel: 0171 837 4481
Principal: Mrs J Almond

PURLEY SCHOOL OF COMMERCE
13 High Street, Purley, Surrey CR2 2AF
Tel: 0181 660 5060/2568
Principal: Miss P W Kent

PURLEY SECRETARIAL & LANGUAGE COLLEGE
14 Brighton Road, Purley, Surrey CR8 3AB
Tel: 0181 660 5060/2568
Principal: Miss P W Kent

QUEEN'S BUSINESS & SECRETARIAL COLLEGE
24 Queensberry Place, London SW7 2DS
Tel: 0171 589 8583/581 8331
Principal: Mrs C Bickford

QUEEN'S MARLBOROUGH COLLEGE
Bateman Street, Cambridge CB2 1LU
Tel: 01223 367016
Principal: Mrs C Bickford

RAVENSCOURT TUTORIAL COLLEGE
28 Studland Street, London W6 0JS
Tel: 0181 846 8542
Principal: Miss P M Saw

REED COLLEGE OF ACCOUNTANCY
The Manor, Moreton-in-Marsh, Gloucestershire GL56 0RZ
Tel: 01608 674224
Principal: David Wilson

SANDRA TUTORIAL COLLEGE OF SECRETARIAL & COMPUTER STUDIES
Sandra House, London EC1R 5ET
Tel: 0171 833 3101
Principal: Mr David

SHACKLETON ASSOCIATES: OFFICE & COMPUTER CENTRE
96 Bridge Street, Peterborough, Cambridgeshire
Tel: 01733 68451
Principal: Ken Shackleton

SIGHT & SOUND EDUCATION LTD
Two Duke Street, Sutton Coldfield, West Midlands B72 1RJ
Tel: 01295 2565300
Principal: Basil Poulopoulos

ST ALDATE'S SECRETARIAL & BUSINESS COLLEGE
Rose Place, Oxford OX1 1SB
Tel: 01865 240963
Principal: Mrs Pauline Martin

ST JAMES'S SECRETARIAL COLLEGE
4 Wetherby Gardens, London SW5 0JN
Tel: 0171 373 3852
Principal: N C E Knight

SWIFT TRAINING CENTRE
70 Queen Street, Newton Abbot, Devon TQ12 7HG
Tel: 01626 208011
Principal: R Flemming

WILMSLOW SECRETARIAL COLLEGE
99 Hawthorn Street, Wilmslow, Cheshire SK9 5EJ
Tel: 01625 525440
Principal: Mrs J Booth

TUTORIAL COLLEGE OF SPEEDWRITING
St Aubin's Road, Jersey, Channel Islands JE2 3LL
Tel: 01534 20295
Principal: Major C G Hall BA

WEST LONDON COLLEGE
Avon House, London W1N 9HA
Tel: 0171 491 1841
Principal: P Rainey MA, MSc, MBCS

THE ZOBEL SECRETARIAL COLLEGE
18 Pembroke Road, Sevenoaks, Kent TN13 1XR
Tel: 01732 451595
Principal: Miss D H C Zobel

Computer, Electronics, Specialist

BABEL TECHNICAL COLLEGE
69 Notting Hill Gate, London W11 3JS
Tel: 0171 221 1483
Principal: M H Kubba BSc, MSc, MACM, MBCS

BOURNEMOUTH COMPUTER & TECHNOLOGY CENTRE
27 Spencer Road, Poole, Dorset BH13 7ET
Tel: 01202 708687
Principal: Mrs R A Marsden

COLLEGE OF DATA PROCESSING
213-215 Tottenham Court Rd., London W1 4US
Tel: 0171 636 2212
Principal: J Kay

KENSINGTON COLLEGE
41 Kensington High Street, London W8 5ED
Tel: 0171 937 8886
Principal: E B Robinson BSc, DipEd

LONDON ELECTRONICS COLLEGE
20 Penywern Road, London SW5 9SU
Tel: 0171 373 8721
Principal: M D Spalding BSc(Hons), MSc, CEng, MIEE, PGCE, MCybSoc, FRSA

THE SCHOOL OF COMPUTER TECHNOLOGY
213-215 Tottenham Court Rd, London W1 4US
Tel: 0171 636 6441/2
Principal: N Kay

WRAY CASTLE COLLEGE
Ambleside, Cumbria LA22 0JB
Tel: 01539 432320
Principal: Ian Gordon

Cookery & Home Economics

COOKERY AT THE GRANGE
Frome, Somerset BA11 3JU
Tel: 01373 836579
Principal: Mrs J Averill

ELIZABETH RUSSELL SCHOOL OF COOKERY
Flat 5, 18 The Grange, London SW19 4PS
Tel: 0181 947 2144
Principals: Miss A Russell & Mrs E Pilon

HARROW HOUSE
1 Silverdale Road, Eastbourne, East Sussex BN20 7AA
Tel: 01323 730851
Principal: Mrs J E Jenion BEd, MIHEC

LE CORDON BLEU CULINARY ACADEMY
114 Marylebone Lane, London W1M 6HH
Tel: 0171 935 3503
Principal: Miss L Gray

★ **LEITH'S SCHOOL OF FOOD & WINE**
21 St Alban's Grove, London W8 5BP
Tel: 0171 229 0177
Principal: Caroline Waldegrave

TANTE MARIE SCHOOL OF COOKERY
Woodham House, Woking, Surrey GU21 4HF
Tel: 01483 726957
Principal: Mrs B A Childs FIHEC

Hairdressing

ALAN D SCHOOL OF HAIRDRESSING
61-62 East Castle Street, London W1P 3RE
Tel: 0171 580 3323
Principal: Tina Jerrom

DOMINO'S ACADEMY OF HAIR & BEAUTY
1 St James's Street, Brighton, East Sussex BN2 1RE
Tel: 01273 681929
Principal: Mrs J A Faulkner

HARPERS HAIRDRESSING SCHOOL
9 Blandford Street, Sunderland, Tyne & Wear SR1 2YE
Tel: 0191 567 9300
Principal: Mr Harper

LILLIAN MAUND HAIR & BEAUTY CENTRE
Bache Hall, Chester, Cheshire CH2 1BR
Tel: 01244 383810
Principal: Mrs Lillian Maund IA, City & Guilds

LOOK & LEARN
62a Silver Street, Doncaster, South Yorkshire DN1 1HT
Tel: 01302 360343
Principal: Ivor D Jones

ROBERT FIELDING SCHOOL OF HAIRDRESSING
61-62 East Castle Street, London W1P 3RE
Tel: 0171 580 3323
Principal: Tina Jerrom

ROBERTO MOURA HAIRDRESSING ACADEMY
22 Park Row, Leeds, West Yorkshire LS1 5JF
Tel: 0113 2436842
Principal: R Moura

SOUTH LONDON COLLEGE OF HAIRDRESSING
26 Lewis Grove, London SE13
Tel: 0181 852 7693
Principal: Mr A Ross

SUPREME SCHOOL OF HAIR & BEAUTY CONSULTANCY
12 West Green Road, London N15 5NN
Tel: 0181 800 7459/802 4599
Principal: Mrs J Sam

VIDAL SASSOON ACADEMY SCHOOL OF HAIRDRESSING
15 Davies Mews, London W1Y 1AS
Tel: 0171 318 5202
Principal: S Ellis

Health & beauty

THE BRITISH SCHOOL OF OSTEOPATHY
1/4 Suffolk Street, London SW1Y 4HG
Tel: 0171 930 9254
Principal: Clive Standen MA, DO, MRO

BISHOP COLLEGE OF BEAUTY THERAPY
32-36 Duke Street, Darlington, County Durham
Tel: 01325 384465/718688
Principal: Ms J Hinton Clifton

BRETLANDS BEAUTY TRAINING CENTRE
Baden-Powell Place, Tunbridge Wells, Kent TN4 8XD
Tel: 01892 533161
Principal: Mrs J Thornycroft CIDESCO, BABTAC, C&G

CAMBRIDGE SCHOOL OF BEAUTY THERAPY
94 High Street, Cambridge CB2 4HJ
Tel: 01223 832228
Principal: Mrs P Keyte

CHAMPNEYS INTERNATIONAL COLLEGE OF HEALTH & BEAUTY
Chesham Road, Tring, Hertfordshire HP23 6HY
Tel: 01442 873326
Principal: Mrs S Page ITEC, CGTC

CHESHIRE SCHOOL OF BEAUTY
17c Church Street, Frodsham, Cheshire WA6 6PN
Tel: 01928 732304
Principal: Mrs L J Hutchinson

EDINBURGH SCHOOL OF NATURAL THERAPY
42 Frederick Street, Edinburgh EH2 1EX
Tel: 0131 557 3901
Principal: W D Austin

HEALTH AND BEAUTY SCHOOL
64 High Street, Wem, Shropshire SY4 5DW
Tel: 01939 232918

HENLOW GRANGE COLLEGE OF HEALTH & BEAUTY
Henlow Grange Health Farm, Henlow, Bedfordshire SG16 6DB
Tel: 01462 811111
Principal: Catherine Turner CIDESCO, BABTAC, FETC, IBSA, MIFA, IHBC

JOAN PRICE'S FACE PLACE BEAUTY SCHOOL
33 Cadogan Street, London SW3 3PP
Tel: 0171 589 4226
Principal: Mrs T Quayyum BABTAC, ITEC, CIDESCO

LANCASHIRE HOLISTIC COLLEGE
Greenbank House, Preston, Lancashire PR1 7BH
Tel: 01772 825177
Principal: Mrs J C Basnyet

LEEDS CENTRAL SCHOOL OF BEAUTY
8 Templar Street, Leeds, West Yorkshire LS2 7NU
Tel: 0113 2434343
Principal: Mrs J Lloyd

LONDON ACADEMY OF HEALTH & BEAUTY
53 Alkham Road, London N16 7AA
Tel: 0181 806 2788
Principal: Mrs Penina Katsch

MARY BOLTON INTERNATIONAL COLLEGE OF BEAUTY
Educational Institute, Nottingham NG5 4GW
Tel: 0115 9621866
Principal: Mrs M Bolton

MARY REID INTERNATIONAL SCHOOL OF BEAUTY
2nd Floor, Edinburgh EH12 1LH
Tel: 0131 225 3167
Principal: Mrs Joan Stewart CIDESCO, CIEL

MILLFIELD SCHOOL OF BEAUTY
Millfield House, Nr Horsham, West Sussex RH1Z 4PR
Tel: 01293 871406
Principal: Mrs C Collyer CertEd, ITEC Hons

NORTHERN INSTITUTE OF MASSAGE
100 Waterloo Road, Blackpool, Lancashire PB4 1AW
Tel: 01253 403548
Principal: E A Caldwell BEd(Hons), LCSP(Phys)

PARK SCHOOL OF BEAUTY THERAPY
Storcroft House, Retford, Nottinghamshire DN22 7EB
Tel: 01777 860377 (707371)
Principal: Ms B Percival ITEC(Hons), CIBTAC, CIDESCO, C&GFECERT

RAWORTH COLLEGE FOR SPORTS THERAPY AND NATURAL MEDICINE
Dorking, Surrey RH4 2HG
Tel: 01306 742150
Principal: Mrs N A Williams

THE RAY COCHRANE BEAUTY SCHOOL
118 Baker Street, London W1M 1LB
Tel: 0171 486 6291
Principal: Miss B Suri CIDESCO, CIBTAC

RENBARDOU SCHOOL OF BEAUTY THERAPY
Acorn House, Croydon, Surrey CR0 6BA
Tel: 0181 686 4781
Principal: Renee Tanner

ROGENE SCHOOL OF BEAUTY THERAPY
Rogene House, Ilford, Essex IG1 1BX
Tel: 0181 478 2728
Principal: Mrs C Gibson

STEINER SCHOOL OF BEAUTY THERAPY
193 Wardour Street, London W1U 3FA
Tel: 0171 434 4534/4564
Principal: Mrs J Wackett

WEST LONDON SCHOOL OF THERAPEUTIC MASSAGE
41a St Luke's Road, London W11 1DD
Tel: 0171 229 4672
Principal: C Chabrier LTPhys, MIPTI

YORKSHIRE COLLEGE OF BEAUTY
The Manor, Leeds, West Yorkshire LS19 7EM
Tel: 0113 2509507
Principal: Mrs C W Tilley BABTAC, CIDESCO, FETeachCert

Hotel Training

HOTEL & TRAVEL TRAINING COLLEGE
287 Oxford Street, London W1R 1LB
Tel: 0171 629 1762
Principal: Dr D A Samarakoon

IHMES INTERNATIONAL HOTEL SCHOOL
Windsor House, Port Erin, Isle of Man IM9 6LA
Tel: 01624 832836
Principal: Edward E Lee CHA, MHCIMA, MIMgt

LAKEFIELD CATERING & EDUCATIONAL CENTRE
41a Maresfield Gardens, London NW3 5RY
Tel: 0171 433 3454
Principal: Miss J E Gardner

Teacher Training (Nursery and Infant)

CHILTERN NURSERY TRAINING COLLEGE
16 Peppard Road, Reading, Berkshire RG4 8JZ
Tel: 01734 471847
Principal: Mrs E Sadek

LONDON MONTESSORI CENTRE LTD
18 Balderton Street, London W1Y 1TG
Tel: 0171 493 0165
Principal: Lauren Joffe BA, MontDip, AdDip

MARIA MONTESSORI TRAINING ORGANISATION
26 Lyndhurst Gardens, London NW3 5NW
Tel: 0171 435 3646
Principal: Mrs L Lawrence

★ **THE NORLAND COLLEGE**
Denford Park, Hungerford, Berkshire RG17 OPQ
Tel: 01488 682252
Principal: Mrs L E Davis MPhil, RGN, FRSH

THE PRINCESS CHRISTIAN COLLEGE
26 Wilbraham Road, Manchester M14 6JX
Tel: 0161 224 4560
Principal: Mrs E Rigby NNEB, SRN, RSCN, CSS, FETC

Other Specialist

ABBEY SCHOOL FOR SPEAKERS
16 Gayfere Street, London SW1P 3HP
Tel: 0171 222 6037
Principal: Thelma Seear MA

ARCHITECTURAL ASSOCIATION SCHOOL OF ARCHITECTURE
34-36 Bedford Square, London WC1B 3ES
Tel: 0171 636 0974
Principal: Mohsen Mostafavi AADipl, RIBA

THE BRITISH ENGINEERIUM
Off Nevill Road, Hove, East Sussex BN3 7QA
Tel: 01273 559583
Principal: J E Minns

BUCKLAND UNIVERSITY COLLEGE
Ewert Place, Oxford OX2 7YT
Tel: 01865 311113
Principal: A Kerr MA

BUILDING CRAFTS COLLEGE
153 Great Titchfield Street, London W1P 7FR
Tel: 0171 636 0480
Principal: P Quick

CABAIR COLLEGE OF AIR TRAINING LTD
Cranfield Airfield, Bedford MK43 0AL
Tel: 01234 751243
Principal: Captain E C Heathcote

CAMBRIDGE CENTRE FOR LANGUAGES
Sawston Hall, Cambridge CB2 4JR
Tel: 01223 835099
Principal: Dr S Bayraktaroglu

CAMPANA INTERNATIONAL COLLEGE
Moor Park House, Farnham, Surrey GU9 8EN
Tel: 01252 727111
Principal: Mrs M A P Frost, LésL

CHELSEA COLLEGE OF ENGINEERING
Shoreham Airport, Shoreham-by-Sea, West Sussex BN4 5FJ
Tel: 01273 461198

COLLEGE OF PETROLEUM & ENERGY STUDIES
Sun Alliance House, Oxford OX1 2QD
Tel: 01865 750181 & 250521
Principal: E I Williamson

COMMERCIAL COLLEGE
18A St Nicholas Street, Bristol BS1 1UB
Tel: 0117 9214612
Principal: Mrs M J Leach

DAVID CHARLESWORTH (FURNITURE & CABINET MAKER)
Harton Manor, Bideford, Devon
Tel: 01237 441288
Principal: D Charlesworth

HOLBORN COLLEGE
200 Greyhound Road, London W14 9RY
Tel: 0171 385 3377
Principal: John Grenier

INNS OF COURT SCHOOL OF LAW
39 Eagle Street, London WC1R 4AJ
Tel: 0171 404 5787
Principal: Mrs M A Phillips

INTERNATIONAL BOATBUILDING COLLEGE
Sea Lake Road, Lowestoft, Suffolk NR32 3LQ
Tel: 01502 569663
Principal: J B R Elliot MITD, MIPTM, CertEd

ISLE OF MAN COLLEGE OF FE
Homefield Road, Douglas, Isle of Man
Tel: 01624 623113
Principal: Mr J R Smith CEng, BSc, MSc, MA, MIMech.Eng

IVOR SPENCER INTERNATIONAL SCHOOL
12 Little Bornes, London SE21 8SE
Tel: 0181 670 5585/8424
Principal: I Spencer

Directory - Professional Schools and Colleges

JOSEPH ALLNATT CENTRE LTD
17 Knyveton Road, Bournemouth, Dorset BH1 3QG
Tel: 01929 422122
Principal: D B Martin FCA

LONDON ACADEMY OF DRESSMAKING
3rd Floor, London W2 4UA
Tel: 0171 727 0221/2850
Principal: Mrs P A Parkinson MA

LONDON INTERNATIONAL FILM SCHOOL
24 Shelton Street, London WC2H 9HP
Tel: 0171 836 9642
Principal: Martin M Amstell

THE LONDON SCHOOL OF INSURANCE
53-55 East Road, London N1 6AH
Tel: 0171 251 5858
Principal: R Sampat BSc, MBIM

MARIE LECKO SCHOOL OF FASHION & DESIGN
12 North Grove, London N6 4SL
Tel: 0181 348 1440
Principal: Mme Marie King Lecko

MASTERKEY
49 North Street, Exeter, Devon EX4 3QR
Tel: 01392 410551
Principal: Sandra Barrell

NATIONAL EXTENSION COLLEGE
18 Brooklands Avenue, Cambridge CB2 2HN
Tel: 01223 316644
Principal: R Morpeth

THE OLD VICARAGE
Marden, Tonbridge, Kent TN12 9AG
Tel: 01622 832200
Principal: Mrs P G Stevens LRAM(S&D)

OUTWARD BOUND TRUST
Chestnut Field, Rugby, Warwickshire CV21 2PJ
Tel: 01990 134227
Principal: I L Fothergill

OXFORD AIR TRAINING SCHOOL
Oxford Airport, Oxford OX5 1RA
Tel: 01865 844268
Principal: Mr Bruce Latton

PARNHAM COLLEGE
Parnham House, Bridport, Dorset DT8 3NA
Tel: 01308 862204
Principal: Robert Ingham DLC, NDD, DipEd

RICHMOND COLLEGE AMERICAN INTERNATIONAL UNIVERSITY
Queen's Road, Richmond, Surrey TW10 6JP
Tel: 0181 940 9762
Principal: Dr W J Petrek BA, STL, PhD

ROYAL SCHOOL OF NEEDLEWORK
Appartment 12A, Hampton Court Palace, Surrey KT8 9AU
Tel: 0181 943 1432
Principal: Mrs E Elvin

THE TOTNES SCHOOL OF GUITARMAKING
Collins Road, Totnes, Devon TQ9 5PJ
Tel: 01803 865255
Principal: N Reed

WELBECK COLLEGE
Worksop, Nottinghamshire S80 3LN
Principal: J K Jones BA

WINDMILL HILL PLACE TENNIS CENTRE
Windmill Hill Place, Hailsham, East Sussex BN27 4RZ
Tel: 01323 832552
Principal: Andrew Waltham

Directory of Colleges of the Arts

Art, Fine Art and Photography

Dance, Drama and Mime

Interior Design and Restoration

Music

Art, Fine Art & Photography

BLAKE COLLEGE
162 New Cavendish Street, London WIM 7FJ
Tel: 0171 636 0658
Principal: D A J Cluckie BA, BSc

BYAM SHAW SCHOOL OF ART
2 Elthorne Road, London N19 4AG
Tel: 0171 281 4111
Principal: A Warman

CHRISTIE'S EDUCATION
63 Old Brompton Road, London SW7 3JS
Tel: 0171 581 3933
Principal: R Cumming

CITY & GUILDS OF LONDON ART SCHOOL
124 Kennington Park Road, London SE11 4DJ
Tel: 0171 735 2306/5210
Principal: Michael Kenny RA

★ **FINE ARTS COLLEGE**
85 Belsize Park Gardens, London NW3 4NJ
Tel: 0171 586 0312
Principals: Candida Cave CFA(Oxon) & Nicholas Cochrane CFA(Oxon)

★ **THE HEATHERLEY SCHOOL OF FINE ART**
Upcerne Road, London SW10 OSH
Tel: 0171 351 4190
Principal: J Walton RP, DFA(Lond)

MODERN ART STUDIES
39 Bedford Square, London WC1B 3EG
Tel: 0171 436 3630
Principal: Jean Hodgins

PHOTOGRAPHIC TRAINING CENTRE
52/54 Kenway Road, London SW5
Tel: 0171 373 4227
Principal: A S Fox

ROYAL ACADEMY SCHOOLS
Burlington House, London W1V 0DS
Tel: 0171 439 7438
Principal: Norman Adams

SOTHEBY'S EDUCATIONAL STUDIES
30 Oxford Street, London W1R 1RE
Tel: 0171 323 5775
Principal: Mrs Anne Ceresole

WOLFSCASTLE POTTERY
'Lordship', Haverfordwest, Pembrokeshire SA62 5LZ
Tel: 01437 741609
Principals: Mr & Mrs P Cunningham

Dance, Drama and Mime

THE ACADEMY DRAMA SCHOOL
189 Whitechaple Road, London E1 1DN
Tel: 0171 377 8735
Principal: T Reynolds RADA

★ **ACADEMY OF LIVE & RECORDED ARTS**
Royal Victoria Building, London SW18 3SX
Tel: 0181 870 6475
Principal: Sorrel Carson

THE BIRMINGHAM THEATRE SCHOOL
The Old Repertory Theatre, Birmingham,
West Midlands B5 4DV
Tel: 0121 643 3300
Principal: C Rozanski BA(Hons)

CAMBRIDGE LANGUAGE & ACTIVITY COURSES
10 Shelford Park Avenue, Cambridge CB2 5LU
Tel: 01223 846348
Principals: Miss E Heath CertEd,RSA,CertTEFL
& Anne George BA,RSA,DipTEFL

CENTRAL SCHOOL OF SPEECH AND DRAMA
Embassy Theatre, London NW3 3HY
Tel: 0171 722 8183
Principal: Mr B Fowler

COLLEGE OF ROYAL ACADEMY OF DANCING
36 Battersea Square, London SW11 3RA
Tel: 0171 223 0091
Principal: Miss S Danby LRAD, ARAD

DOREEN BIRD COLLEGE OF PERFORMING ARTS
Arts - Birkbeck Centre, Sidcup, Kent DA14 4DE
Tel: 0181 300 6004 or 3031
Principal: Miss D Bird

DR ROWE'S TUTORIALS
6 Branksome Avenue, Southampton, Hampshire SO15 5NY
Tel: 01703 773447
Principal: Dr M Rowe BA, BCOMM,
MA, PhD, FRSA, FCollP, MFBE

DRAMA CENTRE
176 Prince of Wales Road, London NW5 3PT
Tel: 0171 267 1177
Principal: C Fettes

DRAMA STUDIO LONDON
Grange Court, London W5 5QN
Tel: 0181 579 3897
Principal: P Layton

EAST 15 ACTING SCHOOL
Hatfields, Loughton, Essex IG10 3RU
Tel: 0181 508 5983
Principal: Mrs M Walker

GUILDFORD SCHOOL OF ACTING
Millmead Terrace, Guildford, Surrey GU2 5AT
Tel: 01483 560701
Principal: G McDougall MA, FRSA

ITALIA CONTI ACADEMY OF THEATRE ART
23 Goswell Road, London EC1M 7AJ
Tel: 0171 608 0047
Principal: C K Vote BA, DipEd

LABAN CENTRE FOR MOVEMENT AND DANCE
Laurie Grove, London SE14 6NH
Tel: 0181 692 4070
Principal: Dr Marion North MA, PhD, Hon D'Arts

LONDON ACADEMY OF MUSIC & DRAMATIC ART
Tower House, London SW5 0SR
Tel: 0171 373 9883
Principal: Peter James

LONDON ACADEMY OF PERFORMING ARTS
2 Effie Road, London SW6 1TB
Tel: 0171 736 0121
Principal: Miss C Hocking RADA

LONDON CONTEMPORARY DANCE SCHOOL
The Place, London WC1H 9AT
Tel: 0171 387 0152
Principal: Dr R Ralph

LONDON STUDIO CENTRE
42-50 York Way, London N1 9AB
Tel: 0171 837 7741
Principal: N Espinosa

MOUNTVIEW THEATRE SCHOOL
104 Crouch Hill, London N8 9EA
Tel: 0181 340 5885/0097
Principal: Peter Coxhead

NORTHERN BALLET SCHOOL
The Dance House, Manchester M1 5QA
Tel: 0161 237 1406
Principal: Miss P McDonald ARAD, LISTD, RAD Major Examiner

OXFORD SCHOOL OF DRAMA
Sansomes Farm Studios, Woodstock, Oxfordshire OX7 1ER
Tel: 01993 812883
Principal: G T R G Peck MA

**RAMBERT SCHOOL OF BALLET
& CONTEMPORARY DANCE**
West London Inst.of HE, Gordon House, Twickenham, Middlesex
Tel: 0181 891 8200
Principal: R McKim

ROSE BRUFORD COLLEGE OF SPEECH & DRAMA
Lamorbey Park, Sidcup, Kent DA15 9DF
Tel: 0181 300 3024
Principal: Robert Ely

ROYAL ACADEMY OF DRAMATIC ART
62-64 Gower Street, London WC1E 6ED
Tel: 0171 636 7076
Principal: N Barter

SHANDY STAGE SCHOOL
56A Livingstone Road, Hove, East Sussex BN3 3WL
Tel: 01273 822244
Principal: Mr Lindsdale

STELLA MANN SCHOOL OF DANCING
343a Finchley Road, London NW3
Tel: 0171 435 9317
Principal: Miss M Breen ARAD, AISTD

VACANI SCHOOL OF DANCING
38-42 Harrington Road, London SW7 3ND
Tel: 0171 589 6110
Principals: Miss E Eden & Miss M Stassinopoulos

WEBBER DOUGLAS ACADEMY OF DRAMATIC ART
30-36 Clareville Street, London SW7 5AP
Tel: 0171 370 4154
Principal: R B Jago

Interior Design and Restoration

THE COUNTRY HOUSE COURSE
Holmstall, Mayfield, East Sussex TN20 6NJ
Tel: 01435 872275
Principal: Mrs M Biron DipIntDes, CertEd, FIDDA

THE DESIGN SCHOOL
United House, London N7 9DP
Tel: 0171 607 5566
Principal: Iris Dunbar BA, FCSD

INCHBALD SCHOOL OF DESIGN
7 Eaton Gate, London SW1 9BA
Tel: 0171 730 5508
Principal: Mrs Jacqueline Duncan FIDDA, FIIDA

KLC DESIGN TRAINING
KLC House, London W14 0AE
Tel: 0171 602 8592
Principal: Mrs Jennifer Gibbs MCSD, FRSA

WEST DEAN COLLEGE
West Dean, Chichester, West Sussex PO18 0QZ
Tel: 01243 811301
Principal: David Leigh

Music

CHETHAM'S SCHOOL OF MUSIC
Long Millgate, Manchester M3 1SB
Tel: 0161 834 9644
Principal: Rev P F Hullah BD, AKC, FRSA

GUILDHALL SCHOOL OF MUSIC & DRAMA
Barbican, London EC2Y 8DT
Tel: 0171 628 2571

ST MARY'S MUSIC SCHOOL
Coates Hall, 25 Grosvenor Crescent, Edinburgh EH12 5EL
Tel: 0131 538 7766
Principal: Mrs J Jennifer Rimer BMus(Hons), LRAM, DipEd

School Examinations in the UK

The General Certificate of Secondary Education (GCSE)

Information supplied by the Department for Education

What is the GCSE?

The General Certificate of Secondary Education (GCSE) was introduced in September 1986 with the first examinations in Summer 1988. It replaces the former GCE O level and CSE examinations and is normally taken by pupils around the age of 16. The great majority of maintained schools in England and Wales, together with independent schools, prepare candidates for the GCSE.

The GCSE is the principal means of assessing the National Curriculum at Key Stage 4. Now syllabuses matched to the revised National Curriculum are being developed for GCSE courses, starting in September 1996.

For GCSE, the examination boards in England and Wales are arranged into five Examining Groups; four in England and one in Wales. There is a similar board in Northern Ireland. These are confederations of the (university-based) GCE Boards and the (Local Education Authority consortia-based) CSE Boards. Each group awards GCSE certificates but the single system is designed to uphold uniform standards in the value of grades and of what is studied in each subject. From 1993 - for first examinations in 1995, the City & Guilds and the Royal Society of Arts Examinations Board will be offering GCSE in Technology (subjects).

Main features of the GCSE

Each Examining Group designs its own syllabuses but they are required to conform to criteria laid down by the School Curriculum Assessment Authority (SCAA), which set out the rules and principles for all courses and all examinations in all subjects. The award of a grade is intended to indicate that a candidate has met the level of knowledge or skill laid down by the Criteria.

The new approaches to assessment are one of the main features which distinguish the GCSE from the old GCE O level and CSE examinations, by placing emphasis on positive achievement. Candidates have the chance to demonstrate what they know and can do, rather than being marked down for inadequacies.

A further feature of the new assessment methods is coursework. Credit is given for assignments set and marked by the teacher, with some external moderation, and the marks awarded form a contribution towards the final grade achieved. The proportion of credit obtained from coursework will be subject to limits laid down by SCAA which come progressively into effect.

Grading

Candidate performance at GCSE is graded on a letter scale from starred A to G.

In accordance with the emphasis on positive achievement, there is now greater use of 'differentiated' examination papers. In most subjects, the scheme of GCSE assessment will involve a series of papers targeted at different ranges of ability levels (tiers) within the A*-G range of the grading scale.

Can anyone take the GCSE?

The GCSE is intended mainly for 16 year-old pupils, but is open to anyone of any age, whether studying full-time or part-time at school, college or privately. For those over 16, one-year GCSE courses are available in schools and colleges.

AS courses

AS courses were introduced to promote greater breadth for those engaged in GCE A level studies. The first AS courses began in September 1987 with the first examinations in summer 1989.

AS courses are designed to require about half the study time of GCE A level courses. What is expected of students taking three A levels and of those taking two A levels and two AS levels should therefore be broadly similar.

AS syllabuses are as intellectually demanding as GCE A levels but take account of shorter teaching and studying time available. The achievement of each grade demands the same quality work as comparable grades in A level examinations, although inevitably less ground is covered.

These courses should increase the range of options open to A level students. For example they might study subjects which contrast with, or complement, their main field of study. Students might decide to take two AS courses in place of one of their intended A levels or one AS exam in addition to three GCE A levels.

For instance, if a student intends to study Economics, Geography and History at A level, he or she might take an AS course in a foreign language or Mathematics or Statistics.

Universities and public sector institutions of higher education are adapting their entrance and course requirements to recognise students' achievements in AS courses.

See also pages 4-6.

GCE A levels

GCE A level courses normally involve two years' study after GCSE. Students generally take two or three subjects, with an examination at the end of the course although a limited number of modular courses is available.

The arrangements for A levels were not affected by the introduction of the GCSE.

The GCE Boards however made some minor changes to A level syllabuses from 1988 so that they follow on from GCSE syllabuses.

Revisions have been made to the A level grading system. They resolve a long-standing problem of a narrow mark range at grade C, which meant that a difference of just a few marks could result in a candidate being awarded either a grade B or a grade D.

Grades A and B are not affected by the changes, nor is the pass/fail boundary. But grades C to E are more evenly distributed, with the result that slightly more candidates obtain grade C and slightly fewer grade E.

The old grade O, equivalent to GCE O level pass, is no longer relevant with the introduction of the GCSE. It has been replaced by a grade N, denoting narrow failure. Candidates given a grade N have come within one grade of passing A level. All candidates below that are marked as U (Unclassified) which replaces F grade and is not certificated.

See also pages 4-6.

The Scottish Certificate of Education

Information supplied by the Scottish Examination Board

The counterpart in Scotland of the GCSE/GCE is the Scottish Certificate of Education (SCE), examinations for which are set on two Grades, Standard and Higher. The Standard Grade is taken at the age of 16+. The Higher Grade represents one further year of study and is taken commonly at the age of 17+ or 18+. In addition, there is a Certificate of Sixth Year Studies (CSYS) which may be taken by a pupil who is, normally, in the sixth year of secondary schooling (18+) and who already possesses a pass on the Higher Grade in the subject concerned.

Examinations for the SCE and the CSYS are conducted by the Scottish Examination Board. Information regarding present and past secondary school examinations in Scotland may be obtained from the Chief Executive, Scottish Examination Board, Ironmills Road, Dalkeith, Midlothian EH22 1LE.

The Standard Grade examinations will be taken, normally, at the end of the fourth year of secondary schooling and the Higher Grade examination may be taken at the end of the fifth or sixth year. (These arrangements reflect the fact that transfer to secondary schooling in Scotland takes place normally at the age of 12+). Standard and Higher Grade examinations are scheduled for May/June each year and may in general be taken by Further Education and External candidates as well as school pupils.

Standard Grade awards are made in terms of a seven-point scale 1-7 where 1 is the highest award. The attainment levels for awards 1-6 are specified by Grade Related Criteria (GRC), details of which may be obtained from the Board. Award 7 indicates completion of an approved course, albeit without satisfaction of the GRC for award point 6. In so far as, in a given subject presentation, the Board's requirements have been met, an aggregate award for the subject will be made and this will be supported on the Certificate by a profile consisting of a grade for each defined element of the subject concerned. An award on the Higher Grade is indicated in terms of one or other of four bands, A, B, C, or D; A indicates a scaled mark of 70% or more; B a scaled mark of 60-69%; C a scaled mark of 50-59%; and D a scaled mark of 40-49%. The C/D interface at Higher Grade represents pass/fail boundary and band D equates to the Compensatory Ordinary Grade award at examinations prior to 1986.

Presentation of school pupils for the Standard and Higher Grade examinations is normally based on a broad curriculum and it is common for university candidates in Scotland to possess four or five passes at Higher Grade, possibly with additional Standard Grade awards. While this breadth of the curriculum, together with the shorter period of secondary schooling in Scotland as compared with England, may present difficulties with regard to the precise comparison of SCE and GCE/GCSE awards in terms of subject content attainment, the two Certificates nevertheless relate to approximately the same ability range of candidates. Accordingly, a Standard Grade award of grade 3 or above has been recognised as equivalent to a GCSE award at grade C or above. The Higher Grade is generally recognised throughout the United Kingdom as performing the same task as the Advanced level of the GCE. The equivalence of particular Higher Grade pass groupings to GCE Advanced level is determined in accordance with commonly accepted formulae, details of which may be obtained by educational and professional bodies and employers from the Scottish Examination Board.

Certificate of Sixth Year Studies

The CSYS is an examination intended for sixth year pupils (age 18+). A candidate may be presented for the CSYS provided that in each subject of presentation a pass on the Higher Grade (or equivalent qualification) is already held. The syllabuses emphasise the requirement of individual study and most subjects include the submission of a Dissertation or Project Report. Results for the CSYS are expressed in terms of a five-point scale of Rankings A-E or are ungraded. Ungraded results are not certificated. While the CSYS was not intended in Scotland to detract from the fundamental position of the Higher Grade as the criterion for selection for tertiary education, performance for the CSYS may be taken account of in connection with admission to universities in Scotland and a number of universities elsewhere in the United Kingdom recognise suitable performance for the CSYS for admission purposes.

Examination dates in Great Britain

Examination dates for the General Certificate of Secondary Education, GCE A level and the Scottish Certificate of Education.

The information was supplied by the examining boards and was accurate at the time of going to press. It is intended as a general guide only, for candidates in the United Kingdom. Dates are subject to variation and should be confirmed.

GCSE Examinations

Northern Examinations and Assessment Board

Devas Street
MANCHESTER M15 6EX

Tel: 0161 953 1180 Fax: 0161 273 7572

Summer 1997: May 6 - June 25

Midland Examining Group

Syndicate Buildings
1 Hills Road
CAMBRIDGE CB1 2EU

Tel: 01223 553311

Summer 1997: May 14 - June 26

University of London Examinations and Assessment Council

Stewart House
32 Russell Square
LONDON WC1B 5DN

Tel: 0171 331 4000

Summer 1997: May 15 - June 25

SEG

Stag Hill House
GUILDFORD
Surrey GU2 5XJ

Tel: 01483 506506

Summer 1997: May 16 - June 27

Welsh Joint Education Committee

245 Western Avenue
CARDIFF CF5 2YX

Tel: 01222 265000

Summer 1997: May 15 - June 24

Northern Ireland Council for the Curriculum, Examinations and Assessment

29 Clarendon Road
BELFAST
Northern Ireland BT1 3BG

Tel: 01232 704666

Summer 1997: May 15 - June 23

GCE A and AS level Examinations

The Associated Examining Board

Stag Hill House
GUILDFORD
Surrey GU2 5XJ

Tel: 01483 506506

Summer 1997: May 20 - June 26

Northern Examinations and Assessment Board

Devas Street,
MANCHESTER M15 6EX

Tel: 0161 953 1180 Fax: 0161 273 7572

Summer 1997: May 16 - June 30

Oxford & Cambridge Examinations and Assessment Council

Syndicate Buildings
1 Hills Road
CAMBRIDGE CB1 2EU

Tel: 01223 553311

Summer 1997: May 19 - June 27

University of London Examinations and Assessment Council

Stewart House
32 Russell Square
LONDON WC1B 5DN

Tel: 0171 331 4000

Summer 1997 (provisional dates): May 19 - June 20

Welsh Joint Education Committee

245 Western Avenue
CARDIFF CF5 2YX

Tel: 01222 265000

Summer 1997: June 2 - June 27

Northern Ireland Council for the Curriculum, Examinations and Assessment

29 Clarendon Road
BELFAST
Northern Ireland BT1 3BG

Tel: 01232 704666

Summer 1997: May 15 - June 23

Scottish Certificate of Education

Scottish Examination Board

Ironmills Road
DALKEITH
Midlothian EH22 1LE

Tel: 0131 663 6601

Summer 1997: May 1 - June 4

The International Baccalaureate Organisation

Information supplied by the IBO

The International Baccalaureate Diploma Programme is a two-year pre-university course for 16-19 year-old students which aims:

> to improve and extend international education and so promote international understanding;
>
> to facilitate student mobility and provide an educational service to the internationally mobile community;
>
> to work in collaboration with national educational systems in developing a rigorous, balanced and international curriculum.

It seeks to achieve these aims through the provision of an internationally recognised pre-university curriculum and access to higher education world-wide. The comprehensive course of study for the Diploma is designed to provide students with a balanced education. The IBO also offers the Middle Years Programme (MYP) serving students in the 11-16 age range.

Curriculum and examination

The Diploma curriculum consists of six subject groups:

Group 1   **Language A1** (first language) including the study of selections from World Literature

Group 2   **Language A2, B** or *ab initio** (second language)

Group 3   **Individuals and Societies:** History, Geography, Economics, Philosophy, Psychology, Social Anthropology, Business and Organisation, Information Technology in a Global Society

Group 4   **Experimental Sciences:** Biology, Chemistry, Applied Chemistry, Physics, Environmental Systems, Design Technology

Group 5   **Mathematics:** Mathematics, Mathematical Studies, Mathematical Methods, Advanced Mathematics

Group 6   **One of the following options:**

    (a)   Art/Design, Music, Theatre Arts, Latin, Classical Greek, Computer Science, Information Technology in a Global Society.

    (b)   A School-Based Syllabus approved by the IBO.

(* for students with no previous experience of learning the language.)

Alternatively a candidate may offer instead of a Group 6 subject a third modern language, a second subject from Individuals and Societies, a second subject from Experimental Sciences or Advanced Mathematics SL.

To be eligible for the award of the Diploma, all candidates must:

1   Offer one subject from each of the above Groups;

2   Offer at least three and not more than four of the six subjects at Higher level and the others at Subsidiary level;
3   Submit an Extended Essay in one of the IBO approved list of subjects;
4   Follow a course in the Theory of Knowledge;
5   Engage in CAS activities representing Creativity, Action and Service.

Candidates may also offer single subjects, for which they will receive a Certificate.

The IB Diploma programme has a definite coherence since it was designed to stress the importance of international understanding. The IB Diploma programme emphasises the importance of breadth and balance within the curriculum by the inclusion of the six different subject groups which reflect five disciplines. In addition, the Theory of Knowledge, an interdisciplinary course together with CAS (Creativity, Action, Service) provide further opportunities for the full development of the student. A degree of specialisation is included within the IB Diploma through the three HL subjects and the Extended Essay which requires a student to embark on some individual research within a chosen discipline.

Special features of the IB Diploma

The special features of the IB Diploma are:

Breadth   Six subjects from five disciplines; Theory of Knowledge; CAS

Specialisation   Three Higher Level Subjects; The Extended Essay

Coherence   A specifically designed Diploma Programme; the subjects are drawn together through Theory of Knowledge

Internationalism Emphasis on international understanding

Academic Affairs Board

A committee comprising representation from the examiners, schools and the IBO administration ensures general oversight of the curriculum. Its responsibility is to advise on basic policy and to commission the work of individual subject committees according to an overall timetable of review and revision.

Assessment and moderation procedures

Consistent with the general and subject specific objectives of the IB Diploma courses which focus on the development of cognitive skills and affective capacities, assessment procedures are designed to emphasise process rather than content, and to achieve a balanced assessment of a candidate's performance. Therefore, a variety of assessment methods are used in order to take account of different learning styles and cultural experience and to ensure that all candidates have the opportunity to demonstrate their abilities. Conventional external examination techniques are complemented by internal assessment of coursework conducted by the teacher who thus contributes to the overall assessment of each candidate.

Assessment within the IB is directed and managed by a partnership of Examiners and IB professional staff, with external consultant support as necessary.

IB Diploma recognition

At both Higher and Subsidiary level, each examined subject is graded on a scale of 1 (minimum) to 7 (maximum). The award of the Diploma requires a minimum of 24 points and satisfactory completion of the Theory of Knowledge course, the Extended Essay and CAS. The Diploma is well-recognised for entry to British universities and has the added advantage of being acceptable as an entry qualification to universities in 95 other countries.

There are currently some 680 schools (comprising almost an equal number of state and private schools) offering the IB programme to students in more than 85 different countries.

For further information on the International Baccalaureate contact:

  Dr Ian Hill
  Regional Director for Europe/Africa/Middle East
  International Baccalaureate Organisation
  Route des Morillons 15
  CH - 1218 Grand-Saconnex
  Geneva
  Switzerland
  Tel: +41 22 791 0274
  Fax: +41 22 791 0277
  E-mail: ianh@ibo.org

Schools affiliated to the International Baccalaureate Organisation in the United Kingdom

Central London

International School of London
(IB No 0057)
139 Gunnersbury Avenue
LONDON W3 8LG
Tel: 0181 992 5823
Fax: 0181 993 7012
Headmaster: Mr Richard Hermon
IB Coordinator: Mr H Davies
Private day school; Mixed

La Retraite Roman Catholic Girls' School
(IB No 0833)
Atkins Road
Clapham Park
LONDON SW12 0AB
Tel: 0181 673 5644
Fax: 0181 675 8577
Headteacher: Mrs Maureen Howie
IB Coordinator: Ms Angela Reeves

Southbank International School
(IB No 0309)
36-40 Kensington Park Road
LONDON W11 3BU
Tel: 0171 229 8230
Fax: 0171 229 3784
Headmaster: Mr M Toubkin
IB Coordinator: Mrs H Simon
Private day school; Mixed

Woodside Park School
(IB No 0865)
Friern Barnet Road
LONDON N11 3DR
Tel: 0181 368 3777
Fax: 0181 368 3220
Principal: Mr Jonathan Evans
IB Coordinator: Mr C Platford

Greater London

Marymount International School
(IB No 0128)
George Road
KINGSTON UPON THAMES
Surrey KT2 7PE
Tel: 0181 949 0571
Fax: 0181 336 2485
Principal: Sister R Sheridan
IB Coordinator: Dr B Johnson
Private day and boarding school; girls only

The American Community Schools, England
Middlesex Campus
(IB No 0152)
108, Vine Lane
Hillingdon
UXBRIDGE
Middlesex UB10 0BE
Tel: 01895 259771
Fax: 01895 256974
Headmaster: Mr B Duncan
IB Coordinator: Mrs R Delshadian
Private day school; Mixed

Surrey Campus
(IB No 0431)
'Heywood'
Portsmouth Road
COBHAM
Surrey KT11 1BL
Tel: 01932 867251
Fax: 01932 869791
Headmaster: Mr T Lehman
IB Coordinator: Mr C Worthington
Private day and boarding school; Mixed

St Dominic's Sixth Form College
(IB No 0141)
Mount Park Avenue
HARROW ON THE HILL
Middlesex HA1 3HX
Tel: 0181 422 8084
Fax: 0181 422 3759
Principal: Mr J Lipscomb
IB Coordinator: Mrs J Lynch
State day school; Mixed

Cambridgeshire

Impington Village College
(IB 0579)
New Road
IMPINGTON
Cambridge CB4 4LX
Tel: 01223 232835
Fax: 01223 234730
Warden: Mrs S West
IB Coordinator: Mr Phil Hind
State college: Day; Mixed

Cheshire

Ridge Danyers College
(IB No 0545)
Cheadle Road
Cheadle Hulme
CHEADLE, Cheshire SK8 5HA
Tel: 0161 485 4372
Fax: 0161 488 4354
Head Teacher: Mr Sandy MacDonald
IB Coordinator: Mrs H Badley-Hurst
State sixth form college; Day; Mixed

Cumbria

Ullswater Community College
(IB No 0687)
Wetheriggs Lane
PENRITH
Cumbria CA11 8NG
Tel: 01768 864377
Fax: 01768 890037
Headmaster: Mr D Robinson
IB Coordinator: Mrs H Lanham
Co-educational comprehensive school; Day

Devon

Exeter College
(IB No 0695)
Hele Road, EXETER
Devon EX4 4JS
Tel: 01392 384020
Fax: 01392 210282
Principal: Dr J G Capey
IB Coordinator: Ms Jane Imrie
State tertiary college; Mixed

Tavistock College
(IB No 0887)
Crowndale Road
TAVISTOCK
Devon PL19 8DD
Tel: 01822 614231
Fax: 01822 612030
Principal: Mr Peter Upton
IB Coordinator: Mr Alan Duncan

Essex

Anglo-European School
(IB No 0078)
Willow Green
INGATESTONE
Essex CM4 ODJ
Tel: 01277 354018
Fax: 01277 355623
Headmaster: Mr R Reed
IB Coordinator: Ms D A Inkersole
State day school; Mixed

Gloucestershire

Cheltenham College
(IB No 0636)
Bath Road
CHELTENHAM
Gloucester GL53 7LD
Tel: 01242 513540
Fax: 01242 577746
Headmaster: Mr P Wilkes
IB Coordinator: Mrs K M Jarman
Private day and boarding; Sixth form girls

Hampshire

Southampton City College
(IB No 0886)
St Mary Street
SOUTHAMPTON
Hampshire SO14 1AR
Tel: 01703 635222
Fax: 01703 6367286
Principal: Dr Patrick Lavery
IB Coordinator: Mr Bill Grant

Hertfordshire

Oaklands College
(IB No 0593)
School of Arts & Sciences
St Peters Road
ST ALBANS
Hertfordshire AL1 3RX
Tel: 01727 847070
Fax: 01727 862413
School Head: Mr P Fielding
IB Coordinator: Mrs J Tidey
State college; Day; Mixed

Kent

Dartford Grammar School
(IB No 0866)
West Hill
DARTFORD
Kent DA1 2HW
Tel: 01322 223039
Fax: 01322 291426
Headteacher: Mr A J Smith
IB Coordinator: Mr Robert Tibbott

Maidstone Grammar School
(IB No 0859)
Barton Road
MAIDSTONE
Kent ME15 7BT
Tel: 01622 752101
Fax: 01622 753680
Headmaster: Mr N A Turrell
IB Coordinator: Dr A W Webb

Sevenoaks School
(IB No 0102)
SEVENOAKS
Kent TN13 1HU
Tel: 01732 455133
Fax: 01732 456143
Headmaster: Mr R Barker
IB Coordinator: Miss J Thomas
Private day and boarding school; Mixed

Merseyside

Broadgreen Community Comprehensive School
(IB No 0639)
Queens Drive
LIVERPOOL
Merseyside L13 5UQ
Tel: 0151 228 6800
Fax: 0151 220 9256
Headmaster: Mr I Andain
IB Coordinator: Mr D Thomas
State comprehensive school; Mixed

Oxfordshire

St Clare's
(IB No 0041)
139 Banbury Road
OXFORD OX2 7AL
Tel: 01865 52031
Fax: 01865 310002
Principal: Mrs M Skarland
IB Coordinator: Mr N Lee
Private day and boarding school; Mixed

The Henley College
(IB No 0557)
Deanfield Avenue
HENLEY-ON-THAMES
Oxfordshire RG9 1UH
Tel: 01491 579988
Fax: 01491 410099
Principal: Mr G Phillips
IB Coordinator: Mr R Milne
State sixth form college; Day; Mixed

West Midlands

The City Technology College, Kingshurst
(IB No 0568)
PO Box 1017
Cooks Lane, Kingshurst
BIRMINGHAM B37 6NZ
Tel: 0121 770 8923
Fax: 0121 770 0879
Principal: Mrs V Bragg
IB Coordinator: Mr Arnet Edwards
Part state/part private financed school; Day; Mixed

Stourbridge College
(IB No 0683)
Hagley Road, Old Swinford
STOURBRIDGE
West Midlands DY8 1QU
Tel: 01384 378531
Fax: 01384 397319
Principal: Mr D Toeman
IB Coordinator: Ms S Firman
State college of further education; Mixed

Worcestershire

Malvern College
(IB No 0641)
College Road
MALVERN
Worcestershire WR14 3DF
Tel: 01684 892333
Fax: 01684 572398
Headmaster: Mr R de C Chapman
IB Coordinator: Dr R Filho
Independent: Boarding; Mixed

North Yorkshire

Yorkshire Coast College
(IB No 0739)
Lady Edith's Drive
SCARBOROUGH
N Yorkshire YO12 5RN
Tel: 01723 372105
Fax: 01723 501918
Principal: Mr S Dey
IB Coordinator: Mrs K Jutsum

Northern Ireland

Lagan College
(IB No 0549)
44 Manse Road
Lisnabreeny
BELFAST
Northern Ireland BT8 4SA
Tel: 01232 401810
Fax: 01232 703269
Principal: Dr B K Lambkin
IB Coordinator: Miss Anne Rowe
Government supported secondary school; Inter-denominational; Day; Mixed

Wales

United World College of the Atlantic
(IB No 0017)
St Donat's Castle
LLANTWIT MAJOR
South Glamorgan CF61 1WF
Tel: 01446 792530
Fax: 01446 794163
Principal: Mr C D O Jenkins
IB Coordinator: Mr R J Fletcher
Boarding school; Mixed; mainly scholarship entry

Swansea College
(IB No 0614)
Tycoch Road
Sketty
SWANSEA
Wales SA2 9EB
Tel: 01792 284094
Fax: 01792 284074
Principal: Mr C Lewis
IB Coordinator: Mrs Helen James
State tertiary college; Day; Mixed

Llandrillo College
(IB No 0640)
Llandudno Road
COLWYN BAY
Clwyd LL28 4HZ
Tel: 01492 546666
Fax: 01492 543052
Headmaster: Mr H Evans
IB Coordinator: Ms C Williams
State college of further education; Mixed

Scotland

American School in Aberdeen
(IB No 0893)
Craigton Road
Cults
ABERDEEN
Grampian AB1 9OD
Tel: 01224 868927
Fax: 01224 869753
Director: Dr Robert N Morrison
IB Coordinator: Mr David Mindorff

Lockerbie Academy
(IB No 0753)
LOCKERBIE
Dumfriesshire DG11 2AL
Tel: 01576 202626
Fax: 01576 203032
Rector: Mr A M Blake
IB Coordinator: Mr G J Herbert

BTEC Qualifications

Information supplied by BTEC

The Business and Technology Education Council (BTEC) approves work-related programmes of study in a wide range of subjects throughout England, Wales and Northern Ireland, and in some countries overseas. It awards qualifications to students who successfully complete these programmes.

BTEC programmes

BTEC programmes are for those preparing for employment as well as people already in work. More than half a million students are now enrolled.

BTEC awards nationally-recognised qualifications in these main occupational areas:

* agriculture
* art and design
* beauty therapy
* business and finance
* caring services
* computing and information systems
* construction
* distribution
* engineering
* health and social care
* home economics
* horticulture
* hospitality and catering
* housing
* information technology
* leisure and tourism
* management
* manufacturing
* media
* performing arts
* science

Programmes leading to BTEC's qualifications are run in colleges, universities and schools throughout England, Wales and Northern Ireland.

Programmes can be studied in different ways, including full-time, day-release, evening, block-release, sandwich and, where appropriate, open- and distance-learning courses. The detailed contents may vary to reflect local and regional needs.

Qualifications and other awards

The main BTEC qualifications are:

* BTEC General National Vocational Qualifications (GNVQs)
* National Certificates/Diplomas
* Higher National Certificates/Diplomas
* BTEC National Vocational Qualifications (NVQs)

In addition, students can take an individual module or study programme to receive a Certificate of Achievement that may provide credit towards one of the qualifications.

Entry requirements and length of courses

The normal entry requirements and lengths for BTEC programmes are as follows. Students may also be admitted with other appropriate qualifications and/or experience.

BTEC National Certificates and Diplomas are nationally-recognised qualifications for technicians, junior administrators, and a range of other occupations.

A student should be at least 16 years old and, for most programmes, must hold a BTEC First Certificate/Diploma or four GCSEs grade C or above, or a suitable alternative qualification. *Length of programme:* Certificate, two years part-time; Diploma, two years full-time, three years part-time or sandwich study.

BTEC Higher National Certificates and Diplomas are qualifications taken in universities and colleges for higher-technician, managerial and supervisory levels.

A student should normally be at least 18 years old and hold an appropriate BTEC National qualification, or an equivalent qualification or suitable GCE A level passes, or relevant work-related experience. The actual requirements depend on the individual programme, and a student entering with A levels may have to take additional bridging studies or a conversion course.

Length of programme: Certificate, two years part-time; Diploma, two years full-time, three years part-time or sandwich study.

For programmes in Design, selection is normally by interview and, in addition to academic requirements, centres will ask to see examples of previous work as evidence of imagination and potential.

BTEC GNVQs are work-related, practical equivalents to GCSEs and A levels. Advanced GNVQs can gain access to university, work or other further study. Foundation and Intermediate GNVQs can lead to work or further courses. Each GNVQ provides a grounding in a broad area of the working world as well as developing core skills of communication, using figures and Information Technology. GNVQs are currently available at Foundation, Intermediate and Advanced Levels in Art & Design, Business, Construction and the Built Environment, Distribution, Engineering, Health & Social Care, Hospitality and Catering, Information Technology, Leisure and Tourism, Management, Manufacturing, Media, and Science. There is also a limited introduction of five further subjects. The BTEC GNVQ Intermediate Level is at the same level as four GCSEs, Advanced Level is equivalent to two A levels. As appropriate GNVQs and NVQs become available, corresponding BTEC Nationals are being phased out over a sensible timescale. BTEC Firsts have already been phased out.

BTEC GNVQs will provide students with a broad-based work-related education. BTEC GNVQs are made up of Mandatory units (which include external written tests) and a range of BTEC-designed Optional and Additional Units. Students will acquire skills, knowledge and understanding of a work-related area and will also have a range of personal, transferable skills, known as core skills.

Length of programme: Students need to be at least 16 years old. BTEC GNVQs at Intermediate Level will normally take one year of full-time study, or longer if part-time. BTEC GNVQs at Advanced Level will normally take two years of full-time study, or longer if part-time.

BTEC NVQs are qualifications which demonstrate that people can successfully complete a range of work-related tasks. Each one is relevant to a particular occupation. NVQs are different from traditional qualifications, such as GCSEs and A levels, as they are concerned with the competence of staff at work rather than academic ability. Each NVQ is structured as a number of units each relating to part of a job.

In each occupational area BTEC NVQs can be awarded at up to five different levels - ranging from routine and straightforward tasks (Level 1) through to complex managerial and professional activities (Level 5). In many areas it is possible to progress from the lower to the higher level of achievement.

For further information, students should contact the centre where they intend to study.

How to apply

For full-time and sandwich Higher National Diploma programmes at colleges within the Universities and Colleges Admissions Service (UCAS), applications should be made through UCAS, PO Box 67, Cheltenham, GL50 3SF.

For Higher National Diplomas in Design, applications should be made through the Art and Design Admissions Registry (ADAR), Penn House, 9 Broad Street, Hereford HR4 9AP.

For all other programmes, applications should be made to the centre offering the programme and not to BTEC.

Grants and sponsorship

Students under 19 will normally have their fees paid by their Local Education Authority.

Mandatory grants are available for students on full-time or sandwich

Higher National Diploma courses, provided certain requirements are met. Students should contact their Local Education Authority for details of these and any discretionary grants.

Recognition

Many professional bodies recognise BTEC's qualifications for entry and exemption. Universities recognise BTEC National qualifications as meeting the general requirements for entry to many degree courses.

For further general information contact:

* BTEC Customer Enquiry Unit
  Central House
  Upper Woburn Place
  London WC1H 0HH
  Tel: 0171 413 8400
* a careers teacher or careers officer
* the local college, polytechnic or university

National Vocational Qualifications (NVQs)

(Information supplied by National Council for Vocational Qualifications (NCVQ))

NVQs are qualifications concerned with work skills. Based on standards of competence set by industry, they have been developed to reform vocational qualifications and to produce one coherent, comprehensive and comprehensible system. Awarding bodies such as RSA, BTEC and City and Guilds are adapting their awards to meet NVQ criteria and now offer many NVQ awards.

The award of an NVQ is based upon the achievement of a particular level of competence in any given area. They are open to everyone; there are no age limits or other restrictions.

NVQs are in each case made up of a number of units which focus on part of a role and set out the standard which must be reached. These units can be built up by a candidate until the full NVQ has been achieved, or can be certificated individually.

Each NVQ has a title and a level which places it within the NVQ framework. The framework specifies five levels of achievement; level 1 is the simplest, covering straightforward tasks and skills; achievement at level 5 requires high level managerial responsibilities.

General National Vocational Qualifications (GNVQs) were introduced more recently in September 1992. These have many of the features of NVQs, but are designed on a broader base, each covering a major category in the NVQ framework, so that students who successfully complete a GNVQ will have gained skills and understanding necessary for a range of occupations. They are intended primarily for students aged 16-19 seeking an alternative to the academic route to qualifications. At Advanced level, the GNVQ is equal to two plus A levels.

GNVQs received a phased introduction in about 100 schools and colleges during 1992-93 and are now generally available in ten broad occupational areas: Science, Construction & the Built Environment, Hospitality & Catering, Leisure & Tourism, Manufacturing, Health & Social Care, Business and Art & Design. Further subjects are in development.

The Government's intention is that NVQs and GNVQs should provide a progressive framework for vocational education and training similar to, and integrated with the framework for academic qualifications of GCSEs, A levels and degree courses.

Further information may be obtained from awarding bodies, local careers offices, colleges of further or higher education, industry training organisations and Training and Enterprise Councils.

The National Council for Vocational Qualifications can also give information and is based at 222 Euston Road, London NW1 2BZ. Tel: 0171 728 1914.

In Scotland there is a similar system of Scottish Vocational Qualifications (SVQs) and General SVQs. Further information may be obtained from SCOTVEC (Scottish Vocational Education Council, Hanover House, 24 Douglas Street, Glasgow G2 7NQ. Tel: 0141 242 2168.

SCOTVEC Awards

Information supplied by SCOTVEC

The Scottish Vocational Education Council (SCOTVEC) was set up in 1985. It is the national body responsible for vocational qualifications in Scotland. SCOTVEC qualifications are designed to be relevant to specific occupations and areas of employment. They cover a wide range of vocational education and training including areas such as accounting, computing, engineering, hotel and catering, secretarial, agricultural and construction.

SCOTVEC awards are open to students of all ages, including those at school. There is no upper age limit.

SCOTVEC Awards

SCOTVEC's qualifications are all based on the same simple idea, that you can build them up bit by bit. The 'building blocks' for each qualification are called units or modules (most of which take about 40 hours to complete) and they can be taken on their own or built up into full awards. This means that students can take a vocational qualification at a pace that suits them. They cover almost every area of employment - from care to communications, tourism to technology - and are suitable for people at all levels, from basic to advanced professional awards.

There are no formal exams - instead students have to show that they have the skills, abilities and knowledge that the award requires.

SCOTVEC's vocational qualifications can be taken at every stage of a person's career. This means that if someone has taken a SCOTVEC award at school they can build on it later in life, for example going on to an HNC or HND at college, or perhaps to an SVQ when they start work. Some HND courses allow the student to enter the third year of a four year Scottish degree.

The main kinds of vocational qualifications offered at school are National Certificates. These are described more fully below.

National Certificate Modules

There are over 3000 National Certificate Modules in many different vocational areas. Modules are based on a combination of theoretical work and assessment of practical skills and you may study for them at your own pace, stopping and starting according to your needs. Here are just some of the areas where modules are available:

Agriculture   Catering
Arts and Crafts   Construction
Business/Management   Education
Care   Engineering

Hairdressing
Information Technology
Languages
Leisure & Tourism
The media

Sales & Marketing
Sports & games
Transport

... and there are many more

Modules can be taken on their own or put together in different combinations to make full National Certificate awards. For example:

GSVQs (General Scottish Vocational Qualifications)

The National Certificates, GSVQs, have been specifically developed to meet the needs of 16-19 year olds and adults returning to education after a gap. There are GSVQs in these broad occupational areas - business, leisure and recreation, hospitality, engineering/technology, arts and social sciences, information technology, land-based industries, science, care, design, construction, travel and tourism, and communication and media - and they are available at three levels of difficulty. They provide the skills and knowledge needed for a broad range of jobs or can act as a bridge to HNCs, HNDs, degrees and further training.

National Certificate clusters

Students at school can do a 'cluster' of three modules in a single vocation area, like home economics or technology. This can help them to direct their school subject choices into a more coherent programme, giving a solid foundation on which to build.

Skillstart

There are two Skillstart awards, both made up of National Certificate Modules specially designed for those who have no existing qualifications. Skillstart 1 offers slower learners, including those with special educational needs, a chance to obtain a qualification which recognises their abilities. Skillstart 2 helps people who have been out of employment for some time improve their career prospects or enter further education or training.

SCOTVEC, Hanover House, 24 Douglas Street, Glasgow G2 7NQ
Telephone 0141 248 7900, Fax 0141 242 2244

RSA Examinations Board

Information supplied by RSA

RSA is one of the largest awarding bodies in Britain, offering a wide range of qualifications in many areas of education and training. Schemes range from the pre-vocational level for people still at school, to postgraduate equivalent qualifications. The schemes are open to anyone; RSA qualifications are taken by students, employees, employers, adult learners and teachers and trainers. The schemes are run in many different centres such as colleges of further education and training centres and are also available in a large number of secondary schools.

The main areas of qualification include Accounting, Administration, Book-keeping, Customer Service, Information Technology, Languages, Retail, Sales, Wholesaling and Warehousing, Secretarial, Finance, Teaching and Training.

RSA qualifications in single subjects (for example, word processing) sometimes involve examinations, which are discussed further under the information on 'Series Examinations' below. Other qualifications lead to a Certificate (often an NVQ) based on course work and assessments. Vocational qualifications within this latter group include general vocational qualifications covering a wide range of occupational areas and teacher/trainer qualifications. These are competence-based, internally assessed and externally moderated by RSA verifiers.

RSA schemes are in many cases accredited as National Vocational Qualifications (NVQs) or have been developed in line with the framework established by the National Council for Vocational Qualifications (NCVQ).

A large part of RSA candidate entry comprises the Series examinations. These include all the text-processing examinations as well as the other business related subjects and languages. Most are available at three stages. Achievement at the most advanced stage indicates an all-round knowledge and understanding of the subject, and in practical skills, a very high degree of proficiency. These examinations are held several times a year and are intended primarily for students on clerical, secretarial and business courses in schools and colleges and are suitable both for those on vocational courses and for those who require a background in the world of business. Courses include:

    Accounting
    Audio-Transcription
    Background to Business
    Book-keeping
    Communication in Business
    Initial Text Processing Skills
    English Language
    Medical Audio-Transcription

Medical Shorthand Speed Test
Numeracy
Practical Book-keeping
Shorthand Transcription
Spreadsheets
Typewriting Skills
Text Processing (French, German)
Word Processing

Languages:

General Communicative Languages
  - German, French, Spanish and Italian
Certificate in Business Language Competence (Basic)
  - German, French, Spanish and Italian
Certificate in Business Language Competence (Survival)
  - German, French, Spanish and Italian
Certificate in Business Language Competence (Threshold)
  - German, French, Spanish and Italian
Certificate in Business Language Competence (Operational)
  - German, French, Spanish and Italian
Certificate in Business Language Competence (Advanced)
  - German, French, Spanish and Italian
Certificate in Business Language Competence
  - Japanese
French for Catering

For students interested in taking an RSA qualification, further information may be obtained from a local RSA centre (probably a local college of further education) or RSA's Customer Information Bureau on 01203 470033.

City & Guilds

Information supplied by City & Guilds

City & Guilds is the UK's leading vocational assessment and awarding body. We offer qualifications in over 500 subjects, at all levels from basic skills to the highest standard of professional achievement. Our qualifications emphasise the practical application of skills and knowledge.

Our range of qualifications includes those which have been designed specifically for young people in the 14-18 age range. GCSEs, GNVQs*, NVQs**, SVQs***, Pitman Qualifications and our own certificates all form part of a nationally recognised framework for education and training.

Young people can study for these qualifications at school, college or at a local training centre. For those in employment, NVQs and SVQs can be taken in the workplace.

GCSEs

We offer a variety of GCSEs in Technology, Design and Technology, and Information Systems.

GNVQs

GNVQs are vocational alternatives to GCSEs and A levels. They are offered at three different levels

- Foundation - broadly equivalent to four GCSEs at grades D to G
- Intermediate - broadly equivalent to five GCSEs at grades A to C
- Advanced - broadly equivalent to two A levels

Normally it would take one year of full time study each to complete the Foundation and Intermediate levels. Advanced level should take two years of full time study.

We offer GNVQs in:

- Art and Design
- Business
- Health and Social Care
- Leisure and Tourism
- Manufacturing
- Construction and the Built Environment
- Hospitality and Catering
- Science
- Retail and Distributive Services
- Engineering
- Information Technology
- Media: Communication and Production
- Management Studies

The following GNVQs are being piloted and should be available from September 1998:

- Land and Environment
- Performing Arts and Entertainment Industries

Each GNVQ includes core skills units in communication, numeracy and information technology.

City & Guilds qualifications

In addition, traditional City & Guilds qualifications are available in subjects as diverse as:

- Communication skills
- Computing
- Engineering
- Graphic design
- Languages
- Media
- Science

Pitman Qualifications

We also offer certification through Pitman Qualifications in many areas including:

- Accounting
- Business Studies
- Shorthand
- Typing
- Wordprocessing

All our qualifications for pupils under 16 have been approved by the Secretary of State for Education. The content has been approved by the Schools Curriculum and Assessment Authority.

A City & Guilds qualification is proof of your practical skills and ability; proof which increasing numbers of employers are looking for.

For further information including a full list of subjects contact:
Customer Services Enquiries Unit,
City & Guilds,
1 Giltspur Street,
London EC1A 9DD

Telephone: 0171 294 2800/1/2/4/5 Facsimile: 0171 294 2405

* General National Vocational Qualifications
** National Vocational Qualifications
*** Scottish Vocational Qualifications

Schools offering entry at 16 to Vocational Courses

ENGLAND

Bedfordshire

Dame Alice Harpur School, Bedford

Berkshire

Hurst Lodge, Sunningdale
Licensed Victuallers' School, Ascot
Luckley-Oakfield School, Wokingham
Padworth College, Reading

Bristol

Badminton School, Bristol

Buckinghamshire

Pipers Corner School, High Wycombe
St Mary's School, Gerrards Cross
Teikyo School UK, Wexham

Cumbria

Lime House School, Carlisle

Devon

Grenville College, Bideford
Magdalen Court School, Exeter
Trinity School, Teignmouth

Dorset

Homefield School (Senior Dept), Christchurch

Gloucestershire

Bredon School, Tewkesbury
Selwyn School, Gloucester
The King's School, Gloucester

Hampshire

St John's College, Southsea
Stanbridge Earls School, Romsey
The Atherley School, Southampton

Hereford & Worcester

Bromsgrove School, Bromsgrove
Holy Trinity School, Kidderminster

Hertfordshire

The Arts Educational School, Tring
The Rickmansworth Masonic School, Rickmansworth

Kent

Bedgebury School, Cranbrook
Combe Bank School, Sevenoaks
Farringtons & Stratford House, Chislehurst
Gad's Hill School, Rochester
West Heath School, Sevenoaks

Lancashire

Arnold School, Blackpool
Elmslie Girls' School, Blackpool
Westholme School, Blackburn

Leicestershire

Burleigh Community College, Loughborough
Our Lady's Convent School, Loughborough

London

Italia Conti Academy of Theatre Art, London EC1M 7AJ
The Arts Educational London Schools, London W4 1LY

Merseyside

Mostyn House School, South Wirral

Norfolk

Hethersett Old Hall School, Norwich
Wymondham College, Wymondham

Northamptonshire

Falcon Manor School, Towcester

Oxfordshire

Cokethorpe School, Witney
Headington School, Oxford
Kingham Hill School, Oxford
Our Lady's Convent Senior School, Abingdon
Sibford School, Banbury
St Mary's School, Wantage

Shropshire

Moreton Hall, Oswestry

Somerset

King's School, Bruton
Sidcot School, Winscombe
Taunton School, Taunton
The Park School, Yeovil
The Royal School, Bath

Staffordshire

Abbots Bromley, Nr Lichfield
Lyncroft House School, Cannock

Suffolk

Framlingham College, Woodbridge
Royal Hospital School, Ipswich

Surrey

Elmhurst Ballet School, Camberley
St Maur's School, Weybridge
The Royal School, Haslemere

East Sussex

Michael Hall School, Forest Row
St Bede's School, Hailsham

West Sussex

Slindon College, Arundel

Warwickshire

The Kingsley School, Leamington Spa

West Midlands
Al-Furqan School, Birmingham
Highclare School, Birmingham
Pattison College, Coventry
The Royal Wolverhampton School, Wolverhampton

Wiltshire
St Mary's School, Calne
Stonar School, Melksham

North Yorkshire
Ashville College, Harrogate
Harrogate Ladies' College, Harrogate
York College for Girls, York

West Yorkshire
Gateways School, Leeds
Woodhouse Grove School, Apperley Bridge

IRELAND
County Antrim
Victoria College, Belfast

SCOTLAND
Aberdeen
St Margaret's School for Girls, Aberdeen

Argyll & Bute
Lomond School, Helensburgh

Clackmannanshire
Dollar Academy, Dollar

Dumbarton & Clydebank
Keil School, Dumbarton

Dumfries & Galloway
Cademuir International School, Thornhill

City of Edinburgh
St Margaret's, Edinburgh
St Mary's Music School, Edinburgh
St Serf's School, Edinburgh
The Mary Erskine School, Edinburgh

Glasgow
Belmont House, Glasgow
Glasgow Academy, Glasgow
Laurel Park School, Glasgow
The Kelvinside Academy, Glasgow
The Park School, Glasgow

South Lanarkshire
Hamilton College, Hamilton

Perthshire & Kinross
Morrison's Academy, Crieff
Rannoch School, Pitlochry
The New School, Dunkeld

Stirlingshire
Queen Victoria School, Dunblane

WALES
Cardiff
New College and School, Cardiff

BELGIUM
The British School of Brussels

Educational Associations

Educational Associations

The Allied Schools
Provision of financial and administrative support services and advice to member schools (Stowe School, Wrekin College, Canford School, Harrogate Ladies' College, Westonbirt School, Riddlesworth Hall School) and of secretariat for the Governing Bodies of those schools.
General Manager, David Harris,
42 South Bar Street, Banbury,
Oxon OX16 9XL
(01295 256441)

The Association of British Riding Schools
An independent body of proprietors and principals of riding establishments, aiming to look after their interests and those of the riding public, to raise standards of management, instruction and animal welfare.
General Secretary, Association of British Riding Schools,
Queens Chambers, 38-40 Queen Street, Penzance,
Cornwall TR18 4BH
(Tel 01736 69440 Fax 01736 51390)

The Association of Heads of Independent Schools
Membership is open to all Heads of Girls' and Co-Educational Junior Independent Schools which are accredited by the ISJC (Independent Schools Joint Council).
Honorary Secretary: Mrs A Holyoak,
Queen's Gate School,
133 Queen's Gate,
London SW7 5LE

The Association of Nursery Training Colleges
For information on Careers in Child Care, Careers as Nannies, Careers as Nursery Workers and on NVQ in Child Care and Education offered in the three independent Nursery Training Colleges, please contact:
The Princess Christian College,
26 Wilbraham Road, Fallowfield,
Manchester M14 6JX
(0161 224 4560)

The Association of Tutors Incorporated

This Association is the professional body to further the interests of tutors. Members include tutors teaching every academic and vocational subject at all levels of education, including tutorial college principals and independent tutors.

Enquiries to: Dr D J Cornelius, PhD, BSc,
Sunnycroft, 63 King Edward Road,
Northampton NN1 5LY
(01604 24171)

The Boarding Schools Association

The BSA is concerned that boarding education remains a healthy and relevant resource readily available to all who want or need it, within the range of educational provision in this country.

General Secretary: Michael Kirk,
Ysgol Naut, Valley Road,
Llanfairfechan,
Gwynedd LL33 0ES

British Association for Commercial and Industrial Education

A member organisation concerned with all aspects of vocational education and training. Further information from:

The Librarian,
British Association for Commercial and Industrial Education,
35 Harbour Exchange Square,
London E14 9GE
(0171 987 8989)

The British Association for Early Childhood Education

A Charitable Association prepared to give advice on matters concerned with the care and education of young children from birth to nine years. Publishes booklets and organises conferences for those interested in Early Years Education.

The Secretary, BAECE Headquarters,
111 City View House,
463 Bethnal Green Road,
London E2 9QY
(0171 739 7594)

The Choir Schools' Association

Schools which educate Cathedral and Collegiate choristers.

The Administrator
The Minster School
Deangate, York YO1 2JA
Tel (01904 625217)
Fax (01904 632418)

Common Entrance Examinations

Details of the Common Entrance examinations, which provide common entrance papers for boys and girls transferring from junior to senior schools at 11+, 12+ and 13+ are available from The Administrator at the address below. Copies of syllabuses and past papers are obtainable from CE Publications Ltd at the same address.

Independent Schools Examinations Board,
Jordan House, Christchurch Road,
New Milton, Hants BH25 6QJ
(01425 621111 Fax: 01425 620044)

CIFE
(Conference for Independent Further Education)

CIFE is the professional association for independent sixth form and tutorial colleges accredited by the British Accreditation Council for Independent Further and Higher Education (BAC) or the Independent Schools Joint Council. Colleges seeking to be accredited by either body within three years can be admitted to candidate membership. Member colleges specialise in preparing students (mainly over statutory school-leaving age) for GCSE and A and A/S Level examinations and for university entrance. The aim of the association is to provide a forum for the exchange of information and ideas, and for the promotion of best practice, and to safeguard adherence to strict standards of professional conduct and ethical propriety. Information published by member colleges as to their exam results is subject to regulation and to validation by BAC as academic auditor to CIFE. Further information from:

Myles Glover MA,
Buckhall Farm,
Bull Lane, Bethersden,
near Ashford,
Kent TN26 3HB
(01233 820 797)

The Dyslexia Institute Ltd

A registered, educational charity which has established teaching, assessment and teacher-training centres throughout England. The aim of these Institutes is to help dyslexics of all ages to overcome their difficulties in learning to read, write and spell and to achieve their potential. (Leaflets supplied with SAE).

Information Officer:
The Dyslexia Institute Head Office,
133 Gresham Road,
Staines TW18 2AJ
(01784 463851)

Girls' Schools Association

130 Regent Road, Leicester LE1 7PG
(Tel: 0116 254 1619 Fax: 0116 255 3792)
(E-mail: gsa@dial.pipex.com)
President: Mrs Jacqueline Lang
General Secretary: Ms Sheila Cooper

The Girls' Schools Association exists to represent the 230 schools whose Heads are in membership. Its direct aim is to promote excellence in the education of girls. This is achieved through a clear understanding of the individual potential of girls and young women. 110,000 pupils are educated in schools which cover day and boarding, large and small, city and country, academically elite and broad based education.
Scholarships, bursaries or Assisted Places are available in most schools.

The Girls Public Day School Trust

26 Queen Anne's Gate,
London SW1H 9AN
Tel: 0171 222 9595

The Trust was founded in 1872 and was a pioneer of education for girls. Today the pupils in its 28 independent schools (listed below) number about 19,000.

BATH HIGH SCHOOL AND THE ROYAL SCHOOL, Bath BA1 5ES
BIRKENHEAD HIGH SCHOOL, 86 Devonshire Place, Birkenhead, Merseyside L43 1TY
BLACKHEATH HIGH SCHOOL, Vanbrugh Park, London SE3 7AG
BRIGHTON AND HOVE HIGH SCHOOL, The Temple, Montpelier Road, Brighton, Sussex BN1 3AT
BROMLEY HIGH SCHOOL, Blackbrook Lane, Bickley, Bromley, Kent BR1 2TW
CROYDON HIGH SCHOOL, Old Farleigh Road, Selsdon, South Croydon CR2 8YB
HEATHFIELD SCHOOL, Beaulieu Drive, Pinner, Middlesex HA5 1NB
HOWELLS SCHOOL, Llandaff, Cardiff CF5 2YD
IPSWICH HIGH SCHOOL, Woolverstone Hall, Ipswich, Suffolk IP4 2UH
KENSINGTON PREPARATORY SCHOOL FOR GIRLS, Fulham Road, London SW6
LIVERPOOL: THE BELVEDERE SCHOOL, 17 Belvidere Road, Princes Park, Liverpool L8 3TF
NEWCASTLE: CENTRAL NEWCASTLE HIGH SCHOOL, Fulham Road, Newcastle upon Tyne NE2 4DS
NORWICH HIGH SCHOOL, 95 Newmarket Road, Norwich, Norfolk NR2 2HU

NOTTINGHAM HIGH SCHOOL FOR GIRLS, 9 Arboretum Street, Nottingham NG1 4JB
NOTTING HILL & EALING HIGH SCHOOL, 2 Cleveland Road, Ealing, London W13 8AX
OXFORD HIGH SCHOOL WITH GREYCOTES & THE SQUIRREL PREP SCHOOLS, Oxford OX2 6XA
PORTSMOUTH HIGH SCHOOL, Kent Road, Southsea, Hampshire PO5 3EQ
PUTNEY HIGH SCHOOL, 35 Putney Hill, London SW15 6BH
SHEFFIELD HIGH SCHOOL, 10 Rutland Park, Sheffield S10 2PE
SHREWSBURY HIGH SCHOOL, 32 Town Walls, Shrewsbury, Shropshire SY1 1TN
SOUTH HAMPSTEAD HIGH SCHOOL, 3 Maresfield Gardens, London NW3 5SS
STREATHAM HILL & CLAPHAM HIGH SCHOOL, Abbotswood Road, London SW16 1AW
SUTTON HIGH SCHOOL, 55 Cheam Road, Sutton, Surrey SM2 2AX
SYDENHAM HIGH SCHOOL, 19 Westwood Hill, London SE26 6BL
WIMBLEDON HIGH SCHOOL, Mansel Road, London SW19 4AB

The schools are not denominational. Entry is by interview and test appropriate to the pupil's age.

All schools have a Junior Department. Kensington is a preparatory school only. The Royal School, Bath has boarding facilities.

The schools participate in the Government's Assisted Places Scheme, offering places at 11+ and at Sixth Form level.

For further details please contact the schools direct, or there is a general prospectus available from the GPDST office giving the addresses of all the schools, together with the current fees, and other general information.

The Girls Public Day School Trust is a charity Reg. No. 1026057 which exists to provide high quality education for girls.

The Governing Bodies Association & The Governing Bodies of Girls Schools Association

The objects of the Association are to advance education in Independent Schools, to discuss matters concerning the policy and administration of Independent Schools, and to encourage co-operation between their governing bodies.

Enquiries to: D G Banwell, BA,
The Coach House, Pickforde Lane, Ticehurst,
East Sussex TN5 7BJ
Telephone & Fax (01580 200855)

The Headmasters' and Headmistresses' Conference (HMC)
Membership (240) consists of Heads of major boys' and co-educational independent schools. The objects of the annual meeting are to discuss matters of common interest to members.
Membership Secretary: R N P Griffiths,
1 Russell House,
Bepton Road, Midhurst,
West Sussex, GU29 9NB
Secretary: V S Anthony
130 Regent Road,
Leicester LE1 7PG

The Incorporated Association of Preparatory Schools
IAPS is the professional association of headmasters and headmistresses of preparatory schools in the UK and overseas. Membership is open to suitably qualified heads and deputy heads of schools accredited by the Independent Schools Joint Council. Further information from:
The General Secretary:
John Morris,
11 Waterloo Place,
Leamington Spa,
Warwickshire CV32 5LA
(01926 887833)

Independent Beauty Schools Association
The functions of the Association are to help maintain high standards of training in the member schools; to liaise with examining boards; to be represented on the Health and Beauty Therapy Training Board. Please write for a list of member schools and a copy of
A Guide to Training In Beauty Therapy.
PO Box 781,
London SW3 2PN

Independent Business Training Association
IBTA has been established as an association of the leading private business and secretarial colleges with the objective of promoting the highest possible standards of commercial training in the UK.
The Association also offers a free advisory service to prospective students to help them select a suitable course and College of study.
Marilyn Coles,
IBTA,
15 King Edward Street,
Oxford, OX1 4HT
(01865 791908)

The Independent Schools Association
Membership is limited to the Heads of Schools which are not under the direct control of the Department for Education & Employment. The Association aims to co-operate with other bodies which stand for professional freedom in education and to maintain for Independent Schools due recognition by government and the general public of their place in the educational life of the nation.
Secretary: Timothy Ham, MA, DipEd,
Boys' British School,
East Street,
Saffron Walden,
Essex CB10 1LS
(01799 523619)

The Independent Schools Bursars' Association
Membership: 600 independent secondary schools. Objectives include promotion of administrative efficiency and exchange of information between member schools.
Secretary: D J Bird,
Woodlands, Closewood Road,
Denmead,
Waterlooville,
Hants PO7 6JD
(01705 264506)

The Independent Schools Careers Organisation
The organisation's objects are: to assist careers staff in schools, to assist employers in making career opportunities and qualifications known, to advise children and their parents on careers, higher education and opportunities available, and to arrange courses for staff and pupils.
Administrative Director,
The Independent Schools Careers Organisation,
12a Princess Way,
Camberley,
Surrey GU15 3SP
(01276 21188 Fax: 01276 691833)

The Independent Schools Information Service
Established by the leading Associations of Independent Schools to provide information about schools to parents and the media.
Director: D J Woodhead,
ISIS National Headquarters,
56 Buckingham Gate,
London SW1E 6AG
(0171 630 8793/4)

The Independent Schools Joint Council

The ISJC considers matters of policy and administration common to its members and when required speaks collectively on their behalf. It represents its constituent members in joint discussions with the Department for Education and with other organisations.

ISJC is a federation of the following associations:

Governing Bodies Association (GBA)
Governing Bodies of Girls' Schools Associations (GBGSA)
Headmasters' and Headmistresses' Conference (HMC)
Girls' Schools Association (GSA)
Society of Headmasters and Headmistresses of Independent Schools (SHMIS)
Incorporated Association of Preparatory Schools (IAPS)
Independent Schools' Association Incorporated (ISAI)
Independent Schools Bursars' Association (ISBA)

Their combined membership comprises about 1,350 schools.

General Secretary: Dr Arthur Hearnden OBE,
Grosvenor Gardens House,
35-37 Grosvenor Gardens,
London SW1W 7BS
(0171 630 0144 Fax: 0171 931 0036)

The Montessori Training Organisation

Affiliated to the Association Montessori Internationale. Further information from:
The Secretary,
The Maria Montessori Training Organisation,
26 Lyndhurst Gardens,
Hampstead,
London NW3 5NW
(0171 435 3646)

The Round Square Schools

An international group of schools following the principles of Kurt Hahn, the founder of Salem School in Germany, and Gordonstoun in Scotland was formed in 1967. The Round Square, named after Gordonstoun's 17th century circular building in the centre of the school, now has 25 member schools in nine countries: Australia, Canada, England, Germany, India, Kenya, Scotland, Switzerland and the United States.

Member schools arrange regular exchange visits for pupils and undertake aid projects in India, Kenya, Venezuela and Eastern Europe. All schools in the group uphold the five principles of outdoor adventure, community service, education for democracy, international understanding and environmental conservation.

The member schools in the United Kingdom are:

GIRLS	CO-EDUCATIONAL
Cobham Hall, Kent	Abbotsholme, Derbyshire
St Anne's, Cumbria	Box Hill, Surrey
Westfield, Newcastle upon Tyne	Gordonstoun, Scotland
	Rannoch, Scotland
	Wellington, Berks

For more information about Round Square Schools, please contact:
Kay Holland, Secretary,
The Round Square, Box Hill School,
Dorking, Surrey RH5 6EA
(01372 377812)

Round Square Office
(01737 246108 Fax: 01737 240416)

The Secondary Heads Association
An association representing the majority of Principals, Heads and Deputy Heads in all types of secondary schools and colleges.
General Secretary: J Sutton, MA, FRSA, FIMgt
130 Regent Road,
Leicester LE1 7PG
(0116 247 1797 Fax: 0116 247 1152)

The Society of Headmasters and Headmistresses of Independent Schools
A society of some 70 schools, most of which have a strong boarding element.
Secretary: I D Cleland, BA, MPhil, DipEd, FRSA
The Coach House, 34A Heath Road,
Upton, Chester CH2 1HX
(01244 379649 Fax: 01244 379649)

Steiner Fellowship
Representing Rudolf Steiner Waldorf Education in the UK and Eire. The 26 schools affiliated to the Fellowship are to be distinguished from the curative homes and schools, also based on the work of Steiner, which are for emotionally disturbed and handicapped children.
The Secretary,
Steiner Schools Fellowship,
Kidbrooke Park, Forest Row,
Sussex RH18 5JB
(01342 822115 Fax: 01342 826004)

UCAS
PO Box 67, Cheltenham GL50 3SF
(01242 222444 Fax: 01242 221622)

WES - World-Wide Education Service, Home School
The WES Home School Service enables parents to teach their own children at home, either overseas or in the UK. Full courses of study or single subjects to support local schooling are available for children aged 3-12 years. All courses are consistent with the National Curriculum. For further information contact:
The World-Wide Education Service,
St George's House,
14-17 Wells Street,
London W1P 3FP
(0171 637 2644 Fax: 0171 637 3411)

WES - World-Wide Education Service Ltd
The objectives of the service, which was established over a century ago, are (1) to provide full professional support to overseas British and International Schools which includes inspection, in-service teacher training, curriculum and management advice, feasibility studies and setting up new schools; (2) to undertake OFSTED UK inspections at both primary and Secondary level and to offer advice and support to UK Schools, particularly to 'clustered' groups; (3) recruitment of teaching staff to overseas schools.
WES World-wide Education Service,
Canada House,
272 Field End Road,
Eastcote,
Middlesex HA4 9NA
(0181 866 4400 Fax: 0181 429 4838)

The Woodard Schools
In 1848 Nathaniel Woodard founded Lancing College and by 1891, when he died, had established seven schools. The Woodard Corporation now has 35 schools throughout the country, including 14 associated or affiliated schools. All have an Anglican foundation and together form the largest group of Church Schools in England and Wales. Further information from:
The Registrar,
The Woodard Schools,
1 The Sanctuary, Westminster,
London SW1P 3JT
(0171 222 5381)

Glossary of Abbreviations

AA	Associate of Arts (USA)
AAS	Associate of Applied Science (USA)
ABA	Associate of Business Administration (USA)
ABAC	Association of Business and Administrative Computing
ABBC	Association of British Chambers of Commerce
ABE	Association of Business Executives
ABIM	Associate of the British Institute of Management
ACA	Association of Certified Accountants
ACCA	Associate of the Association of Certified Accountants
ACEA	Associate of the Association of Cost and Executive Accountants
ACFHE	Association of Colleges for Further and Higher Education
ACIE	Associate of the Cambridge Institute of Education
ACP	Associate of the College of Preceptors
ACRA	Association of College Registrars and Administrators
AEB	Associated Examining Board for the General Certificate of Education
AIB	Associate of the Institute of Bankers
AICS	Associate of the Institute of Chartered Shipbrokers
AMISE	Associated Member of the Institute of Science Education
ARBS	Association of the Recognition of Business Schools
ARCA	Diploma of Associateship of the Royal College of Art
ARELS	Association of Recognised English Language Schools
ARIC	Associateship of the Royal Institute of Chemistry
BA	Bachelor of Arts
BABTAC	British Association of Beauty Therapy and Cosmetology
BAC	British Accreditation Council for Independent Further & Higher Education
BAPHE	British Association of Professional Hairdressing Employers
BApSc	Bachelor of Applied Science
BBA	Bachelor of Business Administration (USA)
BEd	Bachelor of Education
BLitt	Bachelor of Letters
BMTEC	British Management Training Export Council
BSC	British Society of Commerce
BSc	Bachelor of Science
BTEC	Business and Technician Education Council
CAA	Civil Aviation Authority
CACC	Council for the Accreditation of Correspondence Colleges
CAM	Communication Advertising and Marketing Education Foundation
CChem	Chartered Chemist
CFA	Certificate of Fine Art
CGLI	City & Guilds of London Institute
CIBTAC	Confederation of Beauty Therapy and Cosmetology
CIDESCO	Comité International d'Esthetique et de Cosmetologie
CIFE	Conference for Independent Further Education
COIC	Careers and Occupational Information Centre
CPE	Common Professional Examination
CPVE	Certificate in Pre-Vocational Education

Abbreviations

CRAC	Careers Research and Advisory Centre
CSE	Certificate in Secondary Education
CQSW	Certificate of Qualification in Social Work
Cantab	Cambridge University
CertEd	Certificate in Education
DFE	Department for Education
DMS	Diploma in Management Studies
DRS	Diploma of Religious Science
Dip AAe	Diploma Aesthetique
DipBTh	Diploma in Beauty Therapy
DipEd	Diploma in Education
DipTP	Diploma in Town Planning
ECIS	European Council of International Schools
EFL	English as a Foreign Language
ESL	English as a Second Language
FBIM	Fellow of the British Institute of Management
FBIS	Fellow of the British Interplanetary Society
FBSC	Fellow of the British Society of Commerce
FCIS	Fellow of the Institute of Chartered Secretaries and Administrators
FCollP	Fellow of the College of Preceptors
FEDE	Federation of European Schools
FIERE	Fellow of the Institution of Electronics and Radio Engineers
FISTM	Fellow of the Institute of Sales Technology and Management
FITD	Fellow of the Institute of Training & Development
FRES	Fellow of the Royal Entymological Society
FRGS	Fellow of the Royal Geographical Society
FRIC	Fellow of the Royal Institute of Chemistry
FRSA	Fellow of the Royal Society of Arts
FSBT	Fellow of the Society of Teachers in Business Education
FSIAD	Fellow of the Society of Industrial Artists and Designers
FTA	Fellow of the Association of Tutors
FinstPB	Fellow of the Institute of Practitioners of Beauty
GCE	General Certificate of Education
GCSE	General Certificate of Secondary Education
GradIMA	Graduate Member of the Institute of Mathematics & its Application
HC	Hairdressing Council
IA	International Aestheticiennes
IACP	International Association of Cooking Professionals
IAM	Institute of Administrative Management
IAT	Institute of Accounting Technicians
ICSA	Institute of Chartered Secretaries and Administrators
IDDA	Interior Decorators & Designers Association
IDPM	Institute of Data Processing Management
IOB	Institute of Bankers
IOJ	Institute of Journalists
IOM	Institute of Marketing
IPB	Institute of Practitioners in Beauty
ISCO	Independent Schools' Careers Organisation
ISIS	Independent Schools' Information Service
ISJC	Independent Schools' Joint Council

ISTA	Independent Secretarial Training Association
ITEC	International Therapy Examination Council
JMB	Joint Matriculation Board
LCCI	London Chamber of Commerce and Industry
LCP	Licentiate of the College of Preceptors
LCST	Licentiate of the College of Speech Therapists
LISTD	Licentiate of the Imperial Society of Teachers of Dancing
LLB	Bachelor of Laws
LRAM	Licentiate of the Royal Academy of Music
MA	Master of Arts
MBA	Master of Business Administration
MBIM	Member of the British Institute of Management
MCFA	Member of the Cookery and Food Association
MCollP	Member of the College of Preceptors
MEd	Master of Education
MFTComm	Member of the Faculty of Teachers in Commerce
MIHEc	Member of the Institute of Home Economics
MIL	Member of the Institute of Linguists
MIM	Master of International Management
MIT	Member of the Institute of Trichologists
MInstM	Member of the Institute of Marketing
MJI	Member of the Institute of Journalists
MLitt	Master of Letters
MPS	Member of the Pharmaceutical Society of Great Britain
MRAIC	Member of the Royal Architectural Institute of Canada
MRP	Master in Regional Planning
MRSC	Member of the Royal Society of Chemistry
MRTPI	Member of the Royal Town Planning Institute
MSc	Master of Science
MSERT	Member of the Society of Electronic & Radio Technicians
NAFSA	National Association for Foreign Student Affairs (USA)
NNEB	National Nursery Examination Board
Oxon	Oxford
PGCE	Post Graduate Certificate in Education
PhD	Doctor of Philosophy
RIBA	Royal Institute of British Architects
RSA	Royal Society of Arts
S level	GCE Special Paper
SAT	Scholastic Aptitude Test (USA)
SCE	Scottish Certificate of Education
STEP	Second Term Entrance Paper (Cambridge)
SUJB	Southern Universities' Joint Board for School Examinations
TOEFL	Test of English as a Foreign Language
UCCA	Universities Central Council on Admissions
WMEB	West Midlands Examination Board (CSE)
YMCA	Young Men's Christian Association
YMCA	Young Women's Christian Association

COUNTIES AND REGIONS OF BRITAIN

Scotland

52 Aberdeen City
53 Aberdeenshire
54 Angus
55 Argyll & Bute
56 Borders
57 City of Edinburgh
58 City of Glasgow
59 Clackmannanshire
60 Dumbarton & Clydebank
61 Dumfries & Galloway
62 Dundee City
63 East Ayrshire
64 East Dumbartonshire
65 East Lothian
66 East Renfrewshire
67 Falkirk
68 Fife
69 Highland
70 Inverclyde
71 Midlothian
72 Moray
73 North Ayrshire
74 North Lanarkshire
75 Perth & Kinross
76 Renfrewshire
77 South Ayrshire
78 South Lanarkshire
79 Stirling
80 Western Isles
81 West Lothian

England

1 Bedfordshire
2 Berkshire
3 Bristol
4 Buckinghamshire
5 Cambridgeshire
6 Cheshire
7 Cornwall
8 Cumbria
9 Derbyshire
10 Devon
11 Dorset
12 Durham
13 East Riding of Yorkshire
14 East Sussex
15 Essex
16 Gloucestershire
17 Greater London
18 Greater Manchester
19 Hampshire
20 Hereford & Worcester
21 Hertfordshire
22 Kent
23 Lancashire
24 Leicestershire
25 Lincolnshire
26 Merseyside
27 Norfolk
28 North Yorkshire
29 Northamptonshire
30 Northumberland
31 Nottinghamshire
32 Oxfordshire
33 Rutland
34 Shropshire
35 Somerset
36 South Yorkshire
37 Staffordshire
38 Suffolk
39 Surrey
40 Tyne & Wear
41 Warwickshire
42 West Midlands
43 West Sussex
44 West Yorkshire
45 Wiltshire

Northern Ireland

Armagh 46
Antrim 47
Down 48
Fermanagh 49
Londonderry 50
Tyrone 51

Wales

Aberconwy & Colwyn 82
Anglesey 83
Blaenau Gwent 84
Bridgend 85
Caerphilly 86
Cardiff 87
Cardiganshire 88
Carmarthenshire 89
Denbighshire 90
Flintshire 91
Gwynedd 92
Merthyr Tydfil 93
Monmouthshire 94
Neath & Port Talbot 95
Newport 96
Pembrokeshire 97
Powys 98
Rhondda Cynon Taff 99
Swansea 100
Torfaen 101
Vale of Glamorgan 102
Wrexham 103

©R H Publications 1997

Index

A

Abacus College, Oxford 24, D36
Abbey Gate College, Chester D86
Abbey Independent College, Manchester D35
Abbey School for Speakers, London D163
Abbey Tutorial College, Birmingham D36
Abbey Tutorial College, London D34
Abbey Tutorial, Cambridge D32
Abbots Bromley, Nr Lichfield D119
Abbotsholme School, Uttoxeter D120
Abingdon School, Abingdon D115
Academy of Live & Recorded Arts, London D166
Ackworth School, Pontefract D134
Adcote School for Girls, Shrewsbury D117
Akeley Wood School, Buckingham D83
Al-Furqan School, Birmingham D130
Alan D School of Hairdressing, London D161
Albany College, London D34
Albyn School for Girls, Aberdeen D137
Aldenham School, Elstree D97
Alexanders International School, Bawdsey D120
All Hallows College, Lyme Regis D90
Alleyn's School, London 52, D105
American Community School, Uxbridge D112
American Community Schools, Cobham D122
Ampleforth College, York D132
Architectural Assc Sch of Architecture, London D163
Ardingly College, Haywards Heath D127
Arnold School, Blackpool 51, D102
Ashbourne Independent Sixth Form College,
   London W8 . . . . 22, D34
Ashbourne Middle School, London D105
Ashford School, Ashford D100
Ashville College, Harrogate D131
Atlantic College, Barry D145
Austin Friars School, Carlisle D87
Ayton School, Great Ayton D131

B

Babel Technical College, London D160
Bablake School, Coventry D131
Badminton School, Bristol D80
Ballard College, New Milton D94
Bancroft's School, Woodford Green D92
Bangor Grammar School, Bangor D136
Barnard Castle School, Barnard Castle D91
Bartholomews Tutorial College, Brighton D37
Basil Paterson College - Academic, Edinburgh D38
Basil Paterson College, Edinburgh D158

Baston School, Bromley D100
Bath High School GPDST, Bath D118
Batley Grammar School, Batley D134
Battle Abbey School, Battle D125
Beaconhurst School, Stirling D142
Bearwood College, Wokingham D83
Beaulieu Convent School, Jersey D145
Beckenham Secretarial College, Beckenham D158
Bedales School, Petersfield 46, D94
Bedford High School, Bedford D81
Bedford Modern School, Bedford D81
Bedford School, Bedford D81
Bedgebury School, Goudhurst 49, D100
Bedstone College, Bucknell D117
Beechwood Sacred Heart, Tunbridge Wells D102
Belfast Royal Academy, Belfast D135
Bellerbys College Mayfield and Wadhurst, Wadhurst D126
Bellerbys College, Hove 28, D37
Belmont House, Glasgow D140
Bembridge School, Bembridge D99
Benenden School, Cranbrook D100
Bentham Grammar School, Lancaster D103
Berkhamsted School for Girls, Berkhamsted D96
Berkhamsted School, Berkhamsted D96
Bethany School, Cranbrook D100
Bilingual Secretarial College of The French Institute,
   London D158
Birkdale School, Sheffield D133
Birkenhead High School GPDST, Birkenhead D110
Birkenhead School, Birkenhead D110
Bishop Challoner School, Bromley D100
Bishop College of Beauty Therapy, Darlington D161
Bishop's Stortford College, Bishop's Stortford D96
Blackheath High School GPDST, London SE3 . . . . 53, D105
Blake College, London D166
Bloomsbury College, London SW6 . . . . D34
Bloxham School, Banbury D115
Blundell's, Tiverton D89
Bolton School (Boys' Division), Bolton D109
Bolton School (Girls' Division), Bolton D109
Bootham School, York D132
Bosworth Tutorial College, Northampton D36
Bournemouth Computer & Tech Centre, Poole D160
Box Hill School, Dorking D122
Bradfield College, Reading D82
Bradford Girls' Grammar School, Bradford D134
Bradford Grammar School, Bradford D134
Bramdean Grammar School, Exeter D88
Bredon School, Tewkesbury D93
Brentwood School, Brentwood D92
Bretlands Beauty Training Centre, Tunbridge Wells D161

Index

Bridgewater School, Manchester D109
Brierley Price Prior Ltd, London D158
Brighton & Hove High School, Brighton D125
Brighton College, Brighton D125
Bristol Cathedral School, Bristol D80
Bristol Grammar School, Bristol D80
Broadway Secretarial Training Centre, London D158
Brockwood Park Krishnamurti Educ Centre, Bramdean D94
Bromley High School GPDST, Bromley D100
Bromsgrove School, Bromsgrove D95
Brooke House VIth Form College, Market Harborough D34
Brookside Secretarial College, Cambridge D158
Bruton School for Girls, Bruton 68, D118
Bryanston School, Blandford Forum D90
Buckingham College Senior School, Harrow D112
Buckland University College, Oxford D163
Building Crafts College, London D163
Burgess Hill School for Girls (Senior), Burgess Hill D126
Bury Grammar School (Girls), Bury D103
Bury Grammar School, Bury D102
Bury Lawn School, Milton Keynes D84
Business & Office Training Centre, Poole D158
Byam Shaw School of Art, London D166

C

C K H R Immanuel College, Bushey D97
Cabair College of Air Training Ltd, Bedford D163
Cademuir International School, Thornhill D138
Cambridge Arts & Sciences, Cambridge D32
Cambridge Centre for Languages, Cambridge D163
Cambridge Centre for Sixth Form Studies, Cambridge D32
Cambridge Language & Activity Courses, Cambridge D166
Cambridge School of Beauty Therapy, Cambridge D161
Cambridge Secretarial Courses, Cambridge D158
Cambridge Seminars Tutorial College, Cambridge D32
Cambridge Tutors College, Croydon D37
Campana International College, Farnham D163
Campbell College, Belfast D135
Canford School, Wimborne D91
Carmel College, Wallingford D116
Casterton School, Carnforth D87
Caterham School, Caterham 70, D121
Cavendish College, London D158
Cawston College, Norwich D113
Central Newcastle High School, Newcastle upon Tyne D127
Central School of Speech and Drama, London D166
Champneys Int.Coll.of Health & Beauty, Tring D162
Channing School, London N6 .... 53, D105
Charterhouse, Godalming D123
Chase Academy, Cannock D119
Cheadle Hulme School, Cheadle D85
Chelsea College of Engineering, Shoreham-by-Sea D163
Cheltenham College, Cheltenham D93
Cheltenham Ladies' College, Cheltenham D93
Cherwell Tutors, Oxford D36

Cheshire School of Beauty, Frodsham D162
Chetham's School of Music, Manchester D109, D167
Chigwell School, Chigwell D92
Chiltern Nursery Training College, Reading D163
Chilton Cantelo School, Yeovil D119
Christ College, Brecon D144
Christ's College, London D105
Christ's Hospital, Horsham D127
Christie's Education, London D166
Churchers College, Petersfield D94
City & Guilds Of London Art School, London D166
City Business College, London D158
City College of Higher Education, London D158
City of London Freemen's School, Ashtead D121
City of London School for Girls, London EC2 .... D54, D105
City of London School, London D105
Claires Court School, Maidenhead D82
Claremont Fan Court School, Esher D123
Clayesmore School, Blandford Forum D90
Clifton College, Bristol D80
Clifton High School, Bristol D80
Clifton Tutors, Bristol D32
Cobham Hall School, Gravesend D101
Cokethorpe School, Witney D116
Coleraine Academical Institution, Coleraine D136
Colfe's School, London D106
College of Central London D158
College of Data Processing, London D160
College of Petroleum & Energy Studies, Oxford D163
College of Royal Academy of Dancing, London D166
Collingham, Brown & Brown, Oxford 24, D36
Collingham, London D34
Collins Secretarial Training, Epsom D158
Colston's Collegiate School, Bristol D80
Colston's Girls' School, Bristol D80
Combe Bank School, Sevenoaks D101
Commercial College, Bristol D163
Commonweal Lodge School, Purley D124
Concord College, Shrewsbury D117
Cookery At The Grange, Frome D161
Craigholme School, Glasgow D140
Cranbrook School, Cranbrook 50, D100
Cranleigh School, Cranleigh D122
Croft House School, Blandford Forum D90
Croham Hurst School, South Croydon D124
Crown Secretarial College, Westcliff-on-Sea D158
Croydon High School GPDST, South Croydon D124
Culford School, Bury St Edmunds D120

D

D'Overbroeck's College, Oxford 25, D36, 66, D116
Damar Training College, Stockport D158
Dame Alice Harpur School, Bedford D81
Dame Allan's Boys' School, Newcastle upon Tyne ... D127
Dame Allan's Girls' School, Newcastle upon Tyne ... D127

Daniel Stewart's & Melville College, Edinburgh D138
Darul Uloom Leicester, Leicester D104
Dauntsey's School, Devizes D129
David Charlesworth (Furniture & Cabinet Makers),
   Bideford D163
David Game Tutorial College, London D34
Davies, Laing and Dick Independent
   Sixth Form College, W2 .... 23, D35
Davies's College, London D34
Dean Close School, Cheltenham D93
Denstone College, Uttoxeter......................... D120
Derby High School, Derby........................... D88
Dixie Grammar School, Market Bosworth............. D104
Dollar Academy, Dollar D137
Domino's Academy of Hair & Beauty, Brighton.......... D161
Doreen Bird College of Performing, Sidcup D166
Douai School, Reading D82
Dover College, Dover D101
Downe House School, Newbury 41, D82
Downside School, Bath............................. D118
Dr Rowe's Tutorials, Southampton D166
Drama Centre, London D166
Drama Studio London D166
Duff Miller, London D35
Duke of York's Royal Military School, Dover............ D101
Dulwich College, London SE21................... 55, D106
Dunottar School, Reigate D124
Durham High School for Girls, Durham D91
Durham School, Durham........................... D91

E

Ealing College Upper School, London D106
Ealing Tutorial College, London D35
East 15 Acting School, Loughton D166
Eastbourne College, Eastbourne D125
Eastcliffe Grammar School, Newcastle upon Tyne....... D127
Edgbaston Church of England College, Birmingham...... D130
Edgbaston High School for Girls, Birmingham.......... D130
Edgehill College, Bideford........................... D88
Edinburgh School of Natural Therapy, Edinburgh D162
Edinburgh Tutorial College & American School,
   Edinburgh D38
Educare College, Manchester....................... D35
Edward Greene's Tutorial Establishment, Oxford........ D36
Egerton-Rothesay School, Berkhamsted D96
Elizabeth College, Guernsey........................ D145
Elizabeth Russell School of Cookery, London D161
Ellesmere College, Ellesmere....................... D117
Elmhurst Ballet School, Camberley D121
Elmslie Girls' School, Blackpool D102
Eltham College, London D106
Emanuel School, London D106
Embley Park School, Romsey....................... D94
Emile Woolf College, London D158
Epsom College, Epsom............................. D122

Everest Secretarial Training, Bristol D159
Ewell Castle School, Epsom D122
Exeter School, Exeter D89
Exeter Tutorial College, Exeter D33

F

Falcon Manor School, Towcester.................... D114
Farlington School, Horsham 75, D127
Farnborough Hill, Farnborough D94
Farringtons & Stratford House, Chislehurst 50, D100
Felsted School, Dunmow........................... D92
Fernhill School, Glasgow D140
Fettes College, Edinburgh.......................... D138
Feversham College, Bradford D134
Ffynone House School, Swansea D144
Finborough School, Stowmarket D121
Fine Arts College, London NW3 .... D35, 155, D166
Forest Boys School, London D106
Forest Girls School, London D106
Foulks Lynch, London D159
Framlingham College, Woodbridge................. D121
Francis Holland School, London NW1................ D56
Francis Holland School, London SW1W D56
Frensham Heights School, Farnham................. D123
Friends' School, Lisburn, Co Antrim 78, D136
Friends' School, Saffron Walden D92
Fulneck School, Leeds D134
Fyling Hall School, Whitby.......................... D132

G

Gad's Hill School, Rochester D101
Gateways School, Leeds........................... D134
George Heriot's School, Edinburgh.................. D138
George Watson's College, Edinburgh D138
Giggleswick School, Settle D131
Glenalmond College, Perth D141
Gordonstoun, Elgin D141
Gosfield School, Halstead D92
Greenacre School, Banstead....................... D121
Greenfields School Educational Trust Ltd, Forest Row ... D125
Greenhill College, Harrow D35
Greenwich College, London D159
Grenville College, Bideford D88
Gresham's School, Holt............................ D113
Guildford High School, Guildford.................... D123
Guildford School of Acting, Guildford D167
Guildford Secretarial College, Guildford D159
Guildhall School of Music & Drama, London........... D168
Gyosei International School UK, Milton Keynes D84

H

Haberdashers' Aske's School for Girls, Elstree......... 48, D97
Haberdashers' Aske's School, Borehamwood........... D97

Haberdashers' Monmouth School for Girls, Monmouth D144
Haileybury, Hertford. D97
Halliford School, Shepperton 64, D112
Hamilton College, Hamilton. D140
Hampton School, Hampton. D111
Haresfoot Senior School, Berkhamsted D96
Harpers Hairdressing School, Sunderland D161
Harrogate Ladies' College, Harrogate D131
Harrogate Tutorial College, Harrogate 29, D38
Harrow House, Eastbourne. D161
Harrow School, Harrow. D112
Harrow Secretarial College, Harrow D159
Headington School, Oxford. D116
Health and Beauty School, Wem D162
Heathfield School GPDST, Pinner D112
Heathfield School, Ascot 41, D81
Hellenic College of London D106
Henlow Grange College of Health & Beauty, Henlow. D162
Hethersett Old Hall School, Norwich. D113
Highclare School, Birmingham D130
Highgate School, London D106
Hipperholme Grammar School, Halifax D134
Holborn College, London D163
Holy Child School, Birmingham D130
Holy Cross Convent, Gerrards Cross D83
Holy Trinity College, Bromley D100
Holy Trinity School, Kidderminster D95
Homefield School (Prep & Senior Depts), Christchurch. . . . D90
Hotel & Travel Training College, London D162
Hounslow College, Feltham D111
Hove Business College, Hove. D159
Howell's School, Denbigh D143
Howell's School, Llandaff GPDST, Cardiff D142
Hull Grammar School, Kingston-upon-Hull. D133
Hull High School for Girls, Hull D133
Hulme Grammar School for Girls, Oldham D103
Hunterhouse College, Belfast D135
Huron University USA in London D35
Hurst Lodge, Sunningdale. D82
Hurstpierpoint College, Hassocks. D126
Hurtwood House, Dorking. D37
Hurworth House School, Darlington D91
Hutchesons' Grammar School, Glasgow D140
Hymers College, Hull. D133

I

IHMES International Hotel School, Port Erin D162
Ilford Ursuline High School, Ilford D92
Inchbald School of Design, London D167
Inns of Court School of Law, London D163
Institut Francais, London. D159
International Boatbuilding College, Lowestoft D163
International Community School, London. D106
International School of Aberdeen D137
International School of London, London. D106

Ipswich High School GPDST, Ipswich D120
Ipswich School, Ipswich. D120
Irwin College, Leicester D34
Isle of Man College of FE, Douglas D163
Italia Conti Academy of Theatre Art, London. D167
Ivor Spencer International School, London D163

J

James Allen's Girls' School, London SE22 . . . . 57, D107
Jewish High School for Girls, Manchester. D109
JHP Business Centre, Cirencester D159
Joan Price's Face Place Beauty School, London D162
Jordan Commercial College, St Helens D159
Joseph Allnatt Centre, Bournemouth. D164

K

Keil School, Dumbarton. D137
Kelly College, Tavistock. D89
Kensington College of Business, London D159
Kensington College, London D160
Kent College, Canterbury D100
Kent College, Pembury, Tunbridge Wells D102
Kilgraston School, Perthshire 78, D141
Kimbolton School, Huntingdon D84
King Alfred School, London D107
King Edward VI High School for Girls, Birmingham D130
King Edward VI School, Southampton D94
King Edward VII School, Lytham-St-Annes. D103
King Edward's School Bath D118
King Edward's School, Birmingham D130
King Edward's School, Witley, Godalming. 71, D123
King Fahad Academy, London. D107
King Henry VIII School, Coventry D131
King William's College, Castletown D99
King's College School, London D107
King's College, Taunton D118
King's School, Bruton. D118
King's School, Rochester. D101
Kingham Hill School, Oxford D116
Kings Monkton School, Cardiff D143
Kingston Grammar School, Kingston upon Thames D123
Kingswood School, Bath D118
Kingswood Schools, Southport D103
Kirkham Grammar School, Preston. D103
KLC Design Training, London D167

L

La Retraite School, Salisbury D130
La Sagesse High School, Newcastle upon Tyne. D127
Laban Centre for Movement and Dance, London D167
Lagan College, Belfast. D135
Lakefield Catering & Educational Centre, London D163
Lancashire Holistic College, Preston. D162

Lancing College, Lancing D127
Langley School, Norwich. D113
Lansdowne Independent Sixth Form College, London. D35
Lansdowne Secretarial College, London D159
Latymer Upper School, London W6 . . . . 58, D107
Laurel Park School, Glasgow D140
Lavant House Rosemead, Chichester D126
Lawnside, Malvern D95
Laxton School, Peterborough D85
Le Cordon Bleu Culinary Academy, London. D161
Leeds Central School of Beauty, Leeds D162
Leeds Girls' High School, Leeds. D134
Leeds Grammar School, Leeds D134
Leicester Grammar School, Leicester 51, D104
Leicester High School for Girls, Leicester. D104
Leighton Park School, Reading D82
Leith's School of Food and Wine, London W8 . . . . 153, D161
Licensed Victuallers' School, Ascot. D81
Lillian Maund Hair & Beauty Centre, Chester. D161
Lime House School, Carlisle. D87
Lincoln Minster School, Lincoln D105
Liverpool College, Liverpool D110
Llandovery College, Llandovery D143
Lomond School, Helensburgh. D137
London Academy of Administration Studies, London D159
London Academy of Dressmaking, London D164
London Academy of Health & Beauty, London D162
London Academy of Music & Dramatic Art, London D167
London Academy of Performing Arts, London D167
London City College, London D159
London College of English & Advanced Studies, London . . D159
London Contemporary Dance School, London. D167
London Electronics College, London D160
London Executive College, London D159
London International Film School, London D164
London Montessori Centre, London D163
London Studio Centre, London. D167
Longridge Towers School, Berwick-upon-Tweed D114
Look & Learn, Doncaster D161
Lord Wandsworth College, Hook D94
Loreto Convent Grammar School, Altrincham D85
Loretto School, Musselburgh D140
Loughborough Grammar School, Loughborough. 52, D104
Loughborough High School, Loughborough. D104
Lubavitch House Grammar School, London. D107
Lucie Clayton College, London SW7 . . . . 153, D159
Luckley-Oakfield School, Wokingham D83
Luton Office Training College, Luton. D159
Lycée Français Charles de Gaulle, London 58, D107

M

Magdalen College School, Oxford D116
Magdalen Court School, Exeter D89
Maidenhead College Claires Court Girls, Maidenhead D82
Malvern College, Malvern 47, D95, 149

Malvern Girls' College, Malvern. D95
Manchester Grammar School, Manchester. D109
Manchester High School for Girls, Manchester. D110
Manchester Jewish Grammar School, Manchester D110
Mander Portman Woodward (B'ham), Birmingham D36
Mander Portman Woodward, Bristol D32
Mander Portman Woodward, London D35
Maria Montessori Training Organisation, London D163
Marie Lecko School of Fashion & Design, London. D164
Marist Convent Senior School, Ascot D81
Marlborough College, Marlborough. D129
Mary Bolton Int. College of Beauty, Nottingham D162
Mary Reid Int. School of Beauty, Edinburgh D162
Marymount International School, Kingston upon Thames . . D123
Masterkey, Exeter D164
Menorah Grammar School, London D107
Mercelles, Hastings D37
Merchant Taylors' School for Girls, Liverpool D110
Merchant Taylors' School, Liverpool D110
Merchant Taylors' School, Northwood D112
Merchiston Castle School, Edinburgh D138
Methodist College, Belfast. D135
Michael Hall School, Forest Row. D125
Mill Hill School, London NW7 . . . . 59, D107
Millfield School of Beauty, Nr Horsham D162
Millfield, Street D118
Milton Abbey School, Blandford Forum D90
MLS College, Bournemouth. D159
Modern Art Studies, London D166
Modes Study Centre (Science Specialists), Oxford D25
Modes Study Centre, Oxford. D36
Moira House School, Eastbourne D125
Monkton Combe School, Bath. D118
Monmouth School, Monmouth. D144
More House School, London D107
Moreton Hall, Oswestry 67, D117
Morley College, London. D35
Morrison's Academy, Crieff D141
Mostyn House School, South Wirral D111
Mount Carmel School, Alderley Edge D85
Mount St Mary's College, Sheffield D88
Mountview Theatre School, London D167

N

National Extension College, Cambridge D164
New College and School, Cardiff. D143
New College, Cardiff 30, D38
New Hall School, Chelmsford D92
Newcastle-under-Lyme School, Newcastle-under-Lyme . . . D119
Newlands School, Seaford D126
Newton Secretarial School, Chester D159
North Cestrian Grammar School, Altrincham D85
North Foreland Lodge, Basingstoke 46, D94
North London Collegiate School, Edgware D111
North of England College, Leeds. D159

Northampton High School, Northampton D114
Northamptonshire Grammar School, Northampton D114
Northern Ballet School, Manchester D167
Northern Business/Commercial School,
    Kingston upon Hull D159
Northern Institute of Massage, Blackpool D162
Northfield School, Watford D98
Northwood College, Northwood D112
Norwich High School for Girls GPDST, Norwich D113
Norwich School, Norwich D113
Notre Dame School, Lingfield D124
Notre Dame Senior School, Cobham D122
Notting Hill & Ealing High School, London D107
Nottingham High School for Girls GPDST, Nottingham D115
Nottingham High School, Nottingham D115

O

Oakham School, Oakham D104
Oakwood, Purley D124
Ockbrook School, Ockbrook 44, D88
Office Skills Centre UK Ltd, London D159
Old Palace School, Croydon D122
Oswestry School, Oswestry 68, D117
Oundle School, Peterborough D85
Our Lady of Sion School, Worthing D127
Our Lady's Convent School, Loughborough D104
Our Lady's Convent Senior School, Abingdon D115
Our Lady's, Chetwynde School, Barrow-in-Furness D87
Outward Bound Trust, Rugby D164
Oxford & County Business College, Oxford D159
Oxford Air Training School, Oxford D164
Oxford College for Business Studies, Oxford D159
Oxford High School GPDST, Oxford D116
Oxford School of Drama, Woodstock D167
Oxford School of Learning, Oxford D160
Oxford Tutorial College, Oxford 26, D36

P

Padworth College, Reading D32
Pamela Neave Training Centre, Bristol D160
Pangbourne College, Reading D82
Park School for Girls, Ilford D92
Park School of Beauty Therapy, Retford D162
Parker-Rodes Educational Programmes, Broadstairs D34
Parnham College, Bridport D164
Parsons Mead School, Ashtead D121
Peterborough High School, Peterborough D85
Photographic Training Centre, London D166
Pipers Corner School, High Wycombe D83
Pitman Central College, London D160
Plymouth College, Plymouth D89
Plymouth Tutorial College (EGAS), Plymouth D33
Pocklington School, York 76, D132
Polam Hall, Darlington D91

Portland Place School, London D107
Portora Royal School, Enniskillen D136
Portsmouth High School GPDST, Southsea D95
Presentation College, Reading D82
Princethorpe College, Rugby D128
Prior Park College, Bath D118
Prior's Field, Godalming 72, D123
Purley School of Commerce, Purley D160
Purley Secretarial & Language College, Purley D160
Putney High School, London D107

Q

Queen Anne's School, Reading D82
Queen Elizabeth Grammar School, Wakefield D134
Queen Elizabeth's Grammar School, Blackburn D102
Queen Elizabeth's Hospital, Bristol D80
Queen Ethelburga's College, York D132
Queen Margaret's School, York D132
Queen Mary School, Lytham-St-Annes D103
Queen Victoria School, Dunblane D142
Queen's Business & Secretarial College, London D160
Queen's College, London W1 .... 61, D107
Queen's College, Taunton D118
Queen's Gate School, London D107
Queen's Marlborough College, Cambridge D160
Queenswood School, Hatfield D97
Quinton House School, Northampton 65, D114

R

Radley College, Abingdon D115
Rambert School of Ballet & Contemporary Dance,
    Twickenham D167
Rannoch School, Pitlochry D141
Ratcliffe College, Leicester D104
Ravenscourt Tutorial College, London D160
Raworth College for Sports Therapy and
    Natural Medicine, Dorking D162
Read School, Selby D131
Reading Blue Coat School, Sonning-on-Thames D82
Redland High School for Girls, Bristol D80
Reed College of Accountancy, Moreton-in-Marsh D160
Reed's School, Cobham D122
Reigate Grammar School, Reigate D124
Renbardou School of Beauty Therapy, Croydon D162
Rendcomb College, Cirencester D93
Repton School, Repton D88
Richmond College American International University,
    Richmond D164
Rishworth School, Halifax D134
Robert Fielding School of Hairdressing, London D161
Robert Gordons College, Aberdeen D137
Roberto Moura Hairdressing Academy, Leeds D161
Rochester Tutors Independent College, Rochester 21, D34
Rodney School, Newark D115

Index

Roedean School, Brighton D125
Rogene School of Beauty Therapy, Ilford D162
Rose Bruford College of Speech & Drama, Sidcup D167
Rossall School, Fleetwood D103
Rougemont School, Newport D144
Royal Academy of Dramatic Art, London D167
Royal Academy Schools, London D166
Royal Agricultural College, Cirencester D158
Royal Belfast Academical Institution, Belfast D135
Royal Botanic Garden, Edinburgh D158
Royal Grammar School Worcester, Worcester........... D96
Royal Grammar School, Guildford D123
Royal Grammar School, Newcastle upon Tyne D127
Royal Hospital School, Ipswich....................... D120
Royal Russell School, Croydon....................... D122
Royal School, Dungannon D136
Royal School of Needlework, Hampton Court Palace D164
Rudolf Steiner School of Edinburgh D139
Rudolf Steiner School, Kings Langley D97
Rugby School, Rugby D128
Ruthin School, Ruthin D143
Rydal Penhros Senior School Co-Ed Division,
  Colwyn Bay D142
Rydal Penhros Senior School Girls' Division, Colwyn Bay.. D142
Ryde School with Upper Chine, Ryde.................. D99
Ryde School, Ryde D99
Rye St Antony School, Oxford D116

S

Sackville School, Tonbridge D101
Saint Martin's School, Solihull....................... D131
Saint Michael's College, Tenbury Wells D96
Salesian College, Farnborough D94
Sandra Tutorial College of Secretarial &
  Computer Studies, London D160
Sands School, Ashburton D88
Scarborough College, Scarborough D131
Scarisbrick Hall School, Ormskirk.................... D103
Schiller International University, London............... D108
School of Horticulture, Richmond D158
Scottish Agricultural College, Ayr D158
Seaford College, Petworth D127
Sedbergh School, Sedbergh......................... D87
Selwyn School, Gloucester.......................... D93
Sevenoaks School, Sevenoaks....................... D101
Shandy Stage School, Hove D167
Shebbear College, Beaworthy D88
Sheffield High School GPDST, Sheffield........... 77, D133
Shelagar Tutorial Centre, St Leonards-on-Sea D37
Sherborne School for Girls, Sherborne................. D90
Sherborne School, Sherborne D90
Sherrardswood School, Welwyn...................... D98
Shiplake College, Henley-on-Thames D116
Shrewsbury High School GPDST, Shrewsbury D117
Shrewsbury School, Shrewsbury D117

Sibford School, Banbury D115
Sidcot School, Winscombe 69, D119
Sight & Sound Education Ltd, Sutton Coldfield.......... D160
Silcoates School, Wakefield D135
Sir William Perkins's School, Chertsey D121
Slindon College, Arundel D126
Solihull School, Solihull D131
Sotheby's Educational Studies, London D166
South Hampstead High School GPDST, London D108
South London College of Hairdressing, London D161
Southbank International School, London D108
St Albans High School for Girls, St Albans D97
St Albans School, St Albans D98
St Albans Tutors, St Albans D33
St Aldate's Secretarial & Business College, Oxford D160
St Aloysius College, Glasgow D140
St Ambrose College, Altrincham D85
St Andrew's Private Tutorial Centre, Cambridge.......... D32
St Anne's College Grammar School, Lytham-St-Annes D103
St Anne's, Windermere D87
St Antony's-Leweston School, Sherborne.............. D90
St Augustine's Priory, London D108
St Bede's College, Manchester D110
St Bede's School, Hailsham D125
St Bees School, St Bees D87
St Benedict's School, London D108
St Brigids School, Denbigh D143
St Catherine's School, Guildford 74, D123
St Christopher School, Letchworth D97
St Clare's Convent, Porthcawl....................... D142
St Clare's, Oxford............................ D37, D116
St Clotilde's School, Lechlade D93
St Columba's College, St Albans..................... D98
St David's College, Llandudno....................... D144
St David's School, Ashford 65, D111
St David's School, Brecon........................... D144
St Denis and Cranley School, Edinburgh D139
St Dominic's Priory School, Stone.................... D120
St Dominic's School, Brewood....................... D119
St Dunstan's Abbey School, Plymouth D89
St Dunstan's College, London SE6 .... 61, D108
St Edmund's College, Ware..................... 48, D98
St Edmund's School, Canterbury D100
St Edward's College, Liverpool D111
St Edward's School, Cheltenham D93
St Edward's School, Oxford......................... D116
St Elphin's School, Matlock D88
St Felix School, Southwold D121
St Francis' College, Letchworth...................... D97
St George's College, Weybridge D124
St George's School for Girls, Edinburgh D139
St George's School, Ascot.......................... D81
St Gerard's School, Bangor D144
St Helen's School for Girls, Northwood................ D112
St Hilary's School, Alderley Edge D85
St Hilda's School, Whitby....................... 77, D132

St James Independent School for Boys, Twickenham . . 62, D108
St James Independent School for Girls, London W11 . . 62, D108
St James' School, Grimsby D99
St James's and The Abbey, Malvern D96
St James's Secretarial College, London D160
St John's College, Southsea D95
St John's School, Leatherhead D124
St John's Senior School, Enfield D111
St Joseph's College with the School of
   Jesus & Mary, Ipswich D120
St Joseph's College, Stoke-on-Trent D120
St Joseph's Convent School, Reading 42, D82
St Joseph's School, Kenilworth D128
St Lawrence College in Thanet, Ramsgate D101
St Leonards School, St Andrews D139
St Leonards-Mayfield School, Mayfield D126
St Margaret's Exeter D89
St Margaret's School for Girls, Aberdeen D137
St Margaret's School, Watford D98
St Margaret's, Edinburgh D139
St Martha's Senior School, Barnet D96
St Mary's Christian Brothers Grammar School, Belfast D135
St Mary's College, Doncaster D38
St Mary's College, Liverpool D111
St Mary's College, Southampton D95
St Mary's Convent School, Worcester D96
St Mary's Hall, Brighton D125
St Mary's Music School, Edinburgh D139, D168
St Mary's School, Ascot D81
St Mary's School, Calne D129
St Mary's School, Cambridge D84
St Mary's School, Gerrards Cross D83
St Mary's School, Shaftesbury D90
St Mary's School, Wantage 66, D116
St Maur's School, Weybridge D124
St Michael's School, Llanelli D143
St Oswalds, Alnwick D114
St Paul's Girls' School, London D108
St Paul's School, London D108
St Peter's Independent School, Blackthorn D114
St Peter's School, York D132
St Serf's School, Edinburgh D139
St Swithun's School, Winchester 47, D95
St Teresa's School, Dorking D122
Stafford Grammar School, Stafford D119
Stamford High School, Stamford D105
Stamford School, Stamford D105
Stanborough School, Watford D98
Stanbridge Earls School, Romsey D94
Steiner School of Beauty Therapy, London D162
Stella Mann School of Dancing, London D167
Stockport Grammar School, Stockport 42, D86
Stonar School, Melksham D129
Stonyhurst College, Clitheroe D103
Stoodley Knowle School, Torquay D89
Stover School, Newton Abbot D89
Stowe School, Buckingham D83
Strathallan School, Perth D141
Streatham Hill & Clapham High School, London D108
Study Associates International, Epsom D122
Sunderland High School, Sunderland D128
Supreme School of Hair & Beauty Consultancy, London . . . D161
Surbiton High School, Kingston upon Thames D123
Sutton High School (GPDST), Sutton D124
Sutton Valence School with Underhill, Maidstone D101
Swift Training Centre, Newton Abbot D160
Sydenham High School GPDST, London D108

T

Talbot Heath, Bournemouth D90
Tante Marie School of Cookery, Woking D161
TASIS England American School, Egham D122
Tauheedul Islam Girls High School, Blackburn D102
Taunton School, Taunton D118
Teesside High School, Stockton-on-Tees D91
Tettenhall College, Wolverhampton D131
The Abbey College, Malvern D33
The Abbey School, Reading D82
The Academy Drama School, London D166
The Alice Ottley School, Worcester D96
The Arts Educational School, Tring D98
The Atherley School, Southampton D95
The Belvedere School GPDST, Liverpool D110
The Birmingham Theatre School, Birmingham D166
The Bolitho School, Penzance D86
The Brigidine School, Windsor D83
The British Engineerium, Hove D163
The British School of Osteopathy, London D161
The Cambridge Business College, Cambridge D158
The Country House Course, Mayfield D167
The Design School, London D167
The Duchy Grammar School, Truro D86
The Edinburgh Academy, Edinburgh D138
The European School, Abingdon D115
The Glasgow Academy, Glasgow D140
The Godolphin and Latymer School, London W6 . . . . . . 57, D106
The Godolphin School, Salisbury D130
The Grange School, Northwich D86
The Heatherley School of Fine Art, London SW10 . . . . 156, D166
The Hereford Cathedral School, Hereford D95
The High School of Dundee, Dundee D138
The High School of Glasgow, Glasgow D140
The Hulme Grammar School, Oldham D103
The International School of Choueifat UK,
   Marshfield 76, D129
The John Lyon School, Harrow D112
The Kelvinside Academy, Glasgow D140
The King's High School for Girls, Warwick D128
The King's School (HMC), North Shields D128
The King's School, Canterbury D100
The King's School, Chester D86

The King's School, Ely D84
The King's School, Gloucester D93
The King's School, Macclesfield D86
The King's School, Worcester........................ D96
The Kingsley School, Leamington Spa................ D128
The Ladies' College, Guernsey....................... D145
The Lady Eleanor Holles School, Hampton D111
The Leys School, Cambridge D84
The London School of Insurance, London D164
The Mary Erskine School, Edinburgh D138
The Maynard School, Exeter.......................... D89
The Mount School, London NW7 .... 60, D107
The Mount School, York D132
The New School, Dunkeld............................ D141
The Newcastle Upon Tyne Church High School,
    Newcastle upon Tyne............................ D128
The Norland College, Hungerford................ 154, D163
The Old Grammar School, Lewes...................... D125
The Old Vicarage, Tonbridge D34, D164
The Oratory School, Reading D82
The Perse School for Girls, Cambridge D84
The Perse School, Cambridge D84
The Portsmouth Grammar School, Portsmouth D94
The Princess Christian College, Manchester D163
The Princess Helena College, Hitchin D97
The Purcell School, Harrow on the Hill............... D112
The Queen's School, Chester......................... D86
The Ray Cochrane Beauty School, London D162
The Red Maids' School, Bristol...................... D80
The Rickmansworth Masonic School, Rickmansworth.... D97
The Royal Ballet School, London D108
The Royal Horticultural Society's Garden, Woking...... D158
The Royal School, Armagh D136
The Royal School, Bath D118
The Royal School, Hampstead, London D108
The Royal School, Hindhead 73, D123
The Royal Wolverhampton School, Wolverhampton D131
The School of Computer Technology, London D161
The School of St Helen & St Katharine, Abingdon D115
The Totnes School of Guitarmaking, Totnes........... D164
The Tuition Centre, London.......................... D35
The Zobel Secretarial College, Sevenoaks D160
Thetford Grammar School, Thetford.................. D113
Threave School of Horticulture, Castle Douglas....... D158
Tonbridge School, Tonbridge......................... D102
Tor School, Buxton D88
Tormead School, Guildford D123
Tremough Convent School, Penryn D86
Trent College, Nottingham D115
Trinity School, Croydon D122
Trinity School, Teignmouth D89
Truro High School for Girls, Truro 43, D86
Truro School, Truro D86
Tudor Hall School, Banbury D116
Tutorial College of Speedwriting, Jersey D160
Twycross House School, Atherstone D128

U

University College School, London D108
Uppingham School, Rutland D104
Ursuline College, Westgate-on-Sea D102

V

Vacani School of Dancing, London D167
Victoria College Belfast D136
Victoria College, Jersey............................ D145
Vidal Sassoon Academy School of Hairdressing,
    London D161
Virgo Fidelis Convent, London SE19............. 63, D109

W

Wakefield Girls' High School, Wakefield D135
Wallace Tutorial College, Edinburgh D38
Walthamstow Hall, Sevenoaks D101
Warminster School, Warminster D130
Warwick School, Warwick D129
Webber Douglas Academy Dramatic Art, London...... D167
Welbeck College, Worksop D164
Wellingborough School, Wellingborough............. D114
Wellington College, Crowthorne D81
Wellington School, Ayr............................. D137
Wellington School, Wellington D119
Wells Cathedral School, Wells...................... D119
Wentworth College, Bournemouth.................... D90
Wessex Tutors, Southampton D33
Wessex Tutors, Winchester......................... D33
West Buckland School, Barnstaple D88
West Dean College, Chichester..................... D167
West Heath School, Sevenoaks D101
West London College, London D160
West London School of Therapeutic Massage, London.... D162
Westfield School, Newcastle upon Tyne D128
Westholme School, Blackburn....................... D102
Westminster Independent Sixth Form College, London D35
Westminster School, London........................ D109
Westonbirt School, Tetbury D93
Westwing School, Bristol............................ D80
Whitgift School, South Croydon..................... D124
William Hulme's Grammar School, Manchester D110
Wilmslow Secretarial College, Wilmslow.............. D160
Wilton House School, Battle D125
Wimbledon High School, London D109
Winchester College, Winchester..................... D95
Windmill Hill Place Tennis Centre, Hailsham........... D164
Wisbech Grammar School, Wisbech.................. D85
Wispers School, Haslemere D123
Withington Girls' School, Manchester D110
Woldingham School, Woldingham.................... D124
Wolfscastle Pottery, Haverfordwest.................. D166
Wolverhampton Grammar School, Wolverhampton D131

Woodbridge School, Woodbridge D121
Woodhouse Grove School, Apperley Bridge D134
Woodside Park School, London N11 . . . . 109, D150
Worksop College, Worksop. D115
Worth School, Crawley D126
Wray Castle College, Ambleside. D161
Wrekin College, Telford. D117
Wychwood School, Oxford 67, D116
Wycliffe College, Stonehouse 45, D93
Wycombe Abbey School, High Wycombe D83
Wynstones School, Gloucester D93

Y

Yarm School, Yarm D132
Yehudi Menuhin School, Cobham D122
Yorkshire College of Beauty, Leeds. D162
YSV College, Hastings D37